D0277648

STOLEN INNOCENCE

A Mother's Fight for Justice
The Story of Sally Clark

JOHN BATT

EBURY
PRESS

1 3 5 7 9 10 8 6 4 2

First published in 2004 by Ebury Press
Random House, 20 Vauxhall Bridge Road,
London SW1V 2SA
www.randomhouse.co.uk

Random House Australia (Pty) Limited
20 Alfred Street, Milsons Point, Sydney,
New South Wales 2061, Australia

Random House New Zealand Limited
18 Poland Road, Glenfield,
Auckland 10, New Zealand

Random House South Africa (Pty) Limited
Endulini, 5a Jubilee Road,
Parktown 2193, South Africa

The Random House Group Limited Reg. No. 954009

Papers used by Ebury Press are natural, recyclable products made from wood
grown in sustainable forests.

Typeset by SX Composing DTP, Rayleigh, Essex
Printed and bound by in Great Britain
by Clays Ltd, St Ives plc

A CIP catalogue record for this book
is available from the British Library.

ISBN 0-09-190070-0

This book is dedicated to 'Tom'.
I have given him the first copy, on which his real name appears on this page.

'Sally Clark had not killed her sons, they were not murdered . . .
This grotesque miscarriage of justice was the result of flawed
evidence given by forensic scientists.'

Clare Montgomery Q.C., addressing the British Academy of
Forensic Sciences, 18th February 2004

Introduction

Overturning a miscarriage of justice is one of the most difficult tasks in the law; some cases have taken fifty years to put right, some after the innocent have been executed. To do so requires the dedicated effort of many people. Many doctors and scientists contributed their time and skills to the plight of Sally Clark: some were eventually paid, others worked *pro bono*. Most of their contributions are recorded in the following pages. But the main and continuing burden – following an unsuccessful appeal – was borne by the core defence team.

The man with the principal responsibility was Mike Mackey, senior partner of Burton Copeland, solicitors, of Manchester. He had the conduct of the case; he was the linchpin of legal activity. He instructed counsel to try the case in court. If the barristers make a bad mistake, he has unpalatable choices: if persuasion fails, should he go with what they say or tell the client to sack them?

Steve Clark is Sally's husband, and also a lawyer, but with no experience of criminal law. This meant that he and his solicitor wife Sally were in the hands of others, and could have little impact on the way the case was prepared apart from giving a written and detailed account of their lives and the deaths of their two sons. The crux of the trial was the battle of the medical science. Once Sally's first appeal was denied, Steve's role became different, pivotal and crucial; he was her adviser, her lifeline in prison, the father without a mother to bring up their surviving son, the family breadwinner and Sally's main campaigner. He sought and followed up every lead, however unpromising, in order to overturn his wife's conviction, and chased Mackey and me at the slightest sign that we were slacking. In the three years following Sally's conviction, he originated hundreds of e-mails, letters and phone calls.

Sue Stapely, also a solicitor, is now practising as a public relations consultant. To persuade a Court of Appeal that a previous panel of such judges got it wrong, the argument must first be won in the court of public opinion, particularly in the legal press and broadsheets. Sue gave up a successful and financially generous partnership so that she could join another firm, Quiller Consultants, which would allow her one day a week – and however much more it would take – to mastermind the media campaign to free Sally. And do it for nothing: *pro bono*. Her efforts led to the most sustained and effective media campaign in legal memory.

David MacKay, a don at Cambridge, who had never met the Clarks, volunteered to set up the Sally Clark Website, a task that occupied him daily for over three years and produced a model which all others may aspire to.

Marilyn Stowe, a partner in Graham Stowe Bateson in Leeds, offered her services, *pro bono*, to help Sally. She spent some days chasing up various matters with Macclesfield Hospital, where Steve had been given the runaround. Her work was crucial: with no little difficulty, she persuaded Macclesfield Hospital's legal department to find and to hand over the medical notes on the two babies who died. These contained evidence that Harry, the second son, had lethal bacteria in many sites in his body. It had been kept secret from the defence and all the other experts.

Frank Lockyer, Sally's father, is a retired police divisional commander. His knowledge of criminal law and procedure was brought into full play in his daughter's cause. He also maintained a continuing and informative correspondence with over 600 interested well-wishers.

I am a solicitor. I have known Sally Clark since she was five, when she played with my younger daughter, Joanna. I attended her trial with a watching brief for the family. After Sally was convicted, I became part of her legal team and saw her regularly, on professional visits to Bullwood Hall prison. My virtually full-time role was as back-up to Mackey, and to research legal and medical evidence relating to cot deaths.

This is the story of the Sally Clark miscarriage of justice. If I have exaggerated my own role, I apologise to any whose contribution has not been properly recognised. There are three voices in this account of what happened: Sally's, Steve's and mine. In italics, I have added explanations and comments to try to de-mystify the more complicated areas of the law and medicine.

The English criminal justice system is adversarial. In the Sally Clark case the adversaries are as follows:

For the Prosecution	For the Defence

Counsel

Robin Spencer QC	Julian Bevan QC
Michael Chambers	John Kelsey Fry

At the Second Appeal
New Counsel
Clare Montgomery Q.C.
James Gregory

Solicitors

Crown Prosecution Service	Michael Mackey of Burton Copeland, Manchester
	John Batt/Batt Holden, Wimbledon
	Sue Stapely
	Marylin Stowe of Graham, Stowe, Bateson

Experts

Dr Alan Roy Williams, Home Office Pathologist	Professor J.E.M. Berry, Paediatric Pathologist
Professor Michael Green, Forensic Pathologist	Dr Ian Rushton, Paediatric Pathologist
Dr Christine Smith, Neuropathologist	Professor Helen Whitwell, Neuropathologist
Professor Sir Roy Meadow, Paediatrician	Professor Phillip Luthert, Ophthalmic Pathologist
Dr Jean Keeling, Paediatric Pathologist	Professor Timothy David, Paediatrician (appointed by the Family Court)

Experts at the First Appeal

Dr Parsons, Opthalmic Pathologist	Dr Levin, Professor of Ophthalmology
	Dr Ian Evett, Statistician
	Professor A. P. Dawid, Statistician

Experts at the Second Appeal

Dr Wilson, Microbiologist

Dr Nigel Klein,
   Microbiologist

Professor James Morris, Consultant
Pathologist

Dr Roger Byard, Forensic Pathologist

Dr Sam Gullino, Forensic Pathologist

Dr Glyn Walters, Chemical Pathologist

Professor P. Fleming, Paediatrician

Professor R. Hill, Mathematician

Professor Tom Meade, Epidemiologist

Dr R. O. Jenkins, Microbiologist.

Professor Caroline Blackwell, Microbiologist

Professor Jean Golding, Paediatric
   Epidemiologist

Dr Douglas Fleming, General Practitioner

Dr Zakaria Erzinclioglu, Forensic Scientist

Professor Behan, Neurologist

Professor John Menkes, Paediatric
   Neuropathologist

Professor Brian Lowry, Geneticist

Prologue

'I catch my first sight of the white prison van, each prisoner in a separate sweat box. I say: 'Don't double-cuff me. I won't run. When I walk free, it will be as a completely vindicated person.' It has no effect. A security guard says she will try to avoid the press getting a photo of me in handcuffs, then carefully adjusts her make-up for the photographers.

'It is dark outside when I face a barrage of flashbulbs as I am escorted to the van. Prisoners in the other boxes are listening to a radio, about the latest conviction; they are shouting abuse, dotted with foul language, at Sally Clark, unaware that I have just joined them. I try to stay quiet; I am very frightened. My name is repeated, again and again, on the radio. I am crying. The women in the other boxes are convinced that I am guilty.

'At Styal Prison, as I walk through the door I appear on the television screen. Fifty faces stare at me screaming: "Here's the nonce!" "Murderer!" "Die woman, die!" I shall hear those words many times over the coming weeks. I am put in a small holding cell. Other prisoners are banging on the door, shouting more abuse and clambering up to look through the window. I feel like a caged animal.'

In the Beginning . . .

26 January 1998

Midnight. The baby is perfect, naked, alone, still, the definition of vulnerability. He is not asleep. He is lying on his back, on a hospital trolley, in a small white-painted, side room. The police constable mentally braces himself. Two and a half hours earlier, eight-week-old Harry Clark was pronounced dead.

The policeman's job is to inspect the body, to establish, for all time, its exact condition. He is looking for signs of abuse: bruising – particularly around the nose and mouth; blood, cuts, abrasions, broken or dislocated limbs, black or bloodshot eyes, tears in the skin or scalp. He looks carefully from the wisps of hair to the miniature toes. He sees no blemish. He turns Harry and inspects his back from head to heels. There is no mark. He records his findings in his notebook.

He remembers doing something similar for another Clark baby, Christopher, a year or so ago. His, too, was an unblemished body.

27 January 1998

The paediatrician on duty at Accident & Emergency has told the police that the autopsy on baby Harry Clark should be done by a paediatric pathologist; a specialist in baby post-mortems can avoid mistaken findings that would cause unnecessary anguish for already suffering parents. Police choose Home Office pathologist Dr Alan Williams. He is under contract and more available. He is not a paediatric pathologist, of which there is a great shortage. He is nearing retirement.

Some say that pathology is the economics of medicine: for every pathologist there is a different opinion.

Harry Clark's baby body now lies on the steel table of the mortuary. Williams picks up the scalpel to begin the opening.

He identifies retinal haemorrhages. These are classic signs of Shaken Baby Syndrome.

Williams takes Detective Inspector Gardiner to a meeting with his friend and colleague, Professor of Forensic Pathology at Sheffield University, Michael Green, one of the country's leading experts on eyes, and a world authority on babies. He is a favourite on the medical lecture circuit because of his engaging personality and sense of humour. He teaches that many mothers murder their babies and pretend they are cot deaths. He puts the figure at up to 40 per cent of all cot deaths. Until 1990, when parents were advised to put their babies to sleep on their backs, there were 30 cot deaths a week in the UK. Since then, after campaigns, the rate has fallen to about seven a week.

Forty per cent of cot deaths would produce a figure, in the last fifty years, of tens of thousands of mothers who have got away with murdering babies without alerting husbands, siblings, grandparents, friends, neighbours, healthcare professionals, police or coroners. Green's theory may mean that pathologists, who at post-mortem often describe unusual findings as non-specific, will say – not in this case – they are consistent with shaking or smothering. This alerts police.

Green tells Williams and Gardiner that the 'pattern and distribution of retinal haemorrhages' is such that Harry must have been shaken violently, several times. There can now be no doubt: Harry did not die of natural causes, or a cot death. He was murdered.

Williams knows that the mother, Sally Clark, was alone with Harry when he died. Williams remembers that she was also alone with her first baby son, Christopher, when he died. Williams performed the autopsy on him. That was natural causes – or so he thought at the time: a lung infection. This puts a different complexion on that diagnosis.

Williams identifies another five findings in Harry: in addition to retinal haemorrhages, there are two petechiae in Harry's left eyelid – a possible sign of asphyxiation; tears in the brain and haemosiderin in the arachnoid space; haemorrhages in the spinal cord with haemosiderin discoloration. He also finds a fracture of the second right rib and dislocated first right rib. Not only was baby Harry murdered, he was the victim of violent abuse.

These findings are what he might expect if this baby was a typical case of Shaken Baby Syndrome.

Williams takes swabs from eight sites in Harry's body and sends them to Microbiology for 'Culture and Sensitivity'. These are tests that can disclose infection that would not be visible to the naked eye or under the microscope. Many doctors do not have much faith in such tests, preferring naked-eye or microscopic observation as the way to identify infection.

When Williams receives the microbiology report from that department of Macclesfield Hospital there are relevant findings. The bacterium *Staphylococcus aureus* has been isolated in the nose, throat, both bronchi, stomach wall, trachea, lungs and the cerebrospinal fluid. In five of those sites the bacterium is in pure growth form, including the spinal fluid, where there are polymorphs. *Staph. aureus* is a common bacterium, frequently the result of contamination in the non-sterile conditions of a mortuary. Polymorphs – the white blood cells that the body creates, during life, to fight infection – could indicate the body fighting natural disease, but it was not confirmed by histological examination. Some doctors would say they must have got there after death. This bacteria can cause septicimia and meningitis. Williams files the report.

Frank
1950 . . .

On the night beat in Salisbury's St Anne Street, Police Constable Frank Lockyer knows that there is a cup of hot tea to be had at the back door of Number 72. Mrs Yarrow has a daughter, Rosemary, and every copper in Salisbury – all twenty-three of them – is in love with her. Frank is no exception. But their paths will not seriously cross for another forty years.

Frank is a good-looking man, a bit short of hair, but with a fine figure. You might think he was managing director of a public company; you would never mistake him for Mr Plod. He exudes charm, courtesy, consideration for everybody before himself. Within moments of meeting him – unless you are a villain he has caught jemmy-handed – you know you are the most important person he has encountered all day.

He disappointed his father when he did not follow him into farming, choosing, instead, to fight his way into grammar school, *en route* to his chosen career in the Wiltshire Constabulary. His first Chief Constable told the young recruit: 'You have to be a bit of a bastard to do this job. It comes naturally to me. You'll have to work at it.'

Jean Bundy's father is a shepherd in Codford, a village a few miles west of Salisbury. Jean is neat, slim, fair-haired, pretty, with a dance of humour in her eyes, if you are fortunate enough to amuse her. Frank spotted her days ago, through the window of Beynons, in Castle Street, where she is a hairdresser. He does not need a haircut. He enters and sits to wait his turn. Jean does not cut his hair – Frank would not allow a woman to do such a thing! She succumbs to the rather formal charms of this big man and agrees to go out with him.

It is a good match. Soon they are deeply in love. They know how to share the marriage territory, neither trespassing on the other's patch – unless Jean thinks it necessary! They are practical people: they marry – on 4 April – one day before the end of the tax year, to qualify for a marriage rebate of £250, enough to pay for the honeymoon. They catch the train for London and the Strand Palace Hotel, a place that will be eventful many years later for the family.

Frank is a mixture of ambition and dedication. The desire to serve has a lot to do with his choice of career, but he feels he has more to offer than traffic control. By 1962, he has risen to the rank of Inspector and is a sub-divisional commander.

Jean and Frank want a family but it does not happen naturally. Jean needs an operation. It is successful and, by the time their daughter Sally is born, on 15 August 1964, he has become the force training officer and a Chief Inspector in Devizes. In 1969, Frank is promoted to become Chief Superintendent and Commander of the South-West Division of Wiltshire. He is Chief of Police in Salisbury when Sally begins her schooldays.

Sally

Frank and Jean's daughter looks like her mother: lithe, blonde, very pretty, athletic. She has an open face and an eagerness to experience life. Sally's best friend is Anona, who is very bright. They do everything together, including sharing holidays. Frank and Jean worry that Sally is not academically gifted and may be out of her depth at South Wilts Grammar School, but her headmaster, Arthur Stuchey, tells them, 'She will not be the brightest pupil but what she lacks in natural talent she will make up for with hard work.'

They are not alone in underestimating Sally's talent; she keeps it well hidden. Sally enjoys school, particularly the choir and athletics; she proves so adept that she runs for her county. Frank, concerned that her Wiltshire accent needs ironing out, sends her to Miss Moore's speech and drama classes. Sally breezes through her grades to win bronze and silver medals. When she takes her gold – acting Portia and reading Jonathan Livingstone Seagull – she is so good that she is offered a scholarship to RADA, the Royal Academy of Dramatic Art. 'Your eyes could make your fortune on the screen,' she is told. But show business has no allure for Sally. She prefers the idea of academia.

After eight good O-level results, she chooses to study history, geography and economics for A level, brushing aside reservations about their difficulty. She likes them and will make them work, despite her apparent lack of natural talent. To the embarrassment of her teachers, at A level Sally gets two As and a B. They have seriously underestimated her: she will easily qualify for Oxbridge, and would bring prestige to the school by going there. But Sally has sussed out the field: she has chosen industrial geography as her subject and although Exeter has a decent course, she did not like the university itself. Her teachers urge Cambridge on her again. Again she dismisses it because the course at Southampton is better and offers more academic rigour. She would have preferred law, but remembers being told she is not bright enough for that career.

Life is difficult for daughters of coppers because young men are frightened off – especially when Dad is the Chief of Police. Sally is seventeen before Howard Robson takes his chances and asks her out. They do the teenage circuit of cinema, games and dancing but nothing serious comes of it. Howard will go on to become a solicitor.

At Southampton University Sally makes friends easily, enjoying the non-academic side. She still does not let up on work, determined to maintain her record for outperforming her lecturers' forecasts. She also makes her first firm male friend – John Aylward, who is blond and attractive – and for a while imagines that she is in love with him. That passes when she meets dark-haired Adrian Bradley, an open, portly man, with a good sense of humour. He falls for her. They share many interests and it is a comfortable relationship. Frank and Jean like him.

Around this time, Jean Lockyer discovers a lump in her breast. It is cancer. It is a bad shock to Sally too, for they are more like sisters than mother and daughter. But an operation proves successful and Jean makes a slow but good recovery. Regular check-ups are reassuring.

Sally gains a 2.1 in industrial geography, a fine achievement. Yet she is bitterly disappointed: she comes first out of 108 candidates with the highest score ever recorded in that difficult discipline but she wanted – and thought she had made – a 'first'. She missed it by a whisker. Southampton has never awarded a first-class degree in this subject. Sally's is not a modest talent just scraping through her exams by exceptionally hard work; she has serious academic ability and a fine brain: 'Those around me have a career in mind but I don't really know what I want to do. I would say that I drifted into banking. It seemed like a good idea at the time. it is well paid and my studies in human geography gave me an interest in business development.'

Sally decides on a career in corporate finance with a merchant bank. Her first setback is that such banks are only interested in Oxbridge graduates.

In 1985, Frank retires from the police force. The most popular Chief of Police in Salisbury's history, he is offered several jobs. He is appointed a consultant in security for United Provident (soon to become Friends Provident) Insurance Company, and the Dean of Salisbury asks him to take on the directorship of the Cathedral Spire Appeal Fund.

Soon Sally is leapfrogging her peers. Lloyds Bank recognises her ability and she becomes a management trainee at London's Ludgate Hill, with a lending discretion for sums beyond Frank's financial experience. Sally passes the banking exams and leaves Lloyds for Citibank and corporate finance, at last.

Life, for Sally, could not be better, in the spring of 1988. Jean's breast cancer is in remission, the prognosis excellent. Sally loves her job at Citibank, and has just bought a flat in Tooting with her university friend Vicky. Sally and Adrian are still together but there has been no talk of permanent commitment.

Steve

At Citibank, Sally's boss asks her to take an important document to their solicitors, Clifford Chance. She knows of Steve Clark – a junior solicitor there – and that he has just returned from three months' back-packing in

Australia. She is shocked at the effect Steve has on her. Flustered, she is aware of his eyes on her. She has not cheated, and would not cheat, on Adrian but this is something outside her experience, perhaps even her control. She makes two decisions: to find out more about Steve, and to improve his dress sense – his shirt and tie are disgusting!

Sally is a confident person, but she becomes tongue-tied and nervous with a new man. This shyness is a rare reaction for her. 'Goodness knows what he thinks of me!' she thinks.

Pursuing her enquiries, Sally establishes that Steve is single, has no permanent girlfriend and is eligible.

Steve is attracted to Sally. He, too, does his 'due diligence' and is disappointed to find that there *is* a man in her life: that means she's out of bounds.

Sally knows that she has fallen victim to the 'across a crowded room' cliché. One day she asks Steve's opinion about a legal paper.

'It's a difficult point,' he replies.

It isn't.

'Will it take a while?' she asks.

It won't.

'Yes,' says Steve.

'Could you spare the time to do it over a drink?'

Her first impressions are confirmed:

'I can't stop looking at him, then turning my eyes away. I can't stop thinking about him. He takes me to lunch, at Café des Bon Amies, in Covent Garden. That's it. I will have to tell Adrian.

'Lies are not only wrong, but usually unnecessary, and yet I lied to Adrian about that lunch in Covent Garden. I see him after work that evening and tell him. He is badly hurt, but my feeling for Steve is overwhelming me, making me do strange things.'

At the flat, that evening, the tears flow as she tells Vicky: 'I'm not going into anything headlong with Steve. I'm not going out with him every time he rings. I'm going to be young and free and single for a while. Give myself time to think and see who else is out there.'

The phone rings. Steve asks her out tomorrow night. She does not hesitate. 'Where shall we meet?' she asks.

Steve Clark's forebears were all miners. His father, Alan, was academically bright and made his way from a pit village just outside Newcastle, through grammar school to Durham University, where he captained the first XI cricket team. He married Ruth, whose father was a master butcher in South Shields, and who paid for his daughter to be educated privately. It paid off when she was given a place at Durham. On graduating, Alan joined the Rank Organisation and Ruth became a teacher. They bought their first house in north Derbyshire. He is keen on all forms of sport but his first love is cricket.

Alan, inspired by the newly elected Margaret Thatcher, stands as a local councillor. Ruth has four passions: her two sons, Stephen and Geoffrey, tennis and the *Times* crossword, which she completes by 7 a.m. each day. The Clarks live life stripped down to its essentials. Books are very important. Education is all. Ornaments are irrelevant distractions. Stephen is born on 19 October 1961 and his brother, Geoffrey, follows two years later.

Steve is a private man, stoical; he does not show his emotions. His great love is sport, particularly cricket. But he is also something of an artist. His comprehensive used to be a grammar school, but Harold Wilson changed that. Steve's new headmaster believes that competition damages the less able, for life. Against that ethos, Steve makes it into the sixth form and, by dint of hard work, achieves A-level results good enough to give him a shot at Oxbridge – the only member of the sixth form to do so.

Downing College, Cambridge, the best place for law, offers him a place, but a year hence. For his gap year, he tries to get into the army, as a second lieutenant in a good regiment. But what the army really wants is long-term commitment, for at least three years. Steve passes the Regular Commission Board but will not tell the lie many before him have uttered – that he is thinking of signing on for three years – just to get the year's experience. Instead, he spends a year teaching at an all-boys prep school in Lincolnshire, enjoys his work there but does not admire what that school does to its pupils. He learns a lot; not least about himself.

University is two shocks: he finds quite a few of the public school boys 'thick'. However, many are not, and some, including many from grammar schools, are much brighter than Steve. The law is not a burning ambition for him. He drifts into it because nothing else appeals more. He knows that to get a 2.1 in law – and anything less will not give him the best career options – he is going to have to work harder than ever before.

He makes the most of extra-curricular activities. He is captain of the second hockey XI, secretary of the cricket club and president of the College Law Society. He represents the college in a number of other disciplines and makes some good friends. Bright undergraduates are steered towards the Bar. The more middle-of-the-road students, if they do not have rich parents, will probably become solicitors. And that is the path Steve chooses.

He graduates with a 2.1 in law and goes to Law School in Chester, little knowing the significance that city will have in his life some fifteen years later. He is then offered a job interview at City firm Clifford Chance, which gives him his articles of clerkship.

He is dedicated, painstaking in detail and, most important of all in that environment, he will work 16-hour days without demur. In his last six months, he is seconded to a prestigious client, Citibank. He loves it.

Steve has heard that if you become a solicitor you are bound to marry one, because you never meet any real people. He hopes it will not happen to him.

When Sally joins the Citibank meeting, the room suddenly lights up for Steve. His first thought is: 'Where has she been all my life?' His second is: 'I hope she's not a solicitor.'

When Sally phones to tell her friends she has met a City lawyer they are not surprised. They expect her to go for a hot-shot, public school Sloane Ranger. They are astonished when they meet the man with the pronounced north Derbyshire accent and no hint of Sloane tendencies:

> 'Why do I love him so much? Because he is my best friend, my innermost mate. I trust him with my soul. I hate the word "dependable" but he is that rare being, somebody who, if he says he will do something, does it; no matter what gets in the way. He is not dynamic but once set, nothing will divert him.'

Steve Clark is not materialistic but he loves 'punishing the credit card' for Sally. He is not demonstrative, which Sally finds difficult at first. In her family, kisses and hugs are a daily occurrence. She sees his lack of emotion as coldness, and there is even a moment when she thinks he does not like her. But that idea is soon dispelled when he makes her laugh.

Sally is in awe of Steve's methodical approach to life:

'Particularly his ability to work through problems rationally, his common sense and general knowledge. He is very keeled, rarely prone to emotional outbursts. He has an enviable ability to lock problems away in mind boxes, to be opened only when he is ready for them. Steve and I are soul mates first, then lovers, and there is a degree of mutual commitment and trust that is rare in any partnership. About the only thing we disagree about is religion. Steve is a thinking atheist. He has worked it all out: there is no God. When we die, it's goodnight! All over!'

Sally believes in God, which is fortunate, because she will be in need of Him. She grew up with Salisbury Cathedral's miraculous spire dominating the city. That stonemasons in 1100 were capable of building it, to a height of 404 feet, on gravel, with none of today's sophisticated knowledge of load-bearing, is a miracle to her. She wonders how they knew it would not fall down in the first gale.

Sally and Steve

Sally and Steve's busy social life is badly disrupted when Jean Lockyer's breast cancer returns. Sally has taken Steve to Salisbury regularly, and he now knows both parents well. Sally spends every spare moment with her mother. Her father's job was a seven days a week commitment; she rarely spent real time with him except on holidays.

In February 1989, Sally is with her mother at Salisbury Infirmary. Jean Lockyer tells her daughter that Steve is just the man for her. Then she closes her eyes and her breathing stops.

Now Sally clutches the two men in her life. Steve is staunch, unstinting in his love and care for her.

Frank is in a bad way. He cannot imagine life without his Jean; or that such a life would be worth living. She not only meant everything to him, she *did* everything for him. He can't boil an egg or operate a hoover. He has no household skills. He has never done any shopping; he does not know what to buy, where to buy it, or what anything costs. In some ways, he is as helpless as a baby.

Sally is not coping well: 'Steve and I are inseparable. I am having quite a difficult time. Mum and I were more like sisters. I miss her so much. Steve never complains at my mood swings, my anger, the tears.'

When Steve asks Frank's permission to marry his daughter he chooses his moment carefully. They are having a night out at a restaurant, before taking Sally on holiday to the Italian Lakes. He is desperate for a private word with Frank, but Sally will not leave his side. Eventually, nature calls, and Steve follows. As they stand side by side, at the urinal, Frank concentrating on the job in hand, Steve pops the question. Frank is a little shaken: not by the question, but by the venue and the immediate consequences. He weighs up the situation. The answer is not in doubt. He has a high regard for Steve but his first concern is how to shake Steve's hand. Should he put his arm round his shoulder, as those in show business do, and at what point should he do so? He has arrested men for their activities in public toilets! Should they shake hands before or after they have washed hands?

In September 1988, on holiday in Italy, Steve proposes and Sally accepts.

Frank has a good friend in Christopher Benson who is making a mark in the world of property and spends most of his time in London. He is married to Jo, formerly Bundy, and distantly related to Jean Lockyer. Jo Benson is a former mayor of Salisbury. The Benson sons, Charlie and Julian, both barristers, grew up with Sally and her friends. Following Jean's death, 'Aunty' Jo takes on the mother's mantle, helping Sally through the next ten months of preparation for the wedding. Steve teaches Frank how to poach an egg and work a washing machine.

On Saturday, 21 July 1990, traffic stops in the centre of Salisbury as the daughter of the Chief of Police is married at St Thomas's Church. The reception is in a marquee on the magnificent lawns of the Pauls Dene House, Jo Benson's family home. This is the happiest day in Sally's life. But in some ways it is the saddest, because her mother is not there to cry at the lavish society-type wedding Frank knew Jean had always wanted for her daughter.

Sally feels her mother's presence throughout the ceremony: 'not in a spooky way; warming, reassuring. I know she approves and is very proud.'

Sally's female friends tell her that their own wedding days passed in such a haze of panic and apprehension that they can barely recall a single event. Sally is determined that will not happen to her:

'I am at the top table, between Steve and Dad. These are the two men I love more than anything in the world. So then I relax and memorise every detail. Steve went along with a church wedding for my sake. His vows were public promises, made to me, in front of the people who meant most to both of us.'

Sally becomes a solicitor

The crazy idea began in Madrid, at a conference organised by Clifford Chance. As Sally explains: 'Patrick O'Connor, one of the partners, said to me: "You really love the law. Why don't you apply for law school and take the Law Society's finals?" He said it as if you could do it in a few hours at night school. I told him I was too old.

' "You're only twenty-five," he replies; "and you've experience of the real workplace. You'll walk it." But my salary at Citibank is £30,000 a year and I am one step away from becoming a "residential vice-president". That will give me a big pay rise, a subsidised mortgage and company car.'

Sally is like her father, Frank: the cup is always half empty. And Steve had made the point that it was good that she was not a lawyer – they had different interests to talk about at night. Sally is apprehensive as she broaches the subject with her husband. But Steve has seen it coming. Watching her reaction to everything he does, he knows the law is right for her.

It means a change of lifestyle, the loss of her considerable income, no grant, and having to live on Steve's salary alone, for two years. The flash cars and the wild social life turn into nights of hard study, a beat-up Ford Fiesta and a couple of 'Indians' a month, if the bank account can stand it. Sally's girl friends – most of whom are talking about starting families – think she's mad, missing out on everything London has to offer the twenty-somethings, with two incomes. But as Sally says, 'I loved the law as soon as I began studying. It filled me with enthusiasm.'

She is accepted on to a law course at City of London University, and applies to eight City law firms for articles of clerkship. She steers clear of the biggest, which seem to her to turn out only 'production line' lawyers. Six firms of solicitors offer her a traineeship. She chooses Macfarlanes.

For the next two years, Sally pushes herself to limits beyond anything she has known. Steve makes sure she paces herself, eats and sleeps properly; he spends hours testing her on the twenty-three subjects in the Final Exam. He marvels at his wife's enthusiasm and stamina.

As the day of publication of the Law Society finals results approaches, Sally becomes more tense. She knows she has given of her best, but cannot help remembering her grammar school careers adviser telling her she is not bright enough for the law. Also she knows that there are more new solicitors than jobs for them, and fears that the standard is being raised to keep more out.

The results appear in the *Daily Telegraph* and *The Times*. Mainline railway stations get them at about 11 p.m. the night before:

'We set off early for Euston Station, and wait . . . and wait. When the van arrives, Steve is the one who buys tomorrow's *Times*. The look on his face – elation and pride – says it all.

'Every previous exam – at school, the Banking Institute – was for parents, others. This is just for me.'

Steve and Frank sit in the Common Room of the Law Society's Hall in Chancery Lane, as the Master of the Rolls, the judge who is the head of the legal profession, hands Sally her scroll of admission. It is the proudest day of her life. She knows how happy her mother would have been.

Rosemary

Frank Lockyer, Director of the Salisbury Cathedral Spire Appeal Fund, receives a letter from Rosemary Squires – the stage name of the daughter of the tea lady at Number 72 Queen Anne Street, who has become an international jazz singer. She writes that she is 'sorry to hear that the spire is falling down'; she had grown rather fond of it, and would like to sign a covenant to give money to prop it up. Frank replies that he would like to persuade her to give a concert in aid of the Appeal.

They call it 'Jazz at Vespers' and 2,000 people fill the nave. The Dean asks Rosemary to make a CD for sale in aid of the spire, which she does with the BBC Big Band.

As Frank and Rosemary get to know each other, neither has thoughts of marriage. Rosemary has never wanted a family and Frank, who had the perfect marriage to Jean, cannot see himself ever achieving such happiness again. Rumours that they are an item abound in the confines of the small cathedral city. Both confidently deny them. David Edelestein, editor of the *Salisbury Journal*, is one of those who has heard the rumours. Frank assures him there is no truth in them but should it ever come to pass he will be the first to know.

It is not long after that that they decide that marriage would not be such a bad idea. Sally is delighted, and gives Frank her blessing. David Edelestein does them proud. On St Valentine's Day their picture appears on the front page of the *Journal*, surrounded by hearts and flowers. They marry at Salisbury Cathedral on 22 April 1991.

My wife, Jane and I help them celebrate.

Manchester, 1993

Steve is not happy with his prospects of partnership in solicitors Clifford Chance, London. Addleshaws, the biggest firm in Manchester, jump at the chance to take on a 'City Solicitor' of his banking experience, as an immediate partner.

Once Sally is qualified, she joins another law firm as an assistant solicitor. It is soon amalgamated with Addleshaws and she finds herself in the same firm as Steve, but in the corporate finance department. This is something neither of them wanted, but the firm is so big that their paths rarely cross in office hours. They buy Hope Cottage, in Wilmslow, Cheshire. It is a dream come true for Sally.

Their friends are having babies. Sporty convertibles are giving way to Volvo estates; swimming pools fill with floats and rubber rings.

Sally and Steve are regularly asked to be godparents, roles that both of them accept and even Steve takes seriously. They have not started a family yet themselves. Sally explains:

'I want to live a little first, and Steve wants to be sure we have the financial resources to bring up children properly. And my career would be better founded if I spent a couple more years in corporate finance law. But I am conscious of my biological clock and now seems to be a good time to give a baby its best chance. I am not desperately maternal but if I were unable to have babies my life would be incomplete. We are apprehensive because several friends have had difficulty conceiving.'

Christopher 1996

On holiday in the Canary Islands, in the first week of the New Year, Sally becomes pregnant. She takes it as a sign that they are meant to be parents:

'When I tell Steve, a few weeks later, this stoic, reserved man lets his emotions show. Steve's parents are as keen to have the first member of the next generation. But Dad will not have given it much thought, wanting only what I want for myself.

'When everybody we can think of has been told, life seems to fall flat.

'I'm not blooming as I should be. I am disgruntled with my looks and appearance. The mood of despondency and irritability lasts about a month. I take time away from work and the mood soon passes. By many standards, my pregnancy is easy: no morning sickness, no debilitating exhaustion, backache or swelling. I eat well and nutritiously. I take exercise. My only food fetishes are mashed potatoes and chicken tikka sandwiches. I work until 16 August 1996, exactly one month before the baby is due.

'We make elaborate plans for the baby. I can't go part-time because, having been qualified such a short time, I am a "worker bee", unlike Steve, who is a partner, able to delegate work. At home, I go into nesting frenzy, cleaning and re-cleaning anything that doesn't move, preparing the nursery and shopping for the new arrival.

'I am surprised at how much I enjoy antenatal classes and talking babies with mothers from very different backgrounds, comparing breast-feeding with the bottle, "Pampers" nappies versus supermarkets' own brands.

'For as long as I can remember, I have known my first baby would be called Christopher. One Christopher I know is Benson, Dad's friend, who is one of my favourite people. He has been a good friend to me and my mother. He is a man of great charisma, with a gorgeous speaking voice, and although his is now a public company and very successful, he carries his fame and riches modestly. Rather like Dad, he makes people, and especially me, feel important. Although Mum loathed having a middle name, I insist on Joshua for my son. It is a Clark name; Steve's grandfather had the initials C.J.C. Dad is less enthusiastic.'

Frank says it sounds like a toilet cleaner, especially when shortened to Josh.

Match of the Day is a serious time for Steve, whose love of soccer vies with his addiction to cricket. As the signature tune rings out on the television, Sally's labour twinges begin. Steve knows his priorities: 'Let's see how things work out in the second half,' he says.

But the hospital wants them in – now!

Christopher Joshua Clark is born at 2 a.m. on Sunday, 22 September 1996, at St Mary's Children's Hospital, Manchester. He weighs in at 6lb. 4oz. and is two weeks overdue. The birth is rapid and uncontrolled and only painful in the last hour and a half. Steve is there throughout. He is in control, most of the time, encouraging the right breathing exercises and reminding Sally of the antenatal clinic's advice. But at other times he seems strangely vulnerable: 'If I could take the pain away and bear it myself, I would,' he says.

Sally looks at her baby and panics: 'His colour. It's not normal It's . . . it's a bluey pink! Help me, somebody!'

Quickly nurses assure her that everything is fine. They wrap Christopher in a shawl and put him in her arms. Sally sobs with joy and exhaustion. Then she really looks at him:

'He has a fair complexion, unblemished skin, blue eyes, blond hair and perfect features. There is no other word – he is beautiful. When the midwife guides him to my breast and he sucks for the first time, it feels warm and tingly.'

Steve's parents visit their first grandson. Frank arrives too, mainly relieved that his daughter has come through it unscathed. He is apprehensive about holding something so small. 'But you must have held me when I was a baby,' says Sally. Frank says he left that 'sort of thing' to her mother.

'I don't know if I bonded with him immediately or not. I know he is an incredibly lovely baby, too beautiful for a boy; angelic, serene. I spend hours just watching him, astonished that I could have produced something so delicate and lovely.

'"Right", I say to Christopher: "We're both learners at this game. Let's go for it and if I do something wrong you must tell me!"

'It is on the Tuesday evening that he has his first paddy. I am horrified. Every other baby is asleep. I expect nurses to come running to tell me off, but nobody arrives. It is, apparently, normal. I feed him and for the first time, feel him taking a proper full feed. He falls asleep on my breast. I shall never forget how wonderful and special that felt.'

Wednesday, 25 September 1996, is an exciting day for Sally. She is taking her baby to his home for the first time. Steve, naturally fast and aggressive behind the wheel, is driving slowly and steadily, as if to say: 'Be careful! We have something precious aboard.'

Grandparents Alan and Ruth Clark take photographs.

'I show Christopher every room in the house, explaining how everything works. I introduce him to the cats, Treacle and Tabitha, who are not impressed.

'I had dreamed about doing it so many times. Now comes the reality: I take him for his first walk in his pram. My little lad is oblivious to the adventure and sleeps throughout. How proud I am.'

So began the routine millions of mothers have been through. Morning feed. Wash. Dress. Wash and dress herself. Take Christopher downstairs. Put him in his Moses basket. The postman gets fed up trying to feed all the well-wishers' letters through the box. He puts them in a bundle through the cat flap. Soon after birth, Christopher lost some weight, but he is now putting it on again. After a week, the health visitor stops calling:

'Grandmother Ruth Clark's knitting has now reached production-line quantities and her grandson has cardigans, booties, mittens and hats, all in matching colours.

'Christopher has a newly decorated blue and yellow nursery with Noah's Ark curtains, a toy box. His cot is hand-stencilled with animals by Steve, but he sleeps in his Moses basket in our bedroom. We feel closer to our son that way.

'He is a perfect baby, sleeping well, rarely crying. He demands his feeds with clockwork regularity, every four hours. The only time he cries is for a change of nappy or a feed. I do everything for him during the day, but bath-time is all Steve's. He sings to Christopher, who pulls faces. I spend hours in a special rocking chair, feeding Christopher. It is then that I realise what bonding means. Suddenly, there is something more important than anything else: a little person totally dependent on me, and part of me. I love Steve with all my heart, but Christopher is an extension of myself.'

She only has to hear him stir at night and she reaches out, not overly protective, not checking him for no reason, but because of who he is: he has come from her.

Steve sometimes says, 'Leave him. Let him settle,' but Sally cannot do that: 'I cannot bear the thought of leaving my baby on his own when he needs me.'

'Steve takes two weeks' holiday. We do day trips with the baby. We take him to Salisbury, where Frank is more than happy to show off his first grandson. I take Christopher to St Thomas's churchyard and tell him about the person buried there, who would have been his Nana.'

And so the routine continues. Sally feeds her baby. Steve changes Christopher, puts him into bed with Sally, makes the morning tea and leaves for work.

Sally makes many new friends, all with babies. Christopher is the envy of them all. He lies in Sally's arms, sometimes awake, sometimes asleep, but invariably still and serene. He is alert but silent. Everybody says how angelic he is:

'I wonder if he is not too quiet, but still the thought.

'Weekends are busy with two lunchtime parties in November for over forty guests. I love cooking. I have Christopher in his bouncy chair in the kitchen, "supervising" me. I sing to him, carols, nursery rhymes. I wonder if he thinks me a little mad. With Christmas approaching, we have formal photographs taken. The photographer also remarks how angelic the baby is.

'The christening is more important for me than for Steve. We arrange for it to be done by the priest who married us, Tony Watmough, in Salisbury, on 6 January 1997. It will be an afternoon service, with tea for forty guests at the Red Lion Hotel. I post the invitations with Christmas cards. Fiona, my sensible, dependable school friend, and Alison, Steve's style guru friend, also from schooldays, will be god-mothers. Another Christopher, a friend of mine who never remembers any birthday but is married to somebody who does, and Andy, Steve's intellectual supremo friend, are the godfathers. No christening robes have been handed down, so after a great deal of thought I buy cream silk dungarees and a bronze/mustard silk jacket and booties. There is a matching hat, but Steve vetoes it.

'"He looks like Donny Osmond," he says.'

It is a cold and frosty morning, in the first week in December, when they take the 7.25 a.m. train to London: 'a business trip for Steve and a chance for me to show off my baby to our London friends. I feed Christopher in the train, the first time in public.'

The room at the Strand Palace Hotel is small and cramped. Steve has to remind Housekeeping that they have ordered a cot.

Sally's friend, Liz Cox, arrives and they go shopping, leaving Steve in charge of Christopher. Steve catches up on some paperwork. He glances at the baby and sees a trickle of blood from both nostrils. Christopher seems to be swallowing it and struggling to breathe. Steve panics. He mops the baby's face with tissues, then rings for a doctor. First-aid staff arrive while he is splashing water on the baby's face. The bleeding stops. The first-aiders say he looks recovered. They give Steve the number of the hotel doctor, and Steve phones him. He is not bothered. He says that Steve can take the baby to the surgery if he is worried, but there is no need to do so.

Sally is concerned when Steve tells her and Liz what happened, but Sally frequently suffers nosebleeds and, as neither first-aid staff nor the doctor are worried, they decide to take no further action, but to watch Christopher even more carefully. As if that is possible.

Adrian Bradley, Sally's former boyfriend, has met and married Carolyn. They are now both good friends of the Clarks:

'Carolyn brings her three-year-old, Julia, to stay with us. She loves hugging Christopher. Carolyn says: "when you have a baby, your own life takes second place to that of another, for the first time. Your gut instinct is to defend and protect at all costs, because the baby is an extension of yourself and a hurt for him or her, hurts you."

'My feelings exactly, now, but not before I had him. I never thought in such terms, even when I was pregnant, never imagining that I would have such fierce and passionate feelings. By this time, I thought I would be itching to get back to work, and away from nappies and coffee mornings, but the reality is the opposite. I take

Christopher to the office and give him the grand tour. I don't want maternity leave to end, but I have been a solicitor for such a short time and obtaining the qualification meant so much that I could not give it up. The ideal would be to go back part-time, but that is not an option.

'We decide on a childminder rather than a nursery. I interview several and like one in particular; she will stretch her hours if the job demands it.'

Sally makes preparations for Christmas: the decorations, the cake, the mince pies; she wraps presents:

'I spend hours filling a stocking for Steve, from Christopher. That afternoon I go to the postnatal call of the year – a talk on baby massage. I tell Dr Levett about the nosebleed and that the baby has a continuous sniffle and cannot clear his nose of large bogies. He is not bothered by either and advises steam, to keep Christopher with me when I have a bath, and to use a cotton bud to remove the bogies but without putting it up his nose. I walk home from the Health Centre with my friend Tracey.'

Sally will always hate Friday, 13 December:

'It begins with utter normality; no warning of danger. Not a *frisson* of fear of what is to come. I take Christopher, in the pram, to post a parcel to Carolyn – returning some of Julia's toys left behind. At the bakery, I choose the design of the christening cake – a simple fruit filling with white and blue icing. I spend the afternoon cooking. I speak several times to Christopher's father, as usual.

'Steve has moaned about having to go to an office party that night, straight from work. He is not a natural socialiser. I encouraged him to go. My own department's Christmas party is next week.

'I keep Christopher in the bathroom while I take a bath. Afterwards, I put him in the Moses basket, on the floor, in front of the wardrobe, on my side of the bed; I get into bed and watch television. After a while, I go downstairs to make a drink. It takes five to ten minutes, washing-up and waiting for the kettle to boil. I take the drink upstairs and notice, immediately, that Christopher does not look right. His face is a strange dusky grey colour. I pull back the bedclothes. He does not seem to be breathing. I panic, forgetting all I have been told about resuscitation. I dial 999, run downstairs, the baby in my arms.

'I can't open the back door, forgetting that I had locked it before going to bed. I remember that the spare keys are with our neighbours, Peter and Anne. The front door is never used because it is too difficult to open. I run upstairs, hunting for the keys, but still cannot find them.

'The ambulance men are trying to get in. I shout that Christopher has died, yelling at them to get the keys from the neighbours.

'Paramedics try to resuscitate Christopher on the kitchen table, but fail. One asks how I found him.'

In the ambulance Sally is hysterical, repeatedly asking what is wrong, saying over and again: 'Is he dead? Please don't let my baby die!'

At Accident & Emergency, Sally is taken to a side room. A nurse tells her they are trying to save her baby. She is never left alone; a succession of doctors and nurses are with her, all sympathetic. She cannot stop her hysteria. Sally does not know where Steve's party is being held. Frantic attempts are made to reach him.

It is 10 p.m. at the Spanish Restaurant. A waitress calls Steve to the telephone. A nurse at Macclesfield Hospital says:

'Please can you come to us immediately. Your wife needs you.'

It makes no sense to Steve.

'What's the matter?' he demands.

'Your wife needs you,' is all she will say.

'Is Christopher all right?'

'Just get here as quick as you can.'

At the hospital, Steve can get no sense out of Sally.

A doctor takes him on one side and tells him Christopher is dead.

He tries to comfort Sally, but he, himself, feels drained of emotion, cold. He holds Sally in his arms and confirms her worst fear, that her beloved Christopher is 'gone'.

A policeman talks to them.

Steve phones his parents, who immediately drive to the hospital.

Sally keeps demanding:

'What happened? What happened to my beautiful baby boy?'

Medical staff say they did all they could to save him. It is not enough
for Sally, who cries out:

'Why me? Why us? What did we do wrong?'

Doctor Cowan is gentle and understanding with Sally, but she is not
comforted:

'I long for my little boy . . . He needs a feed; my breasts are swollen with
milk. A nurse gives me pills for the pain; tells me to express some milk.
I am not interested. I just want my Christopher back. I keep pretending
that it is all a misunderstanding and that somebody will bring him to
me, alive and well. I express some milk; is there anything more useless
than expressing milk for a dead baby?

'What am I going to do with all the presents? With the one which
says "To Daddy with love from Christopher?"'

Paediatrician Cowan asks her what happened. Sally begins to explain:

'He was with me in the bouncy chair in the bathroom, getting the steam
to ease his congestion . . . ' when another bout of sobbing overtakes her.

The consultant says there will be time for explanations later. They are
asked if they want to say goodbye to Christopher.

'I can't bear the thought of seeing that grey, dusky face again. I will
remember him as the beautiful baby he was.'

Steve goes. He tells Sally he is glad he saw him. Steve is crying; she has
never seen such tears from him.

Steve's parents arrive. Alan Clark has one question above others:

'Where were you, God!'

Sally takes Valium supplied at the hospital, but they are woken at 2 a.m.
by police at the door. Sally answers all their questions and is too distraught
to be angry at their officious, uncaring attitude. They take away the
bouncy chair and Moses basket.

That night, tears, eventually, induce sleep. Steve's parents stay the
night, but leave early; numb, uncomprehending.

'The house is eerily quiet and cold when Steve and I wake up. After that
first day without end, there seems to be no end to the days without
Christopher. There is nothing to do without him. I never sobbed so
badly as on the night he died, but the tears will not stop coming now,
nor the terrible thoughts.

'I would be in bed, watching television, Steve would be at his Christmas party and Christopher would be sleeping peacefully in his Moses basket beside me. We would wake up and all would be well!'

When she was pregnant, feeling particularly hormonal, a major worry was that her baby would be born with a deformity or abnormality; not because she had not taken care of herself, but all their friends had had normal babies and statistically, it was more probable that something would be wrong with her baby. Irrational, maybe, but she cannot stop the thoughts coming:

'When he was born such a perfect baby, I felt that, even though the odds may have been against us, we had pulled it off: that he was so healthy, thriving and well behaved, simply added to our joy. To lose him in such a sudden and cruel way proved my probability theory right!

'We blame ourselves for his death, but never each other.'

Steve has a harrowing guilt at being at a party when his baby died, not because he could have prevented it, but because he was not there for Sally, when she needed him, more than ever before.

And then, for Sally, comes the thought, the unbearable thought:

'My little boy died alone. He couldn't speak, couldn't tell me what was wrong. But did he try to, in other ways? Was his death my fault because I couldn't find the keys? Were those minutes . . . seconds . . . the difference between life and death? If only I had done things differently, he might not have died.

'We do not want visitors, but being alone is worse. The first day, many friends call. They seem like strangers, intruding on our grief. I hate having to tell the terrible truth over and over, making endless cups of tea. I feel I must be composed, show resilience. I have no idea why. Is it just because I can't bear to show the depth of my pain to anybody but Christopher's father?'

Steve Collis, their vicar, calls and is full of comforting words. Sally is grateful that he does not mention God or prayer: she had struggled hard to find her faith again after her mother died. Now this.

'There is nothing wrong with the funeral director. He is discreet and sympathetic. We sit round the kitchen table, discussing the ceremony, putting emotions on hold while we work out the mechanics. Doesn't anybody know my baby is dead? It is too much to bear.'

Steve does the necessary telephoning. Frank cancels the Red Lion, the christening and the guests.

A week later, the coroner's officer calls. Dr Alan Williams, the Home Office pathologist at Macclesfield Hospital, has done the post-mortem; Christopher died of a lower respiratory tract infection, peacefully, in his sleep:

'It is a relief, of sorts. There is a reason he died. We are free to lay him to rest and to be in peace. But there are questions. Where did he catch the infection? Could we have prevented it? Should I have taken him to the doctor when his sniffle developed?

'It is impossible to put into words the depth of despair that Steve and I feel. We are numb, desolate, exhausted and disbelieving. After the numbness and shock come anger and despair. I suffer terribly from the anguish of feeling that, in some way, I could have saved his life or prevented his death. I dwell, ceaselessly, on what I could have done differently:
   – Were there warning signs that he was unwell that I missed?
   – Was there something more I could have done to help prevent his suffering and death?
   – Should I have attempted to resuscitate him?
   – Did my panic, mislaying my keys, being unable to open the door contribute to his death?
'Will the pain of his death ever go away?'

Christopher's funeral takes place on 22 December 1996, at St Anne's Church, Wilmslow. Sally and Steve check with the grandparents. No, they will not be offended if the funeral goes ahead without them. And so it is. Just the mother, the father and Steve Collis, the vicar. No fuss; a very private ceremony:

'I am shaking all over, trying hard to stop myself sobbing out loud. How tiny is the coffin that holds my precious baby! The vicar's words are beautiful, rejoicing in the time we had with Christopher, not dwelling on the injustice, the fragility of life. I approve his reference to angels. Mother and father are beyond consolation but we leave the church feeling that our little boy is at peace.'

Christmas 1996 is an endurance test. Sally and Steve feel more miserable then they have ever been, surrounded by joviality and laughter. Carol singers come to the house. Sally bursts into tears and shuts the door in their faces:

'Why isn't the world mourning Christopher as Steve and I are? We refuse all invitations. We would not want to inflict our grief on other people's joy. And, in these early days, we just need each other.

'I examine my feelings about the house where he died. I do not blame it for killing Christopher. I feel closer to him at Hope Cottage than anywhere else. His nursery is not a shrine to his memory, because he spent no time there, he slept in our bedroom. He was cremated with his toys, just two kept back as a memento. I give the presents under the tree to a children's charity.

'Steve and I resolve that we will go back to work as soon as possible. The thought is that immersing ourselves in work will take our minds off the terrible past. Is this a mistake? For me, I fear the answer may be yes, because it may stifle the grieving process.'

January 1997

There is sun and sea and — more important — nobody they know in Eilat, Israel. Sally and Steve have flown there for peace, relaxation, to reflect and decide how to get through the rest of their lives:

'We are in bed, watching the film *Babe* on satellite television, when I laugh and immediately regret it. I can't stop crying. I am frightened by the fear and guilt. Does the fact that I can laugh, so soon after his death, mean I never loved him?'

Nobody tells her those feelings are normal.

They are pleased they do not enjoy their break, but it serves a purpose. It brings back appetite and sleep. They talk, and decide they will not move house, or out of Wilmslow. Sally will go back to work; it will help her deal with the grief. Another baby? Would that be disrespectful to Christopher's memory? No. They feel they owe it to him to try again, given that the coroner had not mentioned any genetic problem. Christopher had made their lives complete and had awoken in Sally feelings of maternity and bonding she was unaware of. They return to Manchester, tanned, healthy and ready to face the world.

Back at work at Addleshaws, Sally is pitched into a major deal involving the purchase of a number of private hospitals. It means 12- to 14-hour days, work at weekends, non-stop pressure. But she knows that something has gone out of her life. Nothing is the same.

Harry 1997

One Saturday morning, in early May, Sally is at the chemist's shop:

> 'I buy a pregnancy kit. I have had my suspicions for a few days. I test positive. I can't contain my excitement. I rush into the garden to tell Steve. Minutes later, his brother, Geoff, arrives from America. He is barely out of the taxi when I fling myself at him, telling him the news.
>
> 'Later we calm down and begin to think through the problems. We are scared. We know we will need a lot of help looking after baby number two, but we don't want to be over-protective or paranoid. We will explore what killed Christopher and make sure the new baby is kept well away from any infection. There are tears of happiness for the new baby; different from the tears for Christopher, but Hope Cottage no longer feels an empty place.'

They reject bereavement counselling; the thought of opening such recent wounds, to complete strangers, seems wrong. Counsellors are for people who can't cope for themselves, not for people like them:

> 'It works for Steve, but not for me. I am stifling grief under a mountain of paper. Bubbles of bereavement escape to the surface and overwhelm me without warning. I find that a drink helps. It makes me feel better and convinces people around me that I am coping.
>
> 'In a matter of days, drink becomes, not a help, but a problem. I do not know it, but I have developed a dependency on alcohol. I had always

been a prude about people who drink too much. It was a joke among my friends. I believed myself incapable of such stupidity!

'Now, every two weeks or so, when the pressure of work conflicts with the grief I am unable to deal with, I have a drink. I take a half-bottle of vodka into work when I know it will be a difficult day. Occasionally, I buy made up gins-and-tonic from Marks & Spencer. It helps make people see I am coping.'

It becomes obvious to her colleagues in the office that Sally is drinking. The partners send her on early maternity leave:

'I can't understand me. I have been so determined to follow every recommendation of the professionals on how to give my new baby the best start in life, that I cannot believe I'm even capable of drinking anything at all.

'It is not a daily habit, not even regular. But, suddenly, there comes a time when only a drink can help. At home, I do it in secret, fooling myself that Steve is not noticing. It adds to my problems. Until then, I could talk to Steve about anything, knowing he would understand and support me. But, for some reason I can't fathom, I can't let him into the depths of my despair over Christopher's death.'

At first, Steve is impatient, worried about the effect on Sally and on the baby. But he soon realises that Sally needs professional help. She is relieved when he finds out. Now, at last, they face the problem – as they have every other – together. Sally is ashamed that she deceived him:

'I despise liars and now I despise myself.

'We tell the specialist, at Cheadle Royal Hospital, the full story. He is sympathetic and tells me that it is a minor problem on a scale of 1–10, I am not even a 2. With help I will be well again in a fortnight. He recommends controlled drinking and regular counselling with Len Schofield.

'After several weeks, it seems to work. I have a drink at Christmas and again at New Year, but apart from that, do not drink at all during the remainder of my pregnancy or Harry's life.'

Steve and Sally take her second pregnancy as a sign that they are meant to have a family. They opt for the same hospital, the same antenatal clinic, the same consultant, Dr Lieberman; and see it as a plus that their healthcare professionals know what happened to Christopher:

'I have a reasonably easy time; again, no morning sickness, but this baby is bigger and more cumbersome, earlier. At three months a routine blood test shows a risk of Down's syndrome. As an older mother, it is greater. They can test for it by inserting a large needle into my stomach and extracting a small amount of amniotic fluid.

'I am frightened. It is much more painful than giving birth! Then we have to wait ten days for the results to come through, days of misery, unthinkable thoughts and the anaesthesia of alcohol. I make a pact with God – "Make the tests negative and I will give up drinking for ever."'

The result is fine; a huge cloud is lifted. But then comes a question: do they wish to know the sex of the baby? After a lot of talking they go to the hospital together and discover that Sally is carrying another boy:

'We keep the nursery as it was. Christopher had never slept there. We buy a new Moses basket, in yellow with green ducks on it. Bedlinen and bouncy chair are colour co-ordinated. We throw out most of Christopher's clothes, keeping just a few, in a box, in the attic. Christopher's toys will be a legacy to his brother.'

Sally keeps in touch with other mothers, but is sometimes envious of their babies, wondering what Christopher would have been like at their ages. But it soon passes as she becomes engrossed in the preparations for the new baby boy. She realises that no new mum-to-be wants to be talking to the mother who lost her baby to a lung infection. She feels dishonest in pretending to be a first-timer.

In October, Steve tears his Achilles tendon playing badminton. He is in hospital overnight, his leg in plaster. Sally's only concern is how she will get to hospital when the baby is due. They laugh at the spectacle of themselves: he with his leg in plaster, she with a huge belly, trying to look after him.

Even before Steve's injury, they realise they will need help in the house. An agency supplies names. They choose Lesley Kerrigan, a qualified nanny, whose job will be to help out generally.

'On Saturday, 29 November 1997, we drive to St Mary's Hospital for a check-up, expecting to be sent straight home. But I am in the early stages of labour. We watch *Grandstand* on television:

'What is it about my babies and soccer?

'My baby chooses the wrong moment to evacuate his bowels. What looks like a crochet needle is produced to break the waters and bring on the delivery.

'Harry Richard Clark is born half an hour before *Match of the Day* begins on BBC1. He weighs 6lb., which I find insulting, given how large I became. The doctor says, "We're not talking about the size of a Christmas turkey, Mrs Clark!"

'Harry, unlike his brother Christopher, is a funny-looking chap. I love him for it immediately. Nicknames come quickly to mind. I shall call him Ferkin Features or Hairy Harry. As I stare at the scrumpled, wriggling baby, I am relieved he is so different from his brother – ruddy complexion, podgy features, dark brown hair and a birthmark on his left eyelid. It is wonderfully reassuring that he is so different – it means it's impossible that we could lose him as we lost Christopher.'

Normally, a new mother is taken, by wheelchair, from the labour room to the maternity ward, but as Steve's leg is in plaster:

'He is in the wheelchair, carrying Harry. I trudge behind, carrying his crutches. Steve is given a camp bed and the three of us sleep in a row. Steve holds my hand for most of that night, the two of us staring at the precious red bundle. A new beginning. Our lives are back on track. At long last we are a family. When the ward sister enters in the morning, she asks: "Which one of you is the mother?"'

Harry is two weeks premature and he is a hungry baby. Unlike Christopher, he is hard work from day one:

'Christopher hardly ever cried. That Sunday night, I discover what crying really is. I can't bear to see his little face crumpled, his fists clenched and his legs waving about as he cries. I call the midwife, but no, it is just hunger and perhaps wind – perfectly normal. Feeding him solves the problem. Being able to cure his distress is marvellously comforting. It is also reassuring that Harry is obviously a fighter – no lower respiratory infection is going to get the better of him!'

When Steve comes to pick them up, Harry is asleep in his cot. He does not have 'angelic' in his 'make-up box'; instead there is a mischievous face, faking 'butter won't melt in my mouth'!

'He is so cute. We are so proud!

'There is a reality check before we leave: as happens with all parents who lose a baby, a doctor demonstrates resuscitation before we are allowed to take him home. I see only Christopher's face. I watch and listen, intently, as does Steve. We ask questions.

'I find it impossible to practise on the dummy baby; to me, it's Christopher. But Steve does so. I am shocked at how forcefully the baby's chest must be thumped. The doctor tells Steve that he is not using enough force: "a broken rib is better than a dead baby," he says.'

The homecoming is low key. Because Harry was premature, there was no time to alert friends. Sally's father, Frank, and Rosemary happen to be there, passing through from a trip up North.

'Harry is swamped by his coming-out-of-hospital outfit – red with matching Noddy hat, mittens and booties. He looks more like a garden gnome. He provokes smiles from all who see him. He is so unusual, so endearing. My dad – always to the point – says it:

'"He's a funny looking chap."'

It is so obviously true that they all laugh.

Later that day, the health visitor responsible for the Care of Next Infant (CONI) programme briefs them on how to take special care of Harry. They are shown how to attach an electrode to Harry's abdomen for the apnoea alarm. This looks like a pocket calculator and sounds an interrupted bleep as long as he is breathing normally. If he stops breathing, the bleep becomes continuous:

'We are to keep it attached to his body all the time, even when he is awake. We could turn off the interrupted bleep, which is annoying, particularly at bedtime, but we prefer to take no chances. CONI supplies scales and a daily symptom chart. I am determined to do everything by the book. I weigh him every morning. It becomes a game, daily extending the line on the graph as he gains weight. The records will be fed into national records via the computer at Sheffield University.'

Joining CONI gives them priority access to the children's ward at Macclesfield Hospital, their own paediatrician and more frequent and random calls by health visitors, monitoring Harry's progress.

The first night at home with Harry is unremarkable. Sally buys fish and chips and returns to find Steve on the bed, his plaster-cast leg straight out:

'. . . Harry in his arms, having his first lesson in the rules of cricket, Steve explaining that, when he is old enough, he will be expected to play with his dad, as he played with his dad before him.

'Harry makes everybody smile. He could not be more different from his brother. He is much more active and demanding. Christopher seemed to sense that his place was to fit into the family routine. Harry is not like that. The household revolves around his daily needs. The first reason is Harry's strong personality but in addition, there are the pressures Steve and I put on ourselves because of what happened.'

Sally completes the CONI regime meticulously; every daily weight gain or trouble-free symptom diary entry, is a victory. They try not to be obsessive, but Sally still keeps him well away from anybody with the slightest infection or cold.

They realise that relaxed parents make for a relaxed baby, but find it a difficult line to draw. Sally focuses on the fact that Christopher died of a lung infection, nothing genetic. Surely lightning could not strike twice. They keep Harry indoors much more than Christopher, although he has a 'walk', outside, most days:

'The consolation is that there will be an end to it, when Harry is strong enough. I know I will recognise the signs.

'Staying away from friends is isolating, but I make up for it with the telephone. Steve's only criticism is that I am too much at Harry's beck and call, anticipating his needs rather than reacting to them.'

They decide that for at least the first few months Harry will never sleep alone, he will always be in the Moses basket beside their bed. Harry is a hungry baby, taking a feed every two hours or so. Steve would prefer Sally to wait until he cries for a feed, but she reacts as soon as he stirs, putting him immediately to the breast: 'I just want to be a perfect mum and do everything I can to look after him properly.'

When he does cry, her patience amazes Steve. She never loses her cool:

'Steve, on crutches, is dependent on taxis. He tires quickly. We set up a room to which he can bring back work from the office. But he never knows how long he might have to work on any day, or where. He hates missing bath-times with Harry. He can hold him in his arms, but it is not safe to walk with him. He spends far more time with Harry on his lap than ever he did with Christopher.

'Bath-times are quite comic:

'I settle Steve on the floor, with a pillow under his foot, fill the baby bath and put it beside him, with wipes, clean nappies, changes of clothes and assorted lotions and potions. I then hand Harry to him and let him get on with it. It is a special time for both of them. But, unlike with our first-born, I now watch over them – just in case. And there is usually a photo opportunity. I have two "patients" to look after, and that is tiring.'

Lesley Kerrigan begins working for them about a week after they get home: 9.30 a.m. to 4 p.m., five days a week. Two things are out of bounds to Lesley – cooking, and ironing Harry's clothes. Otherwise there is no set routine. Lesley shares all the chores and fits in so well that she becomes more a member of the family than an employee.

Every day, they discuss Harry's progress and laugh at his antics:

'I value Lesley's advice as an experienced nanny. I find it hard to leave Harry alone, tending to take him with me wherever I go, even room to room. I leave Harry with Lesley only twice: the first time for ten minutes, while I go to the butcher, and then for an hour, at the hairdresser's.

Being premature, Harry is below normal weight, but he is soon in the average quartile on the graph, at the lower end. The healthcare professionals call daily at first, but when Harry seems to be developing normally they reduce their vists to twice a week.

Sally and Steve are sound asleep when the apnoea alarm sounds. Immediately Sally is awake, with a sickening dread. She rushes to her baby. But he is sleeping normally, peacefully in his Moses basket.

They are told it must have been a loose connection.

They reposition the electrode on his tummy, believing there is nothing to worry about. But it happens again and again:

'Each time Harry is breathing normally when Lesley or I reach him. Then it settles down and does not go off again until the seventh week, when it keeps sounding. Each check shows him to be normal. And we can find no loose connection. We believe the experts who say it is just a technical fault. The CONI representative says she will find another alarm.'

A routine appointment with paediatrician Dr Spillman reveals an abnormality in Harry's heartbeat. A specialist from Alder Hey Hospital in Liverpool does an echocardiogram on Harry:

'Seeing his tiny body covered in sensors is almost more than I can bear. And the battery of tests they carry out convinces me that something is seriously wrong with my baby. Only one of us is allowed into the room for some of the tests, and it is me, because I will not leave Harry's side. The verdict – a benign heart murmur, which will cause him no trouble – is an enormous relief. I am in tears. Steve, too, is choked.

'One morning, Harry wakes with a slight sniffle, which gets worse during the day. By that evening it is so bad that we call out the emergency night doctor. He is angry. The baby only has a cold: that is not what the emergency service is for! When we explain about Christopher, he apologises. He gives Harry a full examination and prescribes nose drops. The sniffle lingers on.'

The end of the year approaches:

'Understated yet beautiful, is to be the look for Harry's first Christmas: 1997. A large tree is bought and decorated and the excitement builds. Lesley is caught up in it as much as me. Despite the immediate happiness of the moment, there is sadness under the surface, set to overwhelm us at the slightest reminder of Christopher. There seems to be something missing in everything we do. I am assailed by strange thoughts; a mist suddenly clouds my mood.'

Steve says nothing.

Sally is alone with Harry, who is wide awake in his Moses basket as she puts presents under the tree: 'Suddenly I am reminded of doing the same thing last year, and giving them away. The moment passes, but what returns is resigned effort, not spontaneity. It does not happen all the time, just when I least expect it.'

The fear of other babies' colds keeps her away from postnatal clinics until after Christmas, when Harry will be stronger. She is not lonely because there are visitors – friends or health professionals – most days. Old friends from London stay at weekends:

'Christmas Day is perfect. Quiet. Just the three of us: a family at home. Steve and I take it in shifts to open Harry's presents; there are so many of them. We do not sit down for dinner but fit the courses in between Harry's feeds. In the evening the five of us – Sally Steve, Harry and two cats – sit in front of the open fire.

'At last I feel we're back on track! Life can't get much better than this!'

New Year brings more normality. Lesley takes up a new job with a family in Alderley Edge but continues two mornings a week for Sally. Gradually, Sally feels able to get out more, visiting friends for lunch with Harry, taking him to the clinic to be weighed, then for his first postnatal course. The talk is of babies' feet and first shoes; 'Harry gets bored quickly and demands a feed. I approve: it is another difference from Christopher. Harry is much more like other babies.'

For Steve, the plastered leg is still tiring and he gets busier in the office. As a partner in the biggest law practice in Manchester, he is obliged to do his share of networking, which he has been avoiding. He goes back on the marketing trail. Sally is sad to see less of him but glad, for his sake, that his interest in work has reawakened:

'It is not so easy for Steve, who still blames himself for not being at home when Christopher died. He is out a couple of nights until midnight. It does not bother me. When he tells me that he is due to make an overnight stop in Glasgow at the end of the month, I am not worried at being alone with Harry. Steve insists that he will reschedule his trip if I say so. I do not.'

In the New Year they change the routine for Harry, introducing him to formula milk. He does not care for it. The health visitor says he can smell the breast milk he prefers, when Sally gives him the bottle. So Steve takes over the late-night feed with formula, while Sally expresses milk in case he needs a top-up in the night.

During the day, with Harry in the cot beside her, Sally sits at her desk writing thank-you letters for his many presents. She makes them as amusing as she can. She loves kidding her friends by pretending Harry has written them. A favourite line is: 'By day, I like to lie in my cot, sleeping and looking angelic, but at night I like to lie awake and keep Mummy and Daddy awake too.'

They discuss christening. They will leave it until after Easter, when Harry will be stronger. They choose the same four godparents. They had gone to such lengths to sort out the best of their friends for Christopher that they see no reason to change them.

'There is another first for me – on a Saturday, at the end of January 1998, I am going shopping for myself and on my first extended trip away from Harry. I leave expressed milk in the fridge. It is the first time Steve has looked after him on his own, but it is easier since we now have a carrying pouch, which hangs round our necks.

'On the Sunday we march proudly to the pub for lunch, the pace moderated by Steve's crutches. This is the first time we have walked out as a family, with Harry in his pram. What a lovely day it is.'

Monday, 26 January 1998, begins normally. Sally feeds Harry and changes him. Steve, still on crutches, leaves for the office by taxi:

'I prepare mangetout and other vegetables for the dinner party planned with neighbours, Peter and Anne. I take Harry in the pram to the butcher's, where lamb chops – cut and tied exactly as I ordered – are awaiting me. I choose two good bottles from Victoria Wine and more vegetables from the greengrocer. I buy crackers and cheese from the delicatessen and visit Chelsea Flowers, a favourite shop because they always make a fuss of Harry. I order carnations to be picked up after I have had Harry vaccinated. At the baker's, I buy muffins.'

She phones her friend, Anne, but her son, Sam, has a bad cold and Sally will not risk Harry catching anything so she passes up the offer of a coffee. At Anne's doorway, she has a five-minute chat, but will not take her baby into the house. She gives Anne some chocolate muffins as a present. They laugh about how much bigger Sam is than Harry, even though he's only three months older. Sam will be Harry's protector when they go to school together.

That afternoon, health visitor Ann McDougal arrives with the replacement apnoea alarm. She stays about half an hour while Sally feeds Harry. At around 3.50 p.m. Sally leaves for Wilmslow Heath Centre with Harry. The walk takes twenty minutes or so. When the community nurse gives him his jabs, Sally finds it hard holding Harry as needles are inserted into her precious baby. He hardly cries, just a little whimper. The nurse tells her to give him Calpol if the immunisation upsets him. They have been in the waiting room only a few minutes when Dr Case calls Sally for the postnatal check-up.

She examines Sally and talks about how Harry is doing, but does not examine the baby, barely looking at him. She reminds Sally that she is due for a smear test. Sally and Harry leave at about 5.10 p.m.:

'I keep an anxious eye on Harry. He is unusually quiet, lethargic almost; then he falls asleep, a first, when out in the pram. We arrive home at 5.30 p.m. I know he will wake up when I negotiate the backward and forward thrusts necessary to get in the back door: he always does. To my surprise, he does not.'

At about 4.48 p.m., Helen Knowles, the receptionist at Steve's firm, books a taxi to take him to the airport the following morning. Helen enters the booking in the taxi book, which records all staff and partner taxis for each 24-hour period beginning at 7 p.m.

Later, Steve calls for a taxi home. As it is after 7 p.m., the system requires that the entry recording the booking is put on the following day's page: 27 January 1998. Steve arrives home just after 8 p.m.

That evening, Sally is in bed, breast-feeding Harry. Steve is beside her, in his dressing-gown. Harry sucks well but Sally is not sure if he is taking any milk. After a while he stops and Sally hands him to his father. Harry possets a little milk on Steve's shoulder. The baby rests on Steve's knee. Steve pulls funny faces at him. Harry is not interested. He puts Harry in the bouncy chair beside the bed and hobbles downstairs to make the night-time feed. The television is on.

Sally hears Steve clattering about in the kitchen and glances down at Harry:

'Only minutes have passed since Steve left the room. Something is wrong. Harry is too pale and one hand is scrunched up towards his left shoulder. I yell for Steve. Harry often sleeps with his head to one side, but this time it is much further forward. I get out of bed and lift him. His body is limp. I scream for Steve to do something.'

Steve lays him on the bed and begins resuscitation. He is gentle, not wanting to hurt his baby. Then he remembers that this is wrong. He must do it really hard and on a hard surface. He puts him on the wooden floor, and begins pumping again:

'I run downstairs, phone 999. The emergency operator demands to talk to Steve. I shout to him to pick up the phone. In my panic, I put down the receiver, cutting off the call. The operator phones back immediately and coaches Steve through the resuscitation technique.'

He breathes into his son's lungs, then pumps his chest. He does it over and over. Each time there is no response. Panic gives way to despair. Sally cannot believe this is happening again:

'I find the keys to the back door, unlock it and go down the path to the front gate, in my pyjamas. In only a few minutes, the ambulance arrives and the paramedics take over from Steve. I stand, frozen in anguish and horror, helpless when my baby needs me most.

'Harry is not like the placid Christopher: he is a fighter, spirited in character with a zest for life – surely enough to get him through this. The weird thought occurs that as he was gaining weight so well, he must indeed be a fighter. He will not accept death as his brother did. I pray as never before.'

Paramedics carry Harry to the ambulance. Sally goes with them, hysterical all the way, pleading: 'Don't let him die. Don't let him die!' Because of his crutches, Steve follows by taxi.

Harry is taken to the resuscitation room. Sally vents her anger and frustration at the nurse who guides her to the same waiting room as before. They move her to a curtained area at the end of a ward. Here Sally feels too exposed, and is hysterical again. They move her to another waiting room.

Steve arrives; he holds Sally in his arms. The anger leaves her. They cry together. A few minutes later a doctor tells them that Harry is dead.

Sally does not sob uncontrollably, as she had when told that Christopher had died. This time shock affects her differently, and she feels a sense of resignation:

'With Christopher, I just could not accept that he had been taken from us. But Harry was such a fighter, so much more demanding of his mother's time and attention. My feeling is one of desolation. I am numb, dejected. We have lost the battle. We will never be a family. I am defeated. There is no hope.

'I am less vocal in my grief. I am hurt beyond comprehension. I love Steve as much as any woman can love a man. It is total and absolute. Had we never had children, our love for each other would have been enough to ensure a fulfilled and complete life. Now, having been blessed with two wonderful babies, each very different but both equally special in their own ways, and to have had them taken such a cruel way, means that we had been given a taste of family life only to have it wiped out – yet again. Will even our intense love for each other be enough to see us through this?

'Harry was our future. How can there be any future now that he is gone? Why us? What have we done to deserve such pain?'

She knows that neither of them has done anything wrong. They could not have been better parents to their babies. Harry was nurtured, loved, cared for, and he wanted for nothing:

'Nurses tell me I should say goodbye to my son. The thought is unbearable. Harry was my Ferkin Features, with his podgy nose, tiny mouth and funny, screwed-up face. That is how I will remember him: just as he looked when I took him off the breast such a little time ago, handing him to his father, slightly disgruntled, yawning and with a trickle of milk down the side of his chin, so full of warmth, life and contentment – not lying cold, pale and alone in the darkness of a hospital mortuary. That's not my Harry!'

In the taxi, they cling to each other, silent in their grief. Both are in shock. Twenty minutes after they reach home there is a knock at the door. A doctor says he has been sent by the hospital because there is a sick baby at this address. It is incomprehensible. It makes Sally angry:

'How could you have got it so wrong? Our baby died over an hour ago!'

The doctor is taken aback, and then full of apologies. It pushes Sally over the edge into uncontrollable sobbing.

Sally and Steve sit on the sofa, side by side, holding each other, in silence. Sally cannot bear the thought of going to bed and waking up with the Moses basket empty beside her.

'Tomorrow, reality will dawn. I do not want tomorrow.'

After Harry

There are no words of comfort for a mother and father who have just lost their second beloved baby son. Any words, however well-meaning, seem inadequate to Sally and to Steve. Nobody seems to know what to say. This time there are no platitudes from the health professionals attempting to make sense of what happened.

'But they come, and that shows they care. They could easily have justified staying away, or sent a sympathy card, to avoid the awkwardness. The truth is that I am overwhelmed with grief both for Christopher and now Harry. I do not know how to grieve for my two lovely babies. Maybe time and a little peace will help.

'But there is to be no time for grief and no peace at all.'

A midwife tells Sally that she had heard about a second baby death at the health centre and prayed that it was not the Clarks'. 'You are such a loving couple,' she says, 'with so much to offer a baby. You deserved to be parents. Your home has such a warm and loving feeling about it. It was so obvious that Harry was nurtured and cared for and wanted for nothing.'

She talks about the CONI programme: 'You were wonderful about the detail, following all the procedures, recording the many weight changes and daily symptoms, working so well with all of us. We thought we would spot any early signs of trouble. You could not have foreseen what would happen, nor could you have prevented it. You are not to blame, either of you.'

Sally wonders why she feels so inadequate, so lacking as an individual. Her feeling of desolation is all-consuming:

'I am a failure as a wife, as a mother; a freak, whose children die through mystery viruses and infections. Steve and I have always been so healthy. How could we give birth to such sick children? Why could I conceive so easily if my children are to die so suddenly and without warning of any kind? Above all I want an answer to the question: Why did my Harry die?'

Two police officers arrive the next morning. They are expected. They are sympathetic. One asks the questions, the other takes notes. They look at the bedroom; take photographs. They assure the parents it is routine. Neither Sally nor Steve feels alarmed, threatened or uncomfortable:

'We are still in shock. We are not defensive because we have nothing to hide. When Christopher died, I checked with Dad. He assured me a police investigation was normal procedure. I accept that when a baby dies unexpectedly, there must be a thorough investigation, to ensure that there has not been wrongdoing. When two babies have died, even closer scrutiny is needed. Some would say that there should be suspicion, but, surely, it will be objective and not a witch hunt.'

Sally and Steve answer every question as fully and openly as they know how. They do not expect to see the police again.

Now comes the imperative need to know why Harry died. It is a driving force within Sally and will not go away. That obsession gets her through the first few days.

'There are so many unanswered questions. We will never be able to rest or begin to digest and understand what happened until that question is answered. Why did my two babies die? My worst fear is that it is something genetic. That it will happen to every baby we have.

'It is not like the day after Christopher's death. There is no talk or even thought of another baby. After Christopher's death, a planned pregnancy helped ease the sense of loss, and a new baby was a fitting tribute to his brother's life. There are no such thoughts now. Even to consider having another baby would belittle and cheapen Harry, his life and what he meant to us. It would be like saying "well, we've lost another one, let's move on to the next and see how we get on". Impossible!'

The subject of another baby comes up in conversation, but it is academic, in the context of a possible genetic cause of both babies' deaths. If that is what killed their little boys, then not only has it ruined their past, but it could do the same to their future. Sally needs to know now, one way or the other, to avoid prolonging her anguish and mental torture. The longer the delay, the more time there will be for invented explanations. There is no point in speculating. They need the facts, the science of it.

Sally convinces herself it is genetic, but, moments later, refuses to believe it. Christopher died of a specific and known lung infection. If there had been a genetic component in his death, somebody would have told them:

'The cause of Christopher's death shaped the whole emphasis of the way we looked after Harry, to prevent it happening to him. If the pathology was wrong in his case, not only would we feel cheated, because of his death, but because of all the restrictions on Harry during his life. My mind is working overtime and not always logically. I need to know why my babies died.'

The vicar, Steve Collis, is with Sally when Christine Hurst, the coroner's officer, calls. Sally spoke to her after Christopher's death. She is full of sympathy, says she understands the anguish they are going through, and their urgent need to know the cause of Harry's death. She explains that there will be a post-mortem, and says she will tell them the preliminary result as soon as she knows it. She asks about Harry's health in the days before he died. Sally had told Christine Hurst about Christopher's nosebleed; now she tells her about Harry's blocked nose and wheezing and the nose drops prescribed by the emergency doctor; about how scrupulously she carried out the CONI scheme. She tells her about the apnoea alarm, the weight chart and the symptom diary: 'I pleaded with her to ask the pathologist to be vigilant and careful in his investigations. Neither of us could stand not knowing why he died and being left with a mysterious virus or infection, origin unknown.'

Sally touches on genetics, but finds it difficult to talk about, in case it turns out to be true. Mrs Hurst asks Sally if there is any history of babies dying in infancy in either of the families. Sally tells her that her nana on her father's side lost her firstborn, in infancy, but knows of nothing else. Sally agrees to ask again. Mrs Hurst wants a family tree, for each side, detailing names, dates of birth and death and known illnesses.

In the following days, Sally and Steve make many calls to her, chasing for news. She is always polite and sympathetic. Sally feels that Mrs Hurst is on their side, but in the hands of others. She seems as frustrated as they are at the constant need for further tests. But if tests will ultimately be able to tell them how Harry really died, it will have been worth the wait. Mrs Hurst says the delay is in no way unusual. They believe her, but Steve begins to notice evasiveness in Mrs Hurst's replies. He feels she is stalling for time. He cannot think why and does not pass on his fears to Sally.

The Arrest

They come at dawn; two police cars, full of officers, brake in front of Hope Cottage in Wilmslow.

Sally is in the kitchen in her dressing-gown. There is a knock at the front door. She sees two men and three women, thinks they are salespeople. She bangs on the window indicating that they should go to the back door. Detective Inspector Gardiner introduces himself and his police colleagues. Sally invites them in:

'I assume they have the results of Harry's post-mortem. I have no idea why there are so many of them. I just hope the results are conclusive and that finally we are to be given some answers. I show them into the family room. They ask me to get Steve. I think nothing of it and shout for him. He is in the bath. I try conversation, asking them if they want tea or coffee, but they seem reluctant to talk. They refuse drinks. When Steve arrives, Gardiner tells us that there are abnormalities at Harry's post-mortem, which led the experts to the conclusion that he had not died of natural causes but had been unlawfully killed, and that there has been previous abuse. He cautions us and we are arrested in connection with the murder of Harry Clark.'

Steve is very angry: 'You've got to be kidding,' he says. 'Is there to be no end to this nightmare!'

Sally is calm. She assumes it is shock. Although she is tearful and very shaky she tells herself this is police routine:

'They have to do this to satisfy themselves there has been no wrongdoing. If we co-operate completely, answer their questions honestly and thoroughly and tell the truth, we have nothing to fear. I think I am more bewildered than frightened. This has to be either a huge mistake or a fact-gathering exercise. If we go along with them it will sort itself out.'

Lawyers may find it strange that two solicitors, one the daughter of a senior policeman, should be so naïve. Although I am a solicitor, before my involvement in the Sally Clark case I might have said that telling the truth was the sensible thing to do; even when arrested for murder. No longer. Not after what is to happen in this case. If anybody is arrested for anything – but, particularly, if it is for the murder of a baby – they should refuse to answer any questions without a criminal lawyer's advice. The system is skewed against the parent of a baby who dies suddenly. The state has unlimited resources and the hawks of child abuse are so adept at persuading juries to convict people of murders that may not have happened that any answer, however innocent sounding, may be interpreted as incriminating to back a murder charge. Innocence and honesty are no protection against a prosecution for murder that will almost certainly lead to a conviction, and to life imprisonment.

The only way an innocent carer can avoid saying things that may be interpreted as self-incriminating is to refuse to say anything or answer any questions until they have told the whole story to an experienced criminal law solicitor, who will then advise them what, if anything, it is safe to say. This, too, may be interpreted as evidence of guilt, but, with the greatest reluctance, I conclude that it is the lesser of the evils awaiting hapless mothers and fathers; until Sudden Infant Death cases are removed from the grip of the criminal courts altogether.

Sally rationalises the situation:

'The police officers are not frightening or intimidating. Gardiner is a bit abrupt when he cautions us but when he realises his mistake, he will feel awful about what he has done.

'I remember Dad telling me that when officers interview parents following a baby's death they should err on the side of caution, and treat the parents with sympathy and understanding because, whatever the outcome, the death of a baby is a tragedy. In contrast to Gardiner, the other officers treat both of us with respect and even give us a measure of reassurance.'

Sally is not allowed to speak to Steve again. They are escorted to separate bedrooms while they dress. Sally keeps repeating: 'You are making a terrible mistake. We have done nothing to our beloved babies.' It makes no impression. But she does everything she is told to do. Because of what her father was, Sally respects the force he served in. She knows that police officers are human; they make mistakes, but they are only doing their job.

She pleads to go in the same car as Steve. Her request is granted but they are not allowed to talk to each other. They sit, side by side, holding hands tightly. Steve tries to reassure her that it will be OK; they are just helping with inquiries, but he is ashen and very frightened.

Sally is too appalled by the sight of Steve having to turn out his pockets and hand over his belt and shoes laces to concentrate on her own fears. There are in separate cells. Sally pleads to see Steve:

'I promise not to talk to him if that's what you want. I just want to hug him and tell him I love him.

'My request is denied. I need to know how he is. They won't tell me. Surely, the reality of who we are must be obvious to all the police officers; that I am not trying to play mind games or disguise my weaknesses.'

Sally is desperate. She knows she can cope, but only if she is absolutely sure that Steve is all right. Her love for him is such that if he is hurt, she is hurting too. If she can do anything to spare him pain, she will do it, no matter the cost to her. But inside, she knows there is only so much a person can take and she is near saturation.

Is such treatment of a grieving mother and father really necessary. Police could establish, by a few phone calls, that this mother and father have no history of abuse, and that they are admired by doctors, nurses and healthcare professionals for their exceptional and loving dedication to the welfare of their babies. This is a family of lawyers, one a senior police officer's daughter, neither with a criminal record. Even in those isolated cases where somebody has smothered or shaken a baby, is it appropriate to treat grieving parents, of good character, like this.

Any lawyer in his or her right mind knows that before anybody is arrested, there must be evidence that a crime has been committed, and that no questions should be answered until full details of the allegations have been disclosed and a criminal lawyer is present to advise on what should and should not be answered.

But neither Sally nor Steve is thinking straight. They have just suffered the worst tragedy imaginable – the death of a second adored baby – and they have, for the first time in their lives, been arrested, and for murder. This has so shocked their systems that they are incapable of logical, coherent thought, or of recalling even the basics of their training as lawyers.

Sally's and Steve's behaviour has the hallmark of innocence. Their belief that their knowledge that they have not harmed their babies is their protection. It is to be much admired and it is naïve. Many non-lawyers believe that if you have committed no crime you have nothing to fear from the English criminal justice system. The adversarial system makes this the opposite of the reality. The Clarks have everything to fear from the system if they do not take the elementary precaution every lawyer knows is the suspect's only protection against being wrongly convicted: the advice of a criminal lawyer before saying anything.

Sally – unfortunately – has been taught, and believes in, the difference between right and wrong. She knows that it is wrong to tell lies. That she must always be honest and open in her dealings with everybody, especially the police.

She is the first to be interviewed. Detective Sergeant Cantello and Karen, a WPC (also the daughter of a senior police officer) ask the questions. First, they tell her that she can have a lawyer present. Sally's head rings warning bells, but her heart tells her she needs to know, more than anything else, why her babies died. If the questioning will help in this, she will co-operate. She declines the offer. She asks if Steve has called for a solicitor. They do not answer.

Sally works it out as best she can; she has nothing to hide because there is nothing to hide:

'The police cannot have any evidence to implicate me in the death of my baby, because there is nothing. I was with him virtually all his life. I know that neither I, nor anybody else, did anything to harm Harry. All I have to do is to make that plain to them, and they will not fail to see it for themselves. It must be all show, routine, going through the paces to demonstrate to their superiors that they have investigated every possibility.

'Is there a hint of surprise that I don't want the advice of a solicitor? Maybe I am mistaken. Do they think I am not taking the situation sufficiently seriously? If so, they are right. Of course, it is of the utmost importance to establish why Harry died, but the idea that either Steve or I harmed him is so misguided as to be beyond imagining. And so I chat away freely and without any inhibitions. I am not irritable, angry, obstructive. I do not employ selective memory or see reality through rose-tinted glasses. I tell it as it was. Being so open, helping police build a full picture of what life was like at Hope Cottage, in the Clark household, so that they will see the real truth and we can then work together, as a team, to find the cause of Harry's death.'

Sally is selfless. She is always preoccupied with the plight of others, never herself. She is the ideal candidate for a wrongful conviction, as naïve as a ten-year-old. And yet, with her professional hat on, advising others, she is bright and can summon legal precepts to protect her client and fight for him with all her power. But this is different. This is personal.

'A lawyer who acts for himself has a fool for a client' is never truer than where a solicitor knows – rather than having to rely on the word of a client – that she is innocent. In cases like these, there is a double bind: in most murders, it is beyond dispute that somebody has been killed. The search is for who did it. When? Where? How? Does the alibi stand up? In baby smothering or shaking allegations, nobody, except the person under arrest, even knows if a murder has been committed. Certainly nobody in the police, Crown Prosecution Service or Social Services has any means of making certain. No medical expert can possibly know, no matter how eminent, how international his reputation: unless there is a knife through the heart or other obvious death-inducing violence, all he can express is an opinion, which, however honestly held, may be completely wrong. There is no medical test which can prove that a baby has NOT been smothered.

She does not know it but Sally, by answering everything as fully and honestly as she can, is writing the prosecutor's opening speech at her trial, handing him his case against her on a plate. It is not so much what she says as the way unguarded answers may make her look guilty. Phrases may be taken out of context and seen in isolation, when they warrant full explanation. Because the system is adversarial – one side tries to win a game of complicated rules, the other tries to defeat it – it is not a search for truth.

This is not to say that the police have conspired to convict Sally of a crime they know she did not commit; it is simply the way the adversarial system has to be played, if they are to win. Surely the police must have worked out that if Sally and/or Steve had murdered the babies, they would have made a much better fist of it than this, and would never have said a word without a criminal adviser at each shoulder? Innocence and honesty are the handmaidens of miscarriages of justice.

Cantello asks her about the decision to start a family:

'Early in our marriage, Steve made it clear he wanted children, but I was less sure, one way or the other. I wanted to have some experience in my chosen career, first. Later, I began to warm to the idea, but a few more years as a lawyer seemed sensible; but my biological clock was ticking, and I did not want difficulties conceiving.

'I was overjoyed at the news. Those weeks nursing Christopher were some of the happiest; they changed my outlook on life. I admit that I was shocked at how quickly I became pregnant.'

She does not tell them that, from an early age, she had always wanted to have children, because it is not true. Instead, she tells the literal truth.

This is another gift to her prosecutor. She does not realise that this will become a picture of a woman reluctant to have babies, but who was talked into it by her husband. This admission will be interpreted as showing that Sally's pregnancy was an unnecessary interruption in the professional advancement of a career-obsessed lawyer, who resented it because it made her too tired to do her job properly and too cumbersome to portray the right corporate image to her clients. The truth is that — even though she is a lawyer — she knows nothing about the practices of criminal law; she does not know how to play the adversarial game.

Sally did complain to Steve of feeling fat and cumbersome, like a 'pregnant heffalump!' She was not always at ease with her pregnancy, did not feel comfortable in maternity wear, having been used to business suits. Yet there were more occasions when she blossomed, but she is not asked about those. She is no different from her friends who have had babies: none of them felt perfect for nine months, all had peaks and downers. She makes the mistake of accurately describing Christopher and Harry: the beautiful baby against the funny, stubby-featured one who was a bit of a clown; Harry being more demanding than her first son.

She takes them into her world: Harry, the fighter, full of spirit and with the will to live, which Christopher lacked and which might have contributed to his early death. She admits calling Harry 'the little bugger', but omits the explanation that it was a description accompanied by loving laughter. Her prosecutor, Robin Spencer QC, will make a real meal of this motive for murder. She tells police that, at times, she was lonely:

> 'Such was the length of our working day that we had little time to make local friends. Apart from next-door neighbours, Peter and Anne, our socialising was mainly with friends from London at weekends. I sometimes thought: "Here I am, in our ideal house, that I have dreamed of for so long, I should be happy. Why do I feel fed up?"'

She tells them she misses her friends down south every so often. More unguarded comments!

The reality is that when Christopher was born, everything changed. She did begin to meet more people, make more friends. She really enjoyed being a mum. Every day she felt more settled and pleased that they were building a new life in Wilmslow.

> 'When Steve played hockey on Saturday afternoons, I felt lonely, but did not resent him doing it; I encouraged it. I admit that Steve's injury meant that I had the additional burden of looking after him and that was hard work at times, but I had Lesley Kerrigan to do the household chores and Steve being at home, even on crutches, meant he could spend time looking after Harry. That was not a problem, it was a bonus.'

These admissions will be interpreted as those of a harassed mother, pushed over the edge of her ability to cope and murdering her baby as the only way out.

The interview lasts about an hour and a half. The officers are friendly, the atmosphere is relaxed. It does not feel like an official police interview, more like a mutual fact-gathering exercise. They put Sally at her ease. She talks freely. Even when they ask her about the 'injuries' found at Harry's post-mortem, the alarm bells do not ring. She knows that nobody injured him and therefore the injuries cannot exist; somebody must have made a big mistake, which will surely rectify itself on close examination.

The urge to co-operate with authority is compelling: it is irresistible to most ordinary people.It goes against every instinct to prevaricate, to refuse to answer questions. If a suspect has nothing to fear – as she perceives it – asking for a solicitor is as good as an admission of guilt.

Steve is just as bad. He too, has been brought up to respect the law and the police. His parents have taught him and his brother that if they have done nothing wrong, they have nothing to fear from British justice. He, too, is in a state of shock. He, too, has just suffered the death of his second baby son. He has not harmed either child, nor has his wife, yet both are arrested.

They ask Steve if he would like a solicitor present. What does he need a lawyer for? He *is* a lawyer. He has done nothing wrong! If he answers everything, is as open and honest as he can be, they will soon see his innocence and Sally's shining through.

Sally is taken to the holding cell at the local police station:

> 'I sit, staring into space, crying for my little boys, unable to comprehend what is going on. I long to be with Steve when they interview him, not to interrupt, just to give him a hug. After about three hours – which seems more like a week – the police tell me that they have searched Hope Cottage.
> 'Now they will be able to see how much we loved our little boys and what a nice home we had built for them.'

Sally is interviewed again to 'clarify' matters that had come up while talking to Steve.

They ask her to outline the CONI scheme, which she does. They tell her they have found evidence that she was a patient at a clinic and ask her about her alcohol problem, the extent of it and her treatment. Again, no legal alarms ring. She tells them everything.

At 4.30 p.m. she is told she can see Steve; that they are free to go home, released on police bail, but must report to the police station again in two months' time. In her relief at seeing Steve and being able to hold him again, it does not register that they are still under suspicion of killing Harry. Cantello takes them home in his car. Sally is conversational:

'You're not really going to pursue this, are you? We don't need to get ourselves a lawyer?'

He says: 'I should, if I were you.'

Even at this, Sally assumes that he is simply doing his job; it is all a mistake that will pass. Steve is angrier than Sally. Both are in deep shock. Their two baby sons have died. To be accused of killing Harry takes them far beyond shock. It cannot be the real world – it must be a nightmare. They will wake up.

The accusation of murder, against mother and father, urges each of them to think questions of the other. The need does not lessen because each knows he or she is innocent. Sally is the more introspective of the two and her first question is: 'Did Steve kill Harry?'

He could not have done so. She would have seen him do so.

'Is even that thought disloyal to the man I love?'

Lawyers do not think like ordinary people, who might say: 'I know him/her. He/she couldn't have done it.' The legal mind asks the questions they would ask of clients. Trained not to make assumptions, each of them examines the questions carefully. The law is finally of some use to them. They know that if their marriage is to survive what may now come, not only will they have to be exceptionally strong, but each will have to be absolutely certain of the other. They do not ask the questions aloud.

Sally asks herself, 'Is our marriage as perfect as our friends keep telling us?'

'Some say we are the ideal couple. We are not starry-eyed or particularly demonstrative, but our love and commitment is obvious to outsiders. Is it true behind closed doors? We are both independent; neither follows the other with puppy-dog adoration. It is a healthy relationship, built on friendship and respect. We each have strengths and weaknesses. We are two equals, a marriage of two wholes, not two halves. Neither uses the marriage as a prop. Each of us can function well without the marriage, but when we combine, our strength is greater than the sum of the parts. Never has our love and commitment been so tested as following the deaths of two babies, and our arrest for murder. The relationship seems to thrive and get stronger as each new blow hits us. Is that what love is?'

In Sally's eyes, Steve does have one major fault:

'He will not argue. He considers shouting and screaming a waste of energy. I think a good argument clears the air. Steve's answer is to laugh it off, which either defuses the situation or makes it worse, because I am not being taken seriously. All the vases at Hope Cottage are intact and the doors still on their hinges. Boring, but true. Steve is calm, easygoing and even tempered, except when behind the wheel of a car, when he becomes a born-again boy racer. He has a firm opinion about most things but rarely voices it in public. But watching television – sport or politics – he rages and rants. He is reserved but full of inner confidence.

'What some women might find tedious – his quiet, contemplative nature – I find endearing. When we first met, he seemed cold, unemotional, uncomfortable expressing feelings, even to me. He is patient, but not like me. I am one of life's sulkers. I will sulk for hours. I hate to let an issue drop until it is resolved, and to my satisfaction. I don't like losing or being proved wrong. I am also a stomper and flouncer – the adult equivalent of stamping my fist and tossing my ponytail as a schoolgirl.

'As an only child, I was spoilt: not with money because police pay was poor when I was growing up, but Mum and Dad gave me everything I needed, including a firm sense of right and wrong. They taught me to appreciate what I had. I know how lucky I was – compared to some – to be so loved and cherished. Steve was the first man who stood up to me. Previous boyfriends let me control the relationship. Steve never does that. Neither of us is in charge. It is a partnership. Until I met Steve, I would not back down. My love for him has taught me to compromise.

'Looking back, I am surprised that Steve wanted to marry me. The first two years were difficult because I was hurting so much over Mum's illness and death. When we were first dating, I put on an act, pushed my troubles to the rear of my mind and did not allow him too close to me. But Mum's illness soon made him an integral part of the family and I came to lean on him for support and comfort. I was not easy to live with. I was hurting and needed to take it out on somebody: him.

'When Mum died, the problem became Dad, and how he would cope. He became the child. I was his guide. Roles reversed. I found it hard. I was angry at life. Why me? Why Mum? What had we done to deserve such misery! It was almost as if I wanted to drive Steve away – so that he could be free of my moods and get on with his own life. I didn't want his pity, and I didn't want him to see me so continually upset. A lesser man would have walked. I guess he loved me.'

There were arguments in the early years, over Steve's working hours:

> 'I worked regular hours at the bank and did not understand the urgency
> of high-priced deal-based legal work, where the solicitors work round
> the clock. The deal may depend on it, particularly if their client is in
> competition with other bidders. As a junior partner, Steve had not only
> to do his work for the client, he also had to impress the senior partners
> that he was worthy of promotion, of being allowed to acquire equity in
> the firm, a share in its profits.'

When Sally qualifies as a solicitor she soon realises that the reason for the
very high salaries are those very demanding conditions.

When Steve and Sally are released, Sally cannot get out of the place fast
enough. Her first thought, on opening the door of Hope Cottage, is the
cats: 'Strangers have been in their house. Are they all right?' They are.
Next, she looks to see what sort of a mess the police have made of her
meticulously kept home. It could be worse. She expects to feel alienated
and dirty, but there is relief to be at home and together. Tears do not
flow. That, alone, is a surprise to Sally, but the safety of their own four
walls outweighs other emotions and gives them strength and a sense of
security:

> 'We do not spend hours discussing what has just happened, certain the
> police will take the case no further. The officers must know, by now,
> that nothing sinister occurred. But a brief chat with a criminal lawyer
> makes sense, just in case anything further develops.'

Mackey 1998

The Clarks realise they do not know any criminal solicitor. Steve calls his
boss, Tony Kirby, who knows everybody in the Manchester legal circuit;
he tells them that Mike Mackey, of Burton Copeland, is probably the best
criminal lawyer outside London.

They tell nobody else. They do not want to alarm friends and relatives
unnecessarily.

Sally and Steve have an appointment at Mackey's office in Deansgate.

'We enter a smoke-filled office, piled high with "paper in distress".
Sitting at the corner desk is Mike Mackey, surrounded by ashtrays
bulging with dog-ends. My first impression is organised chaos! He is
wearing a boldly striped suit and his sparse black hair is slicked back. He
has a deep, throaty voice with a slight northern drawl; there is a strong
aroma of expensive aftershave. He has a distinct twinkle in his eye, the
look of a salesman. As I sit – on the other side of the desk for a change –
I realise that I have never met a solicitor who just does crime. If he is from
the mould, they are quite different from corporate lawyers; more cynical.
I wonder if a hard crust is necessary to deal with all those professional
villains. Do you have to have a criminal mind to be able to act for them?
I remember, from law school days, that those who were clever wanted a
place in a private criminal practice, and those who weren't so bright
knew their only hope would be the Crown Prosecution Service.'

*A couple of years before the Crown Prosecution Service was brought into existence,
during research for a television series I was involved in, I met lawyers setting it up.
They told me their biggest problem was persuading the Civil Service to pay enough
to attract the best solicitors and barristers; if the scale was set where it needed to be,
thousands of civil servants would have to have a huge pay hike. The bureaucrats
won the argument.*

Mackey gives Sally the impression of a rough diamond:

'But I soon warm to this man. I know, instinctively, that here is
somebody I can trust; if necessary, put my life in his hands. Yes . . . I am
comfortable with that thought. But it won't come to that.'

Mackey recognises the need for confidentiality. News of this must not get
out. It could do both their careers immense harm. Steve does most of the
briefing. Mike is astonished that two lawyers could have opened their
hearts and minds to police without a criminal lawyer present, having been
arrested for murder! Sally feels like a naughty schoolgirl reprimanded by
the headmaster: 'How can they use anything against us, when everything
we told them was the truth?' she asks.

His wry smile is discomfiting.

They spend a couple of hours with Mackey and promise that they will
have no more conversations with police or anybody else unless he is there.

The next problem is that they have booked a week in the Canary Islands. Aware that they are both at breaking point emotionally, they feel they need to get away from Wilmslow and Hope Cottage, in order to think through everything that has happened to them. Mackey persuades the police to vary the bail conditions. They fly away.

It is not an enjoyable holiday:

'We talk continually about what this means for hopes of having a family. Should we take tests, in case it is something genetic? Is there any treatment we could have? If those answers are no, how about adoption? We draw strength from our love for each other. We are a team; for better or worse. We will not let this – whatever it is – defeat us. Together we know we are invincible. I feel the bereavements intensely. I am at such low ebb, I wonder if it will threaten our sanity.

'Throughout the time on Gran Canaria, my hand is constantly in Steve's. We are lost souls. We watch others and envy them their obvious happiness. Christopher would have been a toddler by now, and Harry a babe-in-arms.'

They return rested, having slept properly for the first time since Harry's death. Physically they are in better shape and have a new reservoir of stamina for the weeks ahead. Emotionally, it is another matter; at best, a plaster on a bleeding wound where the healing process has not begun.

But they are still on bail. Slowly it dawns on them that this is not just an investigation; police actually suspect they have harmed the babies. Sally's anger builds:

'Are they keeping us dangling, hoping that one will crack and accuse the other of doing something?' Sally continues reporting to Wilmslow police station. Nothing happens except that, on one occasion, they question her about the death of Christopher. Mackey asks them for the evidence which triggered the necessity for further questioning. They produce new medical reports.

'We have had no prior warning of these and no idea what they mean,' says Mackey. 'Without the opportunity to ask our own experts about them, I advise my client to say "no comment" to every question.'

It is a typical police ambush. Knowing more than the suspect, police can sometimes get damaging admissions – the truth as they see it – not through evasion, but through ignorance of the significance of what is being alleged. It is very different from Sally's previous interviews, and the police are not happy.

The guidelines for officers interviewing suspects created as a result of a Police Research Award Scheme Grant say:

'The point of initial statements is to lock the suspect into explanations that can easily be rebutted at a later stage.'

Sally feels badly about evading questions she sees as harmless, which is exactly what police intended. Mackey is unrepentant.

Sally gets the impression that the police investigation is leading nowhere. As they leave, Mackey tells her he is reasonably certain they will drop the charge in respect of Christopher.

Gradually Sally realises that they are both so consumed with trying to prove that they were good and loving parents to both of their babies that they have lost sight of their main objective – to find out why Christopher and Harry died:

'We are given a number of medical reports. Merely understanding them is daunting. We have to read each sentence over and over, before making any sense. We have to look up strange medical jargon. Our eagerness to understand what we are up against is in danger of laying us open to criticism that we are fighting as lawyers, not as parents. The vulnerability and unpredictability of our situation occupies an increasing amount of our time, preventing us mourning the loss of Christopher and Harry.'

For Sally and Steve, the emphasis has now shifted: from trying to find out why their babies died, to the adversarial situation – adopting a fighting spirit, determined to prove the truth, that neither baby had been deliberately harmed.

Sally writes:

'I am repeatedly called back to Wilmslow police station, only to be bailed again while the police carry out further investigations. We are so preoccupied with proving we didn't harm them that we seem to have no time to pursue the search for what *did* kill them. We thought they knew what had happened to Christopher, but now Harry has died we push hard for an investigation of the genetics. We become embroiled in the medical reports.

'But I am troubled by the thought that our friends might think we have forgotten our grief and are more interested in the medical technicalities. The truth is that the constant pressure of the police investigation hanging over us means we are fighting for our survival. We are grieving parents, who have done nothing but love our babies, being subjected to inhuman treatment. Have the police not interviewed all the healthcare professionals who looked after the family during each baby's short life? Do they not know that, after Harry's birth there were random visits by CONI nurses, who would have known, in an instant, if either of us was harming him?'

Do they think that husband and father, Steve, would so strongly and consistently aid and protect a woman who murdered his sons? If he had the slightest suspicion that she killed his baby, would any father be so supportive? Do they believe that a former Chief of Police would so staunchly back his daughter if she had murdered his grandsons?

Mackey telephones Steve. The case against him is closed. There is no need for him to report to Wilmslow police station. But there is bad news. He goes home early to tell Sally that she, alone, will stand trial for the murder of Christopher and Harry:

'It should be like a bolt from a blue sky, but that is not my reaction. There have been months of scrutiny, strain and pressure. I find myself incredulous and bewildered, but strangely calm, almost apathetic. I still believe that under English law, if you have done nothing wrong, you have nothing to fear. So my feeling is that this is just another – inevitable, it seems – stage in the judicial process, before I am exonerated. It does not occur to me that my future freedom may be in doubt. I am innocent and I believe in the system.'

Steve drives her to the police station. He can hardly contain his anger:

'Our lawyers have advised that there was no prospect of success in bringing a case; it would not happen. How could they have got it so wrong! What is going on?

'I feel impotent. I am completely out of any comfort zone. What is a husband supposed to do! I thought we were meant to protect out wives. How can I protect Sally; from the system? From being abused by the law of the land? It is as if Sally has been kidnapped – by the law – and I have been publicly castrated.'

Sally does not want a scene; she persuades him to stay in the car. Mackey is waiting for her. Detective Inspector Gardiner reads the charge that she murdered Christopher Clark and Harry Clark and asks if she has anything to say.

Sally tries her damndest to maintain her dignity and composure. She will not allow these officers to see how much they are hurting her. But she breaks down in tears: 'Why are you doing this to me? I loved my two little boys with all my heart, I did nothing to harm either of them.'

There is something Steve can do: he will redouble his efforts and find out what killed his sons.

The bail conditions are that she surrender her passport and continue to live at Hope Cottage and must sign on at the police station three times a week. Steve and Sally still tell nobody, so certain are they that, at the next judicial stage, this terrible mistake will be put right. Incredibly, these two talented and highly paid lawyers still believe that innocence and the truth will protect them.

Tom

Sally has strong views on certain aspects of marriage:

'There is no excuse for an unwanted pregnancy. Nobody should be in ignorance of contraception or how to obtain it.

'It is therefore a bit of a shock to find that I am unintentionally pregnant. The health visitor says that my biological system has not righted itself following the two months during which I breast-fed Harry. It is common for women to be "caught out" when breast-feeding.

'Unplanned but not unwanted, it is a sure sign that we were intended to be a family, after all. While on our break in Gran Canaria, I ate

healthily and worked-out hard, as part of the healing process, but also
to get my body back into shape. I wondered, at the time, why so much
dieting and so many sit-ups did not give me a flat tummy; why I could
not reach my target weight or size. I would like to feel thrilled, but
stunned is more like it. On police bail, in the middle of a murder
investigation, the future unreadable, it is not the ideal situation in
which to be expecting a third child. Then there is the dark cloud of daily
fear that a genetic fault will make this baby unhealthy, that it will have
a deficient immune system.

'Do we go ahead with it, disregarding the warning signs that had
gone before? Or do I have an abortion?

'But, surely, Christopher died of a lung infection, and the best guess,
on Harry, is an overreaction to vaccination? Is it right to forgo future
happiness, in a proper family, because of the possibility that there is a
genetic problem?'

It sounds hard and clinical and maybe it is, but these two lawyers are
trained to analyse complex situations and advise others. And that is what
they are doing:

'We don't know what to think; what to feel. If we could set up an ever
more elaborate support network this time, maybe we could go ahead
and prevent a third tragedy. Once over the initial shock, we decide we
must not get too excited. We will take one day at a time.'

They go to see Mackey:

'He is unreadable, when we tell him. His congratulations are immediate
but what is he thinking? Bad timing? Couldn't be worse! Irresponsible,
he probably thinks, but he is our lawyer first, and as such must set the
emotion on one side. Yet he must know, from all our conversations, how
desperate we are to have a family.'

Mackey is concerned with the legal situation. What he wonders about, but
only tells them later, is what effect this news will have on the Crown
Prosecution Service. They have discretion as to whether to launch a
prosecution or not. If they do nothing and Sally's third child dies, there may
be trouble; the CPS may be blamed for its death. If the murder charges *are*

followed through, the new baby will be taken away from Sally. That lets the CPS off the hook. They may be wondering if Sally Clark deliberately engineered her pregnancy as an attempt to curry compassion, make the police take pity on them; to ward off a prosecution for two murders. Mackey believes it will be a factor in making the CPS go ahead with a trial.

Sally has only one real anxiety:

'That others will mistake my strength in going ahead with having the baby, for hardness, when inside I am crying all the time, from the hurt, the fear, the shocks. I love my job, but I want a baby to make my life complete. We decide a break with tradition is necessary, to do everything differently. Macclesfield Hospital is nearer and – given the speed of previous labours – time is likely to be "of the essence", as we lawyers are fond of saying. The midwives we know at Wilmslow Health Centre report to Macclesfield. It is sensible to choose professionals we trust and who know our circumstances.

'I opt for the Domino scheme, where the mother is assigned to a particular midwife, who deals with everything, including the ultimate delivery. Her name is Jo. She is, very simply, a saint. She and her colleagues are told everything and are supportive, compassionate and incredulous that I could even be suspected of harming my babies. They are not blinkered or swayed by the emotion of pity or friendship: their reaction is a professional assessment. My assessment of them is that they cannot be bluffed or conned. I trust them.

'The culmination of the various stresses makes me tire easily, but my blood pressure is normal. We decide against amniocentesis. I want a boy, not as a replacement, but as a brother for Christopher and Harry. It is unlikely because there are so few males in my family history. We try to preserve some sort of normality for the health of the new baby. But the reality is a nightmare.'

The pregnancy means the intervention of the Local Authority Social Services Department and the Family Division of the High Court. The safety of the newborn baby is the main focus. Steve and Sally know that such fears are groundless, but nobody in authority can afford to believe them. So they will have to fight, as never before in their lives, to clear their names and for the right to bring up their own baby.

Steve makes the first move, with Social Services. He wants to prevent the baby being taken away the moment he is born. Mike Mackey introduces them to Iain Hamilton, a family law solicitor, with Jones, Maidment, Wilson in Manchester. Hamilton arranges a meeting with representatives of Social Services, the Police Child Protection Unit and solicitors representing the Local Authority, Steve and Sally, midwives and health visitors. None of them has experience of quite such a situation, particularly Sally: 'We have thought this through carefully, and have devised our own agenda. We know it may look calculating and, maybe, even cold, but the future of our child is at stake.'

Sally and Steve are not typical Social Services customers. There is a sense of unreality; they do not look like baby-killers. There is a feeling that this is only precautionary; that something will happen to make it all go away.

They are assigned their own social worker, Jan Ash, who interviews each of them at length and separately:

'She is sensitive and compassionate throughout, the consummate professional. If there is anything she can do, within the rules, to make my life more bearable, I have the feeling she will do it. We welcome her into our home and see a great deal of her during the coming months but she cannot become a friend; she keeps her professional edge. I respect her for that.

'The first rule is that I must never be alone with the new baby. All contact will have to be supervised by nursing staff. He will be in the Special Care Baby Unit (SCBU), whose doctors and staff will be told everything but keep high levels of confidentiality. To the others in the maternity ward, we will appear to be a normal family. I will remain in hospital for ten days, after which the baby will "be taken to stay with a foster family".'

To 'stay with', rather than be 'taken into foster care' affirms the temporary nature of the arrangement, for Sally:

'I find it difficult to put into words the brutality, the cruelty and the unfairness to which we are now subjected by the system. The unbearable grief of two babies dying is compounded by the shaming indictment that I murdered them. But we have no option but to deal with it. If we fight the system, it will simply put both of us under additional pressure and alienate people who are only doing their jobs – it will only make things worse. But we will not roll over and give in without making our hurt and anger plain. We still hold on hard to the belief that it will soon end.

'Iain Hamilton tells us that we are lucky – yes, lucky – to be allowed two hours a day with our baby. It is far in excess of anything usually on offer when a baby is in foster care. I do not believe that these concessions are because of who we are, as much as the disbelief, of all with whom we have contact, that I have murdered my first two babies.'

Foster parents are special people. Regular heartache is part of the territory. Children who go to them are often emotionally or psychologically scarred; they need love, attention and support. The foster parents have to be party to the turbulent relationship between parents and Social Services. The Clark family presents unusual difficulties. The chosen foster family must be able to cope with the tragedy of the previous deaths, and the upcoming criminal trial, and both parents visiting for two hours every day; and they must supervise contact when a social worker is not available.

The situation becomes ever more bizarre with the passage of time. The people around them are bound to get to know Sally and Steve – and may even like them. They will see who these two people are, what they are made of, their natures, their characters. They will have to assume that one of them – if not both – is a murderer even if their instincts tell them that is impossible.

Sally is determined not to like the foster mother, Linda (not her real name):

'I prepare my emotions for the first meeting with the chosen foster mother, confident that I have my anger in check and that I will not be rude to her face, but I know that I will not be able to disguise the bitter resentment at the intrusion into our family. To my amazement, I find it impossible not to like Linda and her family. Even more astonishing is the fact that she is obviously not "the enemy". Linda makes it plain that, although she has duties to Social Services, and to the parents, her primary responsibility is to the baby. And that disarms me.

'Linda's four-bedroom detached house, in a suburb of Stockport, has a warm feel. She has a lovely husband and family. It is a 20-minute drive from Hope Cottage. The baby's abode-to-be is littered with pictures of former foster children. My son will be Linda's 82nd foster child.'

The 29th of November 1998 would have been Harry's first birthday. It is also the day when Sally is due to give birth to her third child. She sees it as a bad omen:

'In the week leading to that day, I am restless, apprehensive, in dread, but I keep those feelings to myself. The speed of my previous deliveries, with so little pain or discomfort, is at the back of my mind. Doctors and nurses are on stand-by. We work hard on Social Services, to make sure that the Child Protection Unit does not turn up, heavy-handed, to snatch the baby the moment he is born. I have heard frightening stories about that happening. My concerns about the anniversary induce an early labour – at least that is what I feel.'

Early on the Saturday evening, Sally calls Jo, who comes over immediately. Labour is not imminent. She should have a long, hot bath and some sleep. Jo will be on call all weekend and can be at the hospital within minutes:

'*Match of the Day*, on BBC1, is the trigger, yet again, when my waters break in spectacular fashion. It frightens both of us. I still feel no pain as we drive to Macclesfield. Neither of us speaks on the journey. Our minds are awash with emotions, memories and foreboding. But thoughts of Christopher and Harry have now to take second place to the task before me.'

Early labour is confirmed, in a ward so busy that some mothers are in side wards. Steve and Sally have a cubicle to themselves. Sally is relieved to see that nobody knows that they are a special case. Birth is some hours away. Sally sleeps on the bed, Steve on a mattress on the floor. Jo goes home. At 5.30 a.m. the contractions awaken Sally suddenly, with no build-up. Pain, strong and sharp. Jo is summoned. Sally is taken to Delivery. She has developed a special rapport with Jo:

'This labour seems much more controlled, more intimate and more natural. It still hurts, but I can cope, with gas and air. I know I will remember much more this time.'

Her third son is born at 7 a.m. The time is marked by a television set in the corner of the room, which is repeating the previous evening's *Match of the Day*. Recognition is immediate for Sally:

'He is exactly like my Dad. It's the ears!'

The baby cannot be named here, for legal reasons. A High Court injunction prevents him or his whereabouts being identified. We will call him Tom. That is not his real name.

They give Tom a second Christian name, in tribute to their midwife. Their little boy is healthy and beautiful:

> 'He does not have the pale serenity of Christopher or the funny podgy features of Harry; he is our Tom, perfect in every way and gorgeous.
>
> 'For ten minutes, we are left alone. No doctor, no nurse, no social worker, no midwife. Steve and Tom and me. For ten precious minutes there are just the three of us. Whether by design or mistake, those ten minutes give us the illusion that we are a normal loving family, enjoying the ineffable joy of having brought a new life into the world, into the world of our family.'

Never have three people so needed a break – even one as short as ten minutes: 600 seconds out of a lifetime.

> 'Then he is taken away from me. The precious, perfect baby I have borne for nine months and felt the same all-consuming love for the moment he came into this world is taken from my arms – his loving mother's arms – and placed in a Special Baby Care Unit [SCBU]. I am not allowed to see him unsupervised. I stay in a separate room. I have to be watched as I feed him at my breast. I am watched while I change his nappy, while I do anything my baby wants or needs. It is more than distressing, it is an unbearable pain at the core of my being.'

They do not know it, but their future holds, not hope but years of forced separation, shame, fear, mental torture, near-bankruptcy and degradation. Sally Clark, née Lockyer, is, as a solicitor, an officer of the Supreme Court of Judicature of England and Wales, an unlikely candidate to be a serial baby killer. There can be no quarrel with those who prosecute, perhaps even enthusiastically, when the evidence warrants it. But what happens when the most important evidence – from the health care professionals who know nor trust – points to innocence?

If a mother murders her sons, most normal husbands or partners would condemn the killer, as would other close relatives: the health professionals, midwives, practice nurses, doctors and paediatricians. And yet all those potential witnesses speak of Sally's loving care of both babies. Why were, and are, speculative theories preferred to the expertise of those in closest contact with the so-called perpetrators?

Accusing second 'cot death' mothers of killing their babies has become much more frequent in the last few years. The nature of the charge and the state of ignorance about what causes cot deaths means the burden of proof has been allowed to shift.

If a mother is put in the dock and a credible doctor says that in his opinion, the deaths are not natural, juries look to the mother to explain how her babies died. Why babies suddenly stop breathing and die – cot deaths – has defeated the best brains in medical science for over two thousand years. No mother can solve what has defeated so many scientists. It is not surprising that so many juries, in the UK and abroad, convict. These experts and the prosecutors who believe them and present them to juries, bear the responsibility.

Sally knows that in ten days' time she will lose Tom:

'Nothing can stop that. It is not right. It is not justified by the true facts. But nothing can stop it happening. But, also, nothing can stop me making the most of these ten days. I set about laying the foundations of a close and loving bond with Tom. He will not remember his time in hospital, but that does not matter; during the next ten days I will make quite sure he always knows me as his mum.

'If I had to paint a picture of angels, I would think first of the nurses in the SCBU. Their good nature, resilience in the face of pressure and compassion know no bounds. Most of their charges are in incubators – premature, tiny, one-of-twins, unwell or born with deformity. The nurses attend their every need with a level of care and diligence I have never witnessed before. It is clearly a vocation. The money is poor, the working conditions – long hours and the pressure – beyond reason.

'I sit among these "angels" with trepidation. Surely they must feel revulsion at what I am accused of doing. If so, they hide it well and treat me with the same consideration and compassion every parent receives. I am assigned one special nurse, Sue, who supervises what goes on between me and my baby son. Tom weighs in at 6 lb. 15 oz. – about average – and yet he is huge: very active, hungry and rosy-cheeked, compared to other babies in SCBU. I soon establish a firm breast-feeding routine. I sleep in the room next to SCBU and a nurse wakes me every four hours in the night. Every time I am with Tom, Sue is there, supervising. I make a conscious decision not to dwell on the injustice, the hurt, the anger at the way the system is treating us. I put it out of mind, for Tom's sake, and for our own sanity. Sue, for her part, makes a good fist of being an unobtrusive part of the family.'

In view of what had happened to the first babies, the hospital now takes special measures to avoid another cot death. Tom is fitted with a new and more elaborate apnoea alarm. It measures his heart rate, and oxygen saturation levels, as well as his breathing pattern. It has a time-recording device, so that Dr Spillman – the doctor who also cared for Harry – can download what happens every minute in Tom's life. To Sally's consternation, the apnoea alarm goes off. But Tom is fine. After that, it sounds frequently, often when she is breast-feeding him. Once, he even turns slightly blue. But she is assured that that is normal. At one stage, Dr Spillman becomes concerned at Tom's oxygen levels, but concludes that this is the baby adjusting to being out of the womb.

'Most babies are not connected to these alarms,' he says: 'so doctors don't know what to expect, in the first few days of life.'

Sally and Steve trust Dr Spillman, but are still unnerved by what is happening. Steve is there every day. Their special time is when, together, they bathe Tom.

Steve arrives with a present – for Sally:

'I open the small box to reveal a beautiful sapphire eternity ring. There was no time, in the short lives of Christopher and Harry, for Steve to buy me one. This is Tom's seal – the seal of his life: this time, our son will survive.'

Nurse Sue is remarkable in her sensitivity towards Sally and Steve and their relationship with Tom. She makes it clear that, having got to know them, she finds it difficult to believe Sally could have harmed any baby. Sue is special in another sense: she spends all her spare cash on orphans in Romania, and her holidays there, looking after them.

The day of leaving hospital and parting with Tom arrives:

'I try to order my thoughts, my fears, and my consternation. I thought I would never love anybody as I loved Christopher. That first night, when I was alone with him in hospital, and later, at home, breast-feeding him in the rocking chair, I felt complete devotion and the closest of bonds; I would have done anything to protect him and keep him safe. The day I first fed Tom and the last time, now, in hospital, as I put him to my breast, there is the same strength of feeling, except that this time, unbelievably, the feeling that he belongs to me is even stronger, it has a searing edge. And nobody can take that away from me – whatever they may do to me. He is a gift and a treasure. I will fight for him, in any and every way, until my last breath. I did not know such love could exist.

'The prospect of parting from him is heartbreaking; there is a tearing pain, sickness, emptiness. The SCBU nurses watch with concern. There are no words of comfort they can offer; no language for what I feel. I lovingly pack every item of his clothes, every toy, in his little bag. I lay Tom down in his cot and kiss him on the forehead. I gratefully thank each nurse in turn, pausing to give an encouraging smile to Linda and Jan.

'I save the tears for the car journey home, a place I do not want to go. It is not a home without Tom.

'Why is it called Hope Cottage? My life is empty and flat.'

A foster parent is used to children who are mainly kept away from their real parents. To have Sally and Steve, who not only visit for two hours every day, but also so obviously love and care for their baby, want only what is best for him and are also sensitive to the inconvenience they are causing the carer, is unsettling for Linda. They want to be involved in every aspect of his development. She adapts to this situation quickly and caringly. She takes photographs at every significant moment, so that the family album will not have gaps. She telephones Sally when Tom gives his first smile, when he turns himself from his back to his front for the first time. When he first crawls, she also calls. Sally picks the phone up at the first ring:

'The best thing about Linda is that she is not the police, not the Crown Prosecution Service, not Social Services. We now see her as our caretaker for Tom, until he will be returned to his proper home. We do not hate or resent her. We need her. Do we envy her? Of course, but that is a negative thought – not good for Tom. I put it aside.'

The Family Division of the High Court is there to investigate the circumstances of the deaths of Christopher and Harry, in order to decide who will bring up Tom. It does so in secret – in camera – to protect the child. There will be a hearing to determine how the babies died and another to decide who gets custody of Tom.

The prime, but not the only, consideration of the Family Court is the welfare of any children, and the standard of proof is the balance of probabilities. If a credible expert says a subsequent baby has probably been smothered – and no scientific test can prove that a baby has NOT been smothered – what can the judge do, except take any other children away from a suspected mother? There are not many child abuse experts, so the same few appear regularly before the same judges and are, understandably, considered reliable. There are no 'doves' of child abuse; how could any doctor become an expert in children not being abused? The culture, in medicine, of one doctor not criticising another, or blowing whistles, means that flawed theories of abuse are unlikely to be challenged and the judge may have no means of knowing.

The secrecy of the Family Court is absolute – newspaper editors who publish facts covered by an injunction face jail for contempt of court. Family Court miscarriages of justice could go undiscovered and continue indefinitely. I am not the only lawyer who believes that dozens, maybe hundreds, of such miscarriages exist.

A criminal trial is a serious game, to find out which side can win at least ten votes from the jury of twelve, randomly selected people, whose only qualification is that they have been breathing for more than eighteen years. At Sally's trial, each 'team' will call experts, who will be in competition to persuade the jury, first, if any of the medical findings, at post-mortem, are real or imaginary, and, if they exist, what they signify. These jurymen and women have no medical qualification, yet they have to establish the cause of death of Christopher and Harry Clark.

Only if they conclude that the babies' deaths were not due to natural causes, or accident, and that they were murdered, can they then go on to decide if the person in the dock killed them, and if it was murder or manslaughter or infanticide.

In the Family Court, where Tom's custody is decided, the intended aim is to get at the truth. Although the system still has to be adversarial, every effort is made to eliminate adversarial tactics in favour of openness and complete frankness – no secrets about what is going on, even between the family and their solicitors. The Local Authority brings the case for Social Services, which is the applicant. The parents are the respondents. Sally and Steve are assured that their opponents are not in cahoots with the CPS. But

Their first priority is to succeed in the Family Court in getting custody of their own son. That means being open and honest and not creating a climate of distrust and secrecy.

Jan, their social worker, asks searching questions about what happened the night each baby died. How did Harry get a dislocated rib? They do not know. They did nothing to cause such an injury, but pathologist Williams said he felt it – it did not show up on X-ray. Other experts say it does not exist and no healthcare professionals noticed Harry in pain when he was picked up.

Sally and Steve are advised that each must have a separate lawyer in the Family Court. Only Sally is charged with murder. Steve is not charged with anything. Sally cannot be awarded custody unless she is cleared of murder. Steve is not disqualified from custody unless the judge comes to the conclusion that he aided and abetted the babies' murders or turned a blind eye to Sally doing it. This could easily drive a wedge into their relationship, but both are aware of that danger.

The rules of disclosure in the Family Court are strict. Anything they say or write – even to their lawyers – may have to be disclosed to the judge. The danger is that they love each other so much, and this is so obvious, that the judge might think either would say anything to protect the other. Steve is asked many times if he has considered the possibility that Sally harmed his sons. He always answers 'Yes'. He reasons that if he answers no, he may appear to be a 'lapdog', afraid to seem disloyal. Instead he tells the truth: that he has thought about it very carefully. He has known Sally for many years. He has been by her side, in good times and the very worst. He knows her better than anybody else alive. He knows she could not have done such things.

He has to be equally honest about alcohol. He has to persuade Social Services and the judge that if he sees any sign of a danger to Tom, caused by Sally's drinking, he will say so immediately.

Sally and Steve try hard to make Social Services believe the truth: that they genuinely want only what is best for Tom. They see it as essential that Social Services understands that. They seem to make progress until the social workers talk to their lawyers. After every such meeting, they come back more defensive and cautious, their attitudes hardened. Linda comments on it. Sally and Steve resent it.

People ask Sally how she can cope with seeing Tom so rarely:

'It tears me apart every time I have to say goodbye, but because I am innocent, I know it is only a matter of time before we are a family again, and meanwhile, it is preferable to what happened to his two brothers.'

Sally buys all Tom's clothes for him and takes them to Linda. That is a first for her. Foster children often come with nothing and have to be kitted out at Local Authority expense. Sally and Linda share a delight in designer baby outfits. They squeal with pleasure when they dress him in something new. Sally does all Tom's laundry: another first for Linda.

'I want to breast-feed him as long as possible – it's another link. I express milk for feeds when I am not there. The hospital provides a big pump-action expressing machine. I feel like a cow at milking time. Doing it every four hours is exhausting and emotional, because it reinforces the separation and my feelings of emptiness. I cry a lot. Once expressed, it is put into sterilised bottles, labelled, dated and frozen. Our freezer is given over to this one task.

'Christmas 1998 is difficult. I set so much childlike store by it, as did my mum. This time it will be without Tom, because I cannot expect Linda to give up her own big day to us. Steve and I spend a long Christmas Eve with Tom. We open dozens of presents from family and friends. And Linda spoils Tom like he was one of her own.

'We are back on Boxing Day with more presents. I want to scream at Social Services, at the injustice of this torture of an innocent mum. What makes it suddenly bearable is that Linda has shot a long video of Tom's Christmas Day. We will always have that.'

Comes the spring of 1999, and thoughts of a christening. It will not be the same. They will not be in control – others will. But Social Services and Linda are considerate, which emphasises the hurt and frustration Sally feels, because of the limitations that will be imposed. They choose the same godparents: not strange to Sally and Steve, for these are their closest friends, whom they trust to keep a watchful eye on Tom. Steve Collis is still the vicar and understands the need for the ceremony to be low key and discreet. The local and national press are beginning to take an interest. They do not want a bunch of journalists with flashbulbs at the church.

It is a small gathering: Sally, Steve and Tom with Linda and Jan and three of the four godparents, Andy, Alison and Chris and Chris's wife, standing in for the absent Fiona, who had just given birth herself. Sally proudly holds Tom, who is is wearing Dior:

'Baby Dior blue and cream silk shirt and dungarees. He looks handsome and perfect for the occasion. We have a happy, if rather strained, few hours.

When the nightmare is over, we will have a service of thanksgiving to bless Tom's life, followed by a reception, to which all those who miss out this time can come. I am a proud parent and will not forgo any chance to show off Tom. I notice that the godparents handle their rather active godson with some trepidation. Is it because they fear he might die in their arms? Every stranger seems to react in the same way.'

The party comes to an end, and with it comes the realisation that Tom belongs somewhere else. Alone with Steve, Sally is desolate. The tears will not stop. She keeps repeating 'Why me? Why am I being punished so much when I have done nothing wrong?'

It is holiday time for Linda. Tom must go with her. At least she is not going abroad. Sally and Steve take the opportunity to get away themselves, to Salisbury to house-sit for Frank and Rosemary. It is not a happy time. Sally writes: 'I have a physical ache that makes me feel sick. The emptiness because our daily visits to Tom do not happen, overwhelms me. Steve and I are right on the edge.'

They return to face decision time about vaccination: against diphtheria, tetanus and pertussis (whooping cough), with polio. Christopher died twenty-three days after his jabs, but Harry only five hours. Did that have something to do with their deaths? Jan and Linda urge them to have the immunisation. The first shock is that their GP, Dr Case, refuses to vaccinate Tom. She will not give a reason. When Steve asks her if there is a risk that Tom will die, she says only that she will not take the responsibility, given the family history. Consultant Dr Spillman suggests a blood test first, as a precaution. It shows that Tom's white blood cell count is down – his immune system is not working fully. Spillman postpones vaccination.

Any newborn baby has his mother's immune system to protect him at first, but gradually develops his own. In the early stages of this development, the baby may be at risk of infection and as immunisation means introducing infective agents – a mild form of the disease itself – it is better to give the jabs when the immune system is fully functioning. They are usually given at about the time at which most cot deaths happen.

Sally and Steve still can't help wondering if vaccination was the cause of Harry's death.

Six weeks later, Tom's white cell count is still not right. Sally feels bad because it is difficult to get blood from Tom. He screams. Linda and Steve are equally distressed. Weeks go by but eventually his immune system is recovering and Spillman decides to go ahead. Tom is very brave. Sally, Linda and Tom have a hospital room to themselves all day, while Tom is monitored, every hour, by a nurse. Only one of them can stay with the baby overnight and that has to be Linda. Tom is discharged at lunchtime the next day. He is fine. There are two follow-up vaccinations and Sally and Steve are there each time. There is no complication.

They get into a routine, but the goodbyes never become any easier. Tom is a happy baby and brings joy to all who meet him:

'I yearn to have him all the time and still have faith in myself as a mother who would care for him well, given the opportunity. I am allowed one visit, with Tom, each week, at Hope Cottage. I take him into every room, particularly the nursery, which now has his name in coloured letters on the door, introducing him to the home that will soon be his.

'Linda and I take him for walks, in the pram, into the woods, to feed the ducks, which makes Tom giggle. We are allowed other visitors: grandparents, my friend Fiona and her husband, Neil. Gradually, more and more of our friends and relatives are introduced to Tom.'

Steve is not charged with any crime, so he is allowed to take Tom out on his own. They usually go swimming. He does not feel right, doing it without Sally, but it is better than not doing it at all. It would have been so easy for Steve to take Tom home so that they could all be together as a family, and nobody would ever know. But they dare not break the rules, in case all contact is terminated. They will not do anything that will jeopardise their chances of getting Tom back soon.

It is understandable that Sally should feel it is only a short separation.

'What I resent more than anything is the time the system steals from me and my baby; the day-to-day nurture of my only son. The changing of his nappy, pushing the pram out shopping, cooking his tea, running his bath, reading him his bedtime story. I would be happy to do it every hour, if only I could treat him as my own.'

These days are lost for ever. The price Sally and Steve are paying for this wrongful prosecution is terrible, their consequences reaching far into the lives of parents, grandparents, all other members of the family.

Sally and Steve borrow from the bank. The legal fees for cases as complicated as this run to hundreds of thousands of pounds. Sally's first court appearance will be in front of a magistrate, who will decide if there is enough evidence to make her stand trial before a judge and jury. The legal preparations for this are time-consuming and expensive. Sally is sure the magistrate will throw out the case against her.

Sally reports to Wilmslow police station on 29 July 1999. Steve stays in the car. What is about to happen may be a formality, but it is a seminal and frightening moment. The fact that the CPS is now prepared to charge Sally with the worst crime in the book – murder – means that the investigation can no longer be dismissed as something that will go away. Sally is apprehensive, but not afraid:

'Mike Mackey is with me. I hear the words as I am charged with murdering my beloved boys. How can this happen if I have done nothing, absolutely nothing but love them more than my life? They don't seem to register. Mike has told me I can say: "I loved my two little boys with all my heart and did nothing to harm either of them."'

Mackey is still upbeat on the charge relating to Christopher; that should not even go to trial. She may be tried for Harry's death but Mackey sees no prospect of conviction on one charge alone.

Steve is an old-fashioned man. He believes it is the husband's responsibility to keep his wife safe from harm. In this situation, he is emasculated. He can do nothing for the moment, but when the time comes, those responsible will be held to account for their actions.

Sally's bail conditions are the same: that she signs on at the station three times a week, continues to live at Hope Cottage and surrenders her passport. Steve hides his rage as he puts his arms round her.

They have been invited to a wedding in London. Common sense tells them that Sally will never face trial. Such is their faith in the system that they feel the threat must not be allowed to dictate every aspect of their lives; that they should carry on as normally as possible:

'I do not enjoy the wedding, although I am comforted to find myself sitting next to a nanny; a baby died whilst in her care. She was not charged but the mother blames her and wrote nasty letters. She mentions it because she knows I lost two babies; she does not know I have been charged with their murder.'

Steve and Sally do not tell anybody who does not need to know.

Suspects used to complain – not in this case – about being 'fitted up'. The allegation was that unscrupulous officers planted evidence or invented 'verbals' (confessions). It happened, but how often was difficult to tell. Some such incidents result in convictions, some of which are now, belatedly, being quashed. Things were improved by the introduction of the Police and Criminal Evidence Act. All police interviews are now audio-taped.

Mackey does not trust the police ever, unless he has to. The risk to his client is too great. He has seen too many miscarriages of justice ever to assume that the police are interested in anything but getting their chosen perpetrator convicted.

Sir David Napley, probably the best criminal solicitor in our history, maintained that the police had too many powers. Defendants were always at a disadvantage, at risk of a wrongful conviction, from a state with unlimited resources. Was he exaggerating?

Now that Mackey is on the job, I do not think that the system can bring about Sally's conviction for murdering her babies. That is not the emotional reaction of a friend, nor a utopian view of the trial process, but a reasoned evaluation of the evidence.

Clients seldom know the names of any barristers, nor do they know their expertise. It is the job of the solicitor to know who specialises in what part of the law and how good they are. This will be a high-profile case. It will call for a leader – a Queen's Counsel – and a junior. Mackey has known John Kelsey Fry and worked with him on many cases. He thinks he is simply the best junior around for this sort of case. It will not be long before he takes silk – becomes a QC himself. The choice of who should 'lead' – who should do virtually all the advocacy at trial – is more tricky. There are many candidates, but in reality it should be somebody in the top six at the Bar. Ian Burton, Mackey's partner, believes Julian Bevan is the man. He is best known as Senior Treasury Counsel; he spends most of his time prosecuting and is not an obvious choice. But Burton recently briefed him to defend a solicitor on a difficult charge and he was spectacularly successful. Mackey calls their clerks – both barristers are in the same London chambers. They couldn't say no if they wanted to: the cab rank rule. But no barrister in his right mind would want to turn down this sensational headline-grabbing case.

A criminal case begins when police complete an investigation and hand the papers to the Crown Prosecution Service (CPS). This consists mainly of solicitors, but includes some barristers; they are civil servants, paid by the state. Their job is to sift through the evidence that the police have assembled, to see if the essential elements of a crime are present. If they conclude that there is more than a 50 per cent chance of getting a conviction, and it is in the public interest to do so, they will usually consult counsel and if so advised, prepare an indictment containing the details of the charge against the defendant. In this case the CPS alone takes the decision.

If the case is not serious, it may be tried in the magistrates' court. Greater crimes are tried in the Crown Court, before a judge and jury. Before that can happen, a magistrate must be persuaded, at a committal hearing, that there is enough evidence – a prima facie case – to make the defendant answer to the charge at a full trial. Crown prosecutors instruct barristers to appear 'for the Crown', i.e. the state. In complicated cases they can instruct 'premier league' barristers: Queen's Counsel, who are entitled to wear black silk gowns and are known as 'silks'. Junior barristers are instructed to share the workload.

Anybody arrested or suspected of a crime may be interviewed by police and is entitled to have an experienced criminal solicitor present.

Solicitors usually represent defendants in the magistrates' court. The whole cost – prosecution and defence – of most criminal cases is borne by the public purse. The Legal Aid Fund will now only pay the costs incurred by firms which can prove they have criminal law experience; they compete for legal aid contracts.

Barristers practise as self-employed individuals; they are forbidden to work in partnership with others, even other barristers. Solicitors usually band together in partnerships because theirs is the investigative role, calling for more ancillary staff than is required by barristers, whose prime role is advocacy. Barristers practise in offices called chambers, where each has a 'seat' or desk. They share overheads and clerical staff, but never fees. The written instructions from a solicitor to a barrister are called briefs, which is why the criminal community call barristers 'briefs'. The Bar Council lays down extensive and restrictive rules about how they should behave, most famously the 'cab rank' rule: unless a barrister has a very good reason, he or she must accept the next job that is offered, whether it is publicly or privately funded and whether it is for the prosecution or defence and however unsavoury it may be.

The ethics of the Bar are said to ensure the highest standards of behaviour in and out of court. A prosecutor must present the facts impartially and fairly to the jury. Facts that damage or throw doubt on his own case, must be disclosed to the defence. He must test the veracity of the defendant and his witnesses, if necessary by searching cross-examination, but always fairly.

The barristers at the Chester Bar are known to local solicitors as the 'Death or Glory Guys', because of their 100 per cent commitment to every client's cause. Chief crown prosecutors depend, for their career prospects, on getting results: They send a lot of briefs to the Chester Bar.

One of the Chester Bar's newest 'silks' is Robin Spencer QC, a big man, burly, with a great stride as he marches through the court corridors, his silk robes billowing behind him, a harassed-looking junior barrister in his wake.

Chester's Chief Crown Prosecutor is a fan of Spencer's. He sends him the papers on Sally Clark's two babies. It is Spencer's first big case as a silk, and the first time that a lawyer and mother has been charged with a double murder. It is the most important case of his career.

The Committal

On a dual carriageway on the approach to Macclesfield is a 1960s building that has seen better days. It is the magistrates' court, where the bulk of petty crimes and traffic offences are dealt with. More serious crimes, to be tried at the Crown Court, before a jury, have first to be approved for trial by the magistrates here, in a test to see if there is a prima facie case for the defendant to answer.

The first shock, for Sally and Steve, is when a man jumps out of the shrubbery, shooting film of them: the slumbering media has awoken. All hopes of keeping everything under wraps vanishes in a photographer's flash.

The atmosphere in this small courtroom is not tense, as it can be at a trial by jury, mainly because nobody will be convicted or sentenced today. There is no crowd in the public gallery supporting the victims of crime or perceived false accusation. For most in that room, what follows will be a formality, but not for Sally or Steve: their nerves are at screeching point.

Mike Mackey does not believe that there is enough evidence for Sally to be committed to stand trial for Christopher's death. Nor do the barristers.

The room is not nearly big enough to accommodate lawyers, police officers and witnesses; there is no physical separation between them. It feels like an old-fashioned classroom. The defence team members are seated cheek by jowl with those for the prosecution.

Robin Spencer QC is dressed today in a dark suit. Robes are not worn in the lower courts.

Sally is represented by her junior counsel, John Kelsey Fry, who looks more like a film star than a lawyer. He is friendly, and has a highly intelligent face. He exudes concern and confidence. He has one objective: the dismissal of the charge for Christopher's death. The findings of Williams and Green, that there were retinal haemorrhages in Harry, mean that Sally is almost bound to stand trial for his death, but on the first baby, the prosecution case is a legal mess. And if Sally faces a charge on only one count the chances of a conviction are remote and the prosecution will know this. Kelsey Fry has mastered the hundreds of pages of his brief. He knows what every witness, every expert will say, because he has read their statements to police; the most important are firmly at the forefront of his mind. There is nothing he does not know and understand – good and bad – about the case against him. He relishes the challenge. Mike Mackey has instructed him many times before and is a great admirer of his advocacy.

Sally takes her place next to Mackey. Steve is not allowed to be at her side. He is directed to the back of the room.

Michael Green is Professor of Forensic Medicine at Sheffield University. He will say that Harry was shaken and will also explore the evidence for blood in Christopher's lungs, and its significance, if any. He is a good-looking man in his sixties, in a grey suit. His eyes sparkle with humour, even with such serious business at hand. He could be a businessman on an easy assignment. He watches as police carry in a baby's bouncy chair; it is an exhibit.

'I didn't realise that we were that short of chairs,' he says in a loud voice, looking for the laugh.

Sally hears, as do Mackey and Kelsey Fry and Spencer. Steve also hears – and will never forget – the joke made about the bouncy chair in which his baby son Harry died.

The stipendiary magistrate enters. All rise. The lawyers bow to him. He returns the courtesy. He takes his seat, facing them, his clerk in the row below him. A stenographer sets up her machine for a simultaneous note of all that is said.

Most committal proceedings now take the form of a paper review. All prosecution witnesses' statements are filed with the court and served on the defence, who can – but rarely do – submit statements of their own. Advocates then argue to persuade the magistrates to commit the case for trial or dismiss it. In 1999, it was still possible for the defence to demand an 'old-style committal', in which named witnesses for the prosecution could be required to attend and give evidence in person, and so be cross-examined. Mackey has done this and also asked for, and been granted, a legally qualified stipendiary magistrate to hear the case. A lawyer is better qualified to identify a flimsy case and throw it out than lay justices of the peace without legal qualifications.

The first into the witness box is Home Office pathologist Dr Alan Roy Williams. He makes a dishevelled figure. His ill-fitting suit has keys dangling from the belt. His appearance does not inspire confidence in his expertise. He takes the Bible in his right hand and swears to tell the 'truth, the whole truth and nothing but the truth'. He reads the statement he made to police on 8 August 1998 relating to Christopher Clark.

Spencer asks him questions.

Williams: I found a number of . . . fingertip . . . bruises. There is no obvious explanation for them from the child's activity. There is a small split in the fraenulum (under the upper lip) that cannot be readily seen in the photographs. At the time of my post-mortem, I was presented with a young male with no obvious cause of death but with a respiratory tract infection. I thought someone acting enthusiastically could have caused the injury, at the time of resuscitation. In discussion with Professor Green, after Harry Clark's death, I became aware of Beecroft's paper on blood in the lungs and changed my opinion, on Christopher's death, to asphyxia consistent with smothering. The second rib [on Harry] shows callus, evidence of fracture and the first right rib is dislocated. There is no natural cause for these injuries . . .

I gave the cause of death of Harry as Shaken Baby Syndrome. I do not know if the death of Harry assists me in drawing a conclusion in relation to the death of Christopher. If Harry had not died I would not have looked at Christopher's death again.

Kelsey Fry cross-examines Williams about Harry:

Kelsey Fry: Was there any pathological evidence of his being smothered?
Williams: If you accept that his pulmonary collapse was due to resuscitation, no.

Cross-examination continues about his finding of large areas of red blood cells in both of Christopher's lungs. Kelsey Fry's questions focus on how much blood is significant, with Williams reluctant to give any figure.

Eventually he says that 10 per cent or less would not be significant. Williams says that he consulted Green, as a world expert on sudden infant death and particularly the lungs, who made a thorough investigation. He thought they were in agreement about how much blood was there. Kelsey Fry ultimately asks:

If I were to tell you that Professor Green says that there was no more than 5 per cent would you agree with that?

Williams says he cannot disagree because he has not scored it.

Kelsey Fry: If Professor Green is accurate then it would be half your estimate for significance. Am I right?

The Home Office pathologist agrees.

Williams disputes that Christopher's nosebleed at the Strand Palace Hotel could account for the blood in his lungs and he is surprised that Professor Green thinks it might.

Kelsey Fry: Considering, firstly, that there was an infection capable of taking a baby's life, secondly no petechial haemorrhaging and thirdly, if it be the case that there was no significant haemorrhaging in the lungs, would there be any warrant for concluding that Christopher died from smothering?
Williams: In the absence of haemorrhage into the lungs, one would be drawn away from the conclusion I have reached . . .

Green goes into the witness box; takes the oath:

Green: There were a few red cells in Christopher's lungs, less than 5 per cent, a very small number of red cells. The lungs pour forth fluid, rich in red blood cells, in response to a variety of insults. In Christopher there was very little in the way of pouring out of fluid. If ever there is more than 8 per cent . . . airway obstruction must be considered.

He knows of no natural cause for the retinal haemorrhages in Harry's eyes.

Green: The pattern and distribution of the haemorrhages that I saw could not have been produced after death. I believe that he suffered a severe shaking shortly before his death and that this could well have been the cause of it.

However, he gives the cause of death, in each case, as unascertained.

The prosecution case on Christopher is now in tatters. Effectively, Green's evidence means the baby could not have been smothered, as Williams now claims, and Green has said that he does not know why either baby died: that is what unascertained means. Over a snack lunch, Mackey and Kelsey Fry tell Sally and Steve that the Magistrate has no option but to throw out the charge on Christopher. But they have not anticipated the ingenuity of the prosecution.

Professor Sir Roy Meadow is also in his sixties. He too is dark-suited. He has a shadow of a scowl in his face, but a charming, avuncular manner. He is an international expert in child abuse. He was the first person to describe Munchausen's Syndrome by Proxy (MSbP), a condition in which the mother fabricates illness in her child, demanding that ever more elaborate procedures be carried out, in order to appear as a heroine saving a young life.

Children often present with symptoms that are difficult to diagnose and some experts are now beginning to doubt; not that the MSbP exists; the danger is that it may have become an easy diagnosis when obvious causes are eliminated. Hundreds of such cases are reported in every country, every year. Many who are accused of Munchausen vehemently deny the charge (which is now claimed to be a feature of the syndrome itself). These allegations usually end up in the family courts where there is a blanket of secrecy to protect children from publicity. In cases where judges rely, more and more, on a small band of experts, whom they get to know and like, there is a real danger that their knowledge and confidence in them will lead them to prefer their opinions over the parents, and other health professionals' evidence, so possibly leading to miscarriages of justice.

Meadow is editor of the *ABC of Child Abuse* and lectures internationally on the subject. He has lectured judges on how to treat expert evidence. For over twenty years he has been a professional witness in the family and criminal courts testifying in baby murder and child abuse cases. He is one of the most persuasive expert witnesses: regretful at having to make such dreadful allegations; sympathetic towards the mothers who apparently do such things. Most jurors and judges would find it difficult to doubt him.

He is a godsend to prosecutors. He is expensive – but the best always is – and his opinions are always forthright. He can be relied on to see off any barrister with the temerity to question his expertise, generally or specifically. His reputation is so intimidating that few other experts are prepared to 'take him on' in defence of a mother. Meadow's references – his qualifications and published papers – are six pages long.

Meadow was the first president of the Royal College of Paediatrics. He was recommended for his knighthood by Margaret Thatcher.

He knows Dr Alan Williams and Professor Michael Green well. They have shared the witness box, for the prosecution, in a number of cases. Meadow has not met Sally or Steve, nor has he taken detailed histories, either of them or their families. He has seen all this before. He claims to have recorded 81 cases thought to be cot deaths which he subsequently proved to be murder. He has a checklist of features to look for. His report reads: 'Neither baby's death is natural.'

That, to a jury, means murder.

He takes the oath. He reads his written report to the police, which was prepared after studying a number of papers, including Harry's medical records.

Meadow answers questions from Spencer referring to a paper to be published the following September – 'all my own work', he says.

I have never heard an academic use such an expression about his own work.

The paper cites 81 cases in 50 families of children thought to have been cot deaths, but who were subsequently proved, either in the criminal or the family court, to be murder; all cases in which he was involved as an expert, testifying for the prosecution.

Meadow: The aim of the study was to identify features that might help paediatricians differentiate between natural and unnatural deaths.

He is emphatic about Christopher:

Meadow: The absence of fresh blood in his lungs does not have particular significance because I know that children may die from smothering without significant findings at autopsy.

Asked by Kelsey Fry, Meadow replies:

The absence of such blood in the lungs is insignificant to me, as blood is
not always present in the lungs of babies who have died of smothering.
I gain that information from pathologists who have reported their
findings to me at autopsy, including Professor Green. It is not a
controversial statement I make. It is one that is expressed and confirmed
by pathology papers. Professor Green has, in the past, brought to my
attention cases of smothering where there has been no blood found in
the lungs. It is common pathological experience by experienced
pathologists that babies die from smothering without blood being
found in the lungs. I believe Professor Green agrees with that. It would
be incorrect to conclude that the absence of recent significant
haemorrhage pointed away from smothering.

Kelsey Fry is relentless in his cross-examination. He gives Meadow every
chance to change his mind, modify his opinions. Kelsey Fry is
determined there shall be no misunderstanding. Meadow is equally
emphatic:

Meadow: I have material on which I have founded my evidence where
pathologists have found no blood in the lungs. The cases extend back
over a period of 20 years. So far as it is available, I am prepared to supply
this information to the Defence.

Later, he talks about a government report, the *Confidential Enquiry into
Stillbirths and Deaths in Infancy*. He quotes its finding that the percentage
of suspected maltreatment deaths was suggested to be between 8 and 18
per cent.

Meadow: In the event of a family suffering a cot death – a chance of one in
a thousand – research shows the chances of a repeat performance are
effectively the same. I think that one in a million is long odds of this
happening twice.

There is an interesting scene, later, when Meadow's evidence is read out to
him by the clerk, and he is asked to sign it. He denies he ever said that
Green had referred a case of smothering to him where there was no blood
in the lungs.

The stenographer has not only typed the words into the word processor as Meadow said them, but his evidence has been recorded on audio-tape – the so-called live note. Everybody in court heard what he said, including the magistrate, who is nonplussed.

The magistrate's options are not easy. He could conclude that Meadow's denial of what he said makes his evidence, generally, unreliable and tell the prosecution that he is inclined to disregard the whole of Meadow's evidence. Spencer could then try to argue for its retention. It is difficult to regard Meadow's reaction as inadvertent; Kelsey Fry gave him too many opportunities to back off from what he was saying. The magistrate could leave the statement unsigned and let the trial judge make of it what he will.

He adjourns for lunch. Meadow approaches the defence team and says to Sally: 'This is terrible for me, it must be awful for you.'

Steve's instinct is to hit him; as is Mackey's, but his legal training 'beats him to the punch'. He tells Meadow to go away.

When the case resumes, the magistrate, surprisingly, decides to nego-tiate with Meadow. The following handwritten note – signed by the magistrate – appears at the end of the official transcript of Meadow's deposition:

> Prior to signing the Deposition the witness indicated that he would only sign the document if it was made clear that he has no recollection of Professor Green referring a case of smothering where there has been no blood found in the lungs.

Only two prosecution experts have given a sinister cause of death for both babies: Williams says Harry was shaken to death but not smothered, and that Christopher originally died of a respiratory infection. However, following Harry's death, Williams rejected that in favour of smothering, on which he now admits to have serious doubts. Meadow says neither death was natural, and – on the point about blood in the lungs and smothering, he denied saying what everybody in court heard him say. There are two tests the magistrate must apply in deciding whether to send Sally for trial by jury: Is there a prima facie case to answer? If there is, is the evidence such that a jury, properly directed, could convict? If, in his judgement, the answer to either of these is no, in either case, he should refuse to commit Sally for trial on that charge.

It is not perhaps surprising that Kelsey Fry and Mackey tell Sally and Steve that the charge that Christopher was murdered lacks all credibility: no jury would convict. And – standing alone – no jury, once they have heard the defence, should convict on Harry. Legally, the stipendiary magistrate should, in my opinion, throw out the case on Christopher. Admittedly, Sally would still stand trial on Harry, but if there is only one charge, it is doubtful that even Spencer would rate his chances of getting a conviction.

But it is unusual for a magistrate to throw out a murder charge at the committal stage, particularly when the accused is a lawyer: the accusation of protecting one's own is too easily made. And there is nothing to stop Spencer preferring a Bill of Indictment, taking the case direct to the Crown Court and asking that judge to order Sally to stand trial. A magistrate may decide that the prosecution has done enough to justify sending the case to the Crown Court and let the judge throw it out for lack of evidence. If he feels differently. Failing that, the jury can make the decision.

The committal proceedings take two days. Kelsey Fry does a wonderful job; Mackey has chosen well. Meadow's credibility is seriously in issue. Green's evidence is full of holes. Williams originally certified Christopher's as a natural death. There are grave doubts as to whether he was killed at all. Kelsey Fry has articulated, with great skill, the argument that there is no justification for making Sally stand trial before a judge and jury for murdering her firstborn. Harry is more difficult to dismiss because two doctors, Williams and Green, say he has the classic signs of a shaken baby. It must be doubtful, in the extreme, if any prosecutor would expect a guilty verdict if Sally were tried on one charge alone: Harry.

But the magistrate decides – for reasons that only he can know – that there is a case to answer against Sally on both counts. He commits Sally Clark to stand trial, at Chester Crown Court, for the murder of her sons Christopher and Harry.

Introduction to Murder

My grandfather, Edward John Batt, was Headmaster of St Thomas's School in Salisbury; my father and uncle were mayors of the city. I grew up and qualified there as a solicitor. That's how I know Sally and her family. I opened a law office there, Batt Broadbent, in 1964.

My first involvement in the Sally Clark case is in August 1999.

After a meeting in the city, I am looking forward to a leisurely cup of tea with old friends; Sally's father and stepmother, Frank and Rosemary Lockyer. They live on the edge of a village just outside the main part of the town, in one of a cluster of new-build, cottage-style homes. It is in a delightful setting with a small, lovingly tended garden. I spend forty-five minutes boring them with news of my family and the parish pump politics of the village where I live, and then ask:

'How's Sally?'

My family had lost touch with her since she moved to Manchester and it was a while since I had last spoken to Frank.

'Not too good,' says Frank. 'The second baby died, too.'

I did not even know about the first one. I am still trying to work out what to say when Frank adds: 'And she's been charged with their murder.'

His statements do not seem to register. The lawyer in me takes over, searching for rational explanations of the inexplicable: either Sally killed them because of postnatal depression, or there's been an almighty cock-up. Nothing makes sense. I could not imagine the Sally I've known since she was five, who played with my own daughter Joanna, committing the premeditated killing of her babies – that is what murders are. How can there be evidence for murder?

I hear the story, as they know it; and they know only the bare outlines at that stage.

'How can I help?' I ask.

They tell me that Sally is in good legal hands and the outcome is not in doubt, because she is innocent and therefore will be found not guilty. Their solicitor is Mike Mackey of Burton Copeland, a Manchester firm that only does criminal work. Julian Bevan QC is her leading barrister. I know he is in the top six, but he's a prosecutor. But why should Sally's solicitor choose the country's most experienced prosecutor to defend such a high-profile case? I do not voice that concern.

I drive home, a bit like Alice in Wonderland, trying to think too many impossible things at once.

A few days later, I meet Frank for lunch. I tell him I have checked up on Mackey and Bevan and my sources tell me they are simply the best. He tells me that his lawyer friends are surprised at the choice of Bevan. Although Frank is now retired, it is not that long ago that he was responsible for all the prosecutions in his bailiwick and he has considerable experience as an advocate in magistrates' courts.

My former partner Derek Holden, a circuit judge for many years, knows Bevan's work well. He has appeared before him many times. He discounted any reservations based on the fact that Bevan usually prosecutes: 'If you're one of the best, as he is,' he said, 'you can do either. It makes no difference.'

Frank tells me that the trial is now set down for 11 October 1999 in Chester, and that – honouring Sally's wish – he will not be there. I offer to go in his place. (As a solicitor, I can hold a 'watching brief' as it's called when a lawyer represents somebody, in this case the defendant's father, who is not a party to the proceedings but has an interest in the case.)

'I can sit near Sally: at least a friendly face.'

'Absolutely out of the question,' says Frank. 'A most generous offer, which we could not possibly accept.'

'At least put it to Sally and Steve,' I say. 'Let them decide.'

'If you insist,' Frank replies, 'but I know their answer will be the same as mine.'

In September, I fly to Manchester to meet Sally and Steve and stay the night. Steve meets me at the airport.

Steve Clark is a tall, thin man who obviously takes his fitness seriously; I think of Jonathan Edwardes, the Olympic champion: they are the same build, with the same short greying hair. There is a neatness and vitality about him which bodes well for his job as a lawyer. Can I imagine him as a banking solicitor? Yes. He is a stickler for detail and capable of compartmentalising different areas of responsibility. He will need that talent in the years to come.

Hope Cottage looks as it sounds: two storeys, white-painted with black window frames, it is straight out of a fairy tale. No wonder Sally fell in love with it. Inside, it is black-beamed, flagstoned on different levels with a warm, welcoming kitchen. It is neat and yet the atmosphere is friendly and relaxing. It is impossible to imagine that two babies were murdered in such a place. Sally's mother, Jean, who died nine years ago, would have loved it.

Sally gives me a hug. 'I can bear anything except . . . I feel so ashamed; ashamed of what Mum must think of me,' she says.

'Wherever she is,' I reply, 'she knows you haven't done these things, so you can put that out of your mind.'

I repeat my offer to be at the trial.

'We couldn't ask that of you!' says Sally firmly.

'I could,' says no nonsense Steve. ' We need all the help we can get.'

I have had time to think about it. As a consultant with my old firm in Wimbledon, Batt Holden, I am able to pick and choose my clients. I work mainly from home. I will only stay in Chester for the first two weeks of the trial. This will be the worst time for Sally because Steve will not be allowed in court until after he has given evidence. I shall be beside her when the bad things from the prosecution come out. When that's over, she will give her evidence, and after that Steve will take the stand and can stay at the back of the court for the rest of the trial. My job will be over.

I have done no criminal law for years but I was a prosecutor for Army Legal Services during my National Service, and for the next ten years I did crime in private practice. I defended a couple of murders, some complex fraud cases at the Old Bailey, and learned how to think on my feet defending motorists and shoplifters before the local magistrates. I'm out of date, but at least I know the language and I haven't forgotten the basics. Criminal work is said to be easy because there is little law involved: the battles are about the facts. I suspect that this case may turn out to be a bit more complicated than that.

I could not go back on my offer, even if I wanted to. These two people may be lawyers but they are entering a world of which they know little, in which their lives will be exposed in headlines. They need support.

'Of course I mean it,' I say. 'I promise I won't get in the way. I will not embarrass you. I'll just takes notes so that I can keep Frank in touch . . .'

'We can't afford to pay you,' says Steve.

'I'm not working for you. This is for Frank. We'll work something out. We're only talking about a couple of weeks of my time.'

They tell me about the case and arrange for me to meet Mike Mackey at his London office.

On 4 August 1999 a meeting takes place between Professor J.E.M. Berry, a paediatric pathologist who will give evidence for Sally, Dr Alan Williams and Professor Timothy David, a consultant paediatrician appointed by the Family Division to investigate the deaths of the two Clark babies. Williams offers to show David the retinal haemorrhages he identified in slides of Harry's eyes, the classic sign of the shaken baby. Professor Green has described the pattern and distribution of these haemorrhages. The three of them view the slides under microscope ports. After Williams has left the meeting, Berry says to David:

'Not only were the haemorrhages not haemorrhages, the tissue he described as retina was not the retina but the choroid, which is a layer of tissue which is adherent to the outer layers of the retina. I am embarrassed that a professional colleague could make such a mistake.'

'Mike Mackey has the face of an angel that has just been charged with assault and battery,' journalist John Sweeney writes in the *Oldie* magazine. It is not a bad description of the man who greets me at 51 Lincoln's Inn Place, in London. He looks me up and down.

Have his worst premonitions just been realised? 'Some London toff, who knows nothing about anything, here to get in my hair, screwing up the most important job of my career?' I have no reason to believe that that was Mackey's reaction, but it would have been mine, were the roles reversed.

I get off on the wrong foot right away:

'I have done a couple of murders, so this won't be the first time . . .'

'I've defended forty,' is Mackey's response.

I hasten to say that I won't interfere. I'll just be taking notes – for Frank.

'Right,' says Mackey, clearly not believing a word I have said. 'What do you want to know?'

'Everything.'

Mackey talks, non-stop, for two hours. He has an impressive command of the facts, the law and the medicine. I understand what he says about the facts and the law; the medicine might as well be in Esperanto. What does get through to me is that the case effectively began when pathologist Williams identified retinal haemorrhages in Harry, the second baby to die, and Professor Green confirmed them. Williams then tore up the natural cause of death for Christopher Clark fourteen months earlier and said he must have been smothered. And no two medical experts seem to be able to agree about anything. The medical evidence will be the mother of all battles for weeks, the only certainty being that the jury will understand practically none of it.

I ask him about pre-trial submissions. His eyebrows shoot up. I can see him thinking: 'This guy's been talking to somebody who knows a thing or two. More trouble!' Out loud he says, nonchalantly,

'Yeah! A couple: alcohol and similar fact.'

Normally, crimes committed on different occasions, even if by the same person, cannot be tried together because of the prejudice created by the very fact that two crimes are alleged. But if there are similar facts pointing to guilt, which the prosecution can persuade the judge are so similar as to be beyond coincidence, he may order that they be tried together.

'What did the judge decide?' I ask.

'May I call you John?'

'Of course.'

'You know about alcohol?' he asks.

'I didn't know Sally had a problem.'

'She had treatment for it.'

'So it was serious . . .'

This is news to me. Sally with an alcohol problem? It does not fit the Sally I know.

'Everything went wrong from day one,' says Mackey. 'The clients are lawyers, for God's sake! They let the police do anything they wanted –

search the house . . . That turned up receipts for the alcohol treatment.'

Mackey lights a cigarette and continues.

'Alcohol says guilty to a jury. A whiff will put everything else out of their minds. On a charge like this . . . So this was one submission we had to win. Bevan was brilliant: he persuaded the judge that as there was no evidence that she was drinking at the time of either baby's death, the prosecution could not make it part of their case.'

'The judge ruled it out completely?' I ask.

'Yes, but on the condition that we do not put Sally forward as a perfect mother. If we even suggest it, the prosecution can counter-attack with alcohol.'

I agree with Mackay that a jury might be side-tracked by alcohol but the loss of character witnesses seems a devastating trade-off especially as alcohol was irrelevant: character evidence is so important to Sally's innocence. And wouldn't the jury expect to hear it?

'No character witnesses at all?' I say.

There are dozens of people, even some of the great and good, who could testify to what a wonderful person and mother she is. Such witnesses can make the difference between a guilty and a not guilty verdict.

'None!' say Mackey.

'What!'

'Think about it,' he says. 'She's been in treatment . . . If we try to say that there's no blemish on her character we would be misleading the jury. The judge says we may call two healthcare professionals to say how good a mother she was with Christopher and Harry. That's factual observation. But go beyond that and the issue of alcohol's out of the bottle.'

This is like fighting the duel with a revolver on one side and a water pistol on the other:

'Can't you challenge it? Appeal the judge's decision?'

'I happen to think the decision's right, in law,' says Mackey.

A good defence lawyer recognises when it is pointless to fight a well-founded decision made against his client.

'In my opinion,' he continues, 'the Court of Appeal would back the judge's decision. Bevan agrees.'

'What did the judge decide on similar facts?' I ask.

Mackey lights another cigarette.

'The prosecution started with thirteen. All pointing to guilt, they said. Bevan did another great job getting it down to seven.'

'What are they?' I ask.

'Same age for both babies: 11 weeks and 8 weeks. Both discovered unconscious by the mother in the bedroom, allegedly in the bouncy chair. Both died at 9.30 at night, after a feed. In each case, Steve either away from home or about to go away. Evidence of previous abuse on each baby. And evidence of recently inflicted deliberate injury in both cases.'

I protest: 'It's ridiculous to call them facts pointing to guilt – most of them! Where else is a baby going to be at nine o'clock at night? Who does a baby spend 90 per cent of its life with. And what abuse and injury?'

'You weren't listening: Christopher had a nick in the fraenulum – the membrane under the upper lip. It's often the result of abuse, and there were bruises on his legs . . . '

'Not when the copper examined the body two hours after he died.'

'These are allegations,' Mackey says, patiently; 'not proven facts. And in Harry, a fractured rib and another dislocated were found. Both disputed by our experts.'

'Surely,' I say, 'the other points are appealable!'

'No. It's the judge's discretion. And the judge says that's enough. The jury will hear both cases together.'

Mackey's had enough of me.

'Sally and Steve want this over with,' he says. 'But you haven't heard the best bit. My experts have been telling me they can't see any retinal haemorrhages in Harry, but none of them is an expert in eyes. I eventually found the best man on babies' eyes, at Moorfields Eye Hospital, Professor Philip Luthert. He says he can't see any haemorrhages either. Green says Luthert hasn't seen all the slides.

'Talk about panic! I was in the middle of trying to firm up on the evidence from the Strand Palace Hotel about Christopher's nosebleed – the prosecution claim it never happened, but that's another story – when this lot happened. I've had to drop everything. I've been chasing up and down the country for days. Retinal haemorrhages are a classic sign of Shaken Baby Syndrome. If a baby's got 'em, he's been shaken. If he's got 'em bad enough, he's been shaken to death. Rely on it!'

'Does Sally admit shaking Harry?' I ask.

'Never! I think I've found all the slides. Professor Emery had a couple;

he did a second post-mortem on Harry for us. They're coming down by
courier at 5 p.m. to Moorfields. If Luthert is right, Professor Green is in
trouble. He's coming to London tomorrow. They'll look at all the slides
together. I shall be there! If Green sees what Luthert has seen, he will have
to concede that he was wrong and that there are no retinal haemorrhages.
The case is all over. Sally walks.'

'But she's charged with two murders. What about baby Christopher?' I
say.

'Nothing to worry about,' says Mackey. 'Dr Williams said natural
causes originally. He only changed that to smothering because of the
retinal haemorrhages in Harry. If they go, their case on both babies goes
up in smoke.'

'Who is Emery?' I ask.

'Maybe the best paediatric pathologist of his generation. His papers on
cot death are quoted all the time.'

'What did he find at post-mortem?'

'Nothing conclusive,' Mackey replies. 'He would have called Harry's a
cot death.'

'That's very good news for Sally.'

'We may not call him. He's eighty, and a bit frail . . .'

I am trying to make some sense out of all this when Mackey adds:

'And the trial starts Monday!'

Over a drink in High Holborn afterwards, Mackey lets drop: 'You're the
reason I'm in this bloody business.'

I plead not guilty. How could I be?

'I got hooked,' says Mackey, taking another draw on his nicotine, 'on
The Main Chance television series in the seventies. I'm right you wrote
it?'

'Something like that,' I said.

*Although Sally's problem with alcohol predated the boys' deaths, all witnesses (both
lay and expert) agreed that she was not drinking when her babies died and that it
had not contributed to either son's death. That was the reason the judge ruled that
the jury should not hear about it. In practical terms it will hog-tie her on character
evidence and could affect the experts if they knew about it: if any of them were
beginning to wonder if they might just be helping send an innocent grieving mother
to prison, alcohol could have reassured them.*

Sally and Steve are on the bed at Hope Cottage, watching television. They know how important the meeting at Moorfields is and can hardly breathe, waiting for Mackey to call them.

Mackey has been waiting outside Moorfields for the courier for two hours.

This could be make-or-break time for Sally's defence. There must be no room for argument about what happens – be it good or bad; no dispute about who says what to whom. Suzanne Moore, an assistant solicitor at Burton Copeland, has been waiting with Mackey. Bevan wants a second witness. Mackey throws away his empty pack of cigarettes and opens another. He is lighting up his twenty-first unfiltered-tip when the courier arrives. Mackey signs for the package and takes it inside.

Mackey and Moore enter the laboratory. Luthert looks up; Mackey nods. Green has the look of somebody who is about to be vindicated. The microscope has three view ports – tubes jutting out to enable three people to look at the same thing simultaneously.

At Hope Cottage, Channel 4 News takes its first commercial break. Sally looks at Steve. Steve looks at Sally.

'Coffee? Tea?'

She shakes her head.

In the laboratory, Green examines every slide; there are seven. It takes a while but ultimately he agrees that these are the ones he originally examined. One by one they are put under the microscope. Mackey is shown how to look through a port; he has no idea what he is looking at or what he is looking for. Green and Luthert take their places at their ports. The process begins, slide after slide. Mackey does not understand what Luthert and Green are discussing. He cannot even guess if Luthert is being proved right or wrong. Suzanne Moore writes down every word anybody says; spelling the medical terms is a problem.

It looks as if Green is in the clear when he says: 'There are the macrophages. Exactly as I described!'

Luthert says: 'But this was a rapid vaginal delivery.'

Green is astonished. 'Nobody told me that!' he says.

'The macrophages are birth related,' says Luthert.

'What does that mean?' Mackey asks himself. It would seem to be good news: Green just lost a point.

It seems to take for ever, but probably no more than twenty minutes, for Green to admit that there are no retinal haemorrhages in Harry Clark. 'I am going to make a telephone call,' he tells Mackey: 'to counsel for the Crown. I shall tell him that the findings in Harry's eyes have to be discounted, but, of course, you will understand that this will have to remain confidential.'

Nothing about this meeting is confidential! Mackey is there, with a witness to everything that goes on, and Green must know this.

'You will put this in writing,' is all Mackey says.

'Of course.'

Suzanne Moore writes it all down.

'Would you excuse me for one moment?' asks Mackey.

They all nod as he leaves the room. In the corridor he takes out his mobile.

The telephone rings in the Clarks' bedroom. Sally and Steve look at each other. Steve answers it and listens. They are both in tears as Steve says: 'Well done! Thanks, Mike.'

He replaces the receiver and turns to Sally:

'Green agrees with Luthert. He says Harry was never shaken.'

They have been so cruelly buoyed by expectations that Sally's innocence will be recognised, only to have those hopes dashed, that their reaction is not ecstatic, but the numbness feels a little lighter. At least the police can no longer say that Sally or anybody else has shaken Harry! Their subconscious minds register rather more as Steve and Sally Clark have their first untroubled sleep in almost two years.

Lies and Statistics

Sally and Steve have had a winding-down weekend. Their lawyers have told them the case against her has collapsed because of Green, and the most likely thing to happen is that there will be no trial.

Sally feels a whole range of emotions going into court, but of one thing she is certain: 'I will never be found guilty.'

There were occasions leading up to today when she sought reassurances from Steve but that was no more than cuddling up to him in bed and saying 'I'm not going to prison, am I?' More a need for comfort than ever really believing it would happen:

'I was irritated when Mackey tried to tell me what to wear in court, that I should try to look "Mumsy" and not wear a business suit. I suppose that comes from my naïve belief that my innocence will be glaringly obvious for all to see, so why should I try to put on a particular image? Who am I trying to kid!'

It never occurred to her that she would be portrayed in the press as a career woman who never wanted children, and that a smart suit confirms that image.

The rush of cameramen as they walk across the car park is frightening:

'We had decided, rightly or wrongly, that we would deal with it by adopting a stiff upper lip approach, hold our heads up high and walk straight through them.'

Sally has also not realised that Steve will not be there in court until after he has given evidence – and that could be days, even weeks away. And nothing had prepared her for the daunting crush of people in the public gallery.

Mackey advised Sally and Steve to pay a visit to Chester Crown Court, to familiarise themselves with the courtroom and what it feels like. It was wise advice. Neither has seen the inside of a criminal court. They were as intimidated as any non-lawyer would be.

Although Sally and Steve are both lawyers, they are told, by Mackey, to keep well away from both Bevan and Kelsey Fry:

'They know what they are doing. Leave them alone to get on with their jobs.'

To Steve, it is a weird experience: they are the clients, paying the bills, the victims of the bizarre twists of legal fortune, of the dirty tricks perpetrated time and time again; Sally may go to prison for life; Steve may lose his job and have to bring up Tom on his own, without a mother, and yet she and Steve seem able to contribute little that will affect the outcome.

Mackey drops the bomb that the trial is to go ahead and that the prosecution has changed the cause of Harry's death to shaking and or smothering.

Sally is outraged: 'How can they do that! How? How?'

For nearly two years the charge Sally faced was that she had shaken Harry to death. It was only following confirmation of that by Green, that Williams changed the reason he had originally given for Christopher's death: from 'natural causes' to smothering. And, at committal, Williams specifically said that there was no evidence that Harry had been smothered. The prosecution experts, to a man, backed shaking, either as a cause of death or findings consistent with shaking.

Sally and Steve have accepted that there was some evidence that Harry had been shaken because Williams, backed up by Green, said so. Their only question was, how did it happen? But now, over the weekend, the prosecution has got together with its experts and decided it's shaking and/or smothering! And it appears there is no way that Bevan can stop them doing this. Mackey says it happens all the time, the prosecution changing the basis on which a case is constructed at the last minute. And Sally now has only a matter of minutes to decide how to answer it, what to say, how to prove it cannot be true. Mackey adds, as an afterthought:

'They are having trouble with Williams. He flatly disagrees with Green. Insists there are still retinal haemorrhages! So the cause of Harry's death is now smothering and/or shaking.'

Sally and Steve were at a conference, discussing her case with Kelsey Fry, the previous Wednesday, when a prosecution fax came through saying Meadow would be giving statistics of 1:73 million as the chance of two cot deaths in a family like Sally's. At committal he said it was 1:1 million. Kelsey Fry did not seem unduly bothered; neither was Bevan. 'Statistics are just calculations: they prove nothing,' they said. 'Silly numbers that will be meaningless to a jury.' Sally and Steve do not take much persuading that this must be the case when such expensive lawyers say so.

Ordinary people understand odds. Every lottery punter knows that the chance of winning the jackpot is 14 million to one. Meadow's odds are five times that! Ten years writing legal drama for television has given me some insights into what ordinary viewers like and think. It is a different wavelength from the rarefied 'common room' isolation of the Bar. My conscience tells me this is a dangerous number.

There are about 11,000 barristers, one-third of them women, distributed throughout the country, most of them based in or linked to London. It is a club-like community; barristers are not supposed to talk to the client except through a solicitor. They are never allowed to talk to factual witnesses apart from their own clients. Solicitors tend to assume that, because counsel appear before juries all the time, they can 'read' those who sit on them.

THE MAIN CHANCE and JUSTICE, television series based firmly in the law, and with which I was involved, attracted an audience of about ten million viewers each week. We learned, very fast, what turned on an audience of ordinary people — the sort of people who watch prime-time TV and sit on juries. I have no doubt that 1:73 million would be a clincher for them; I fear it might be the same for Sally's jury.

Chester Crown Court occupies the original site of the castle built by William the Conqueror in 1069. The new buildings were completed in 1813 and Wellington's victory at Waterloo is commemorated with illuminated laurels over the entrance. The courtroom is semicircular with a large pediment supported by twelve huge stone columns, each weighing 15 tons and 22 feet in height, brought from the quarry eight miles distant by a six-wheeled carriage drawn by sixteen horses. The colonnade forms a crescent leading away from the Bench where once sat the hanging Judge Jeffreys. Dark oak panelling predominates, creating a sombre, intimidating feel. The dock faces the judge; there is one door leading into the court and another leading to the cells below. The witness box is to the judge's right and the jury has its own enclosure and separate entrance away to his left. The press benches are aligned with the witness box. The front pew faces the judge and will house the 'silks', Spencer and Bevan. Behind them will sit the junior barristers, Kelsey Fry for Sally and Michael Chambers for the prosecution. I shall sit within whispering distance of Sally.

She has been on bail ever since she was first charged and can expect it to be continued during the trial so that she can leave the dock to have lunch with Steve. She will sleep at home. Only if she is convicted will she be taken into custody in the cells below. If that should happen, it could be twenty years before she knows freedom again.

My reaction to the new charge of smothering is that the defence must make a submission to the judge that there is now no prima facie case for Sally to answer, or that no jury properly instructed could convict. Bevan says that if he had been prosecuting, he would have stopped the prosecution; and nobody is better qualified to make that call. Green's latest admission that Harry was not shaken blows their case away. The prosecution have already had to change the cause of death of Christopher; surely the judge will see that it would be cruel and unjust to make Sally go through a three-week murder trial after they've now done the same with Harry.

But Mackey says these ideas are years out of date. Such changes, of even the most basic facts alleged against the guy in the dock, are made, just like that! It is a commonplace. How can there be any justice in allowing the prosecution – which for two years relied on Harry's shaking to justify charging Sally with two murders – to change the whole basis of the case for murder of baby Harry over the weekend? Medically, smothering is a different mechanism of death, and Williams said there was no evidence for it at committal.

A submission seems to me such an imperative that I ring my former partner, Judge Derek Holden, yet again. He says that if he was the presiding judge, he would probably throw the case out. I wonder if the chief crown prosecutor's instructions to his leading counsel endorse Spencer's decision to continue the trial.

One thing is certain: there must be an adjournment, to enable Sally's experts to examine and report on the new allegation that Harry was smothered. But even that assumption turns out to be wrong. Nothing in this case is straightforward. There are unacceptable consequences of an adjournment.

The case is listed to last three weeks. The next time our judge – Mr Justice Harrison – can sit for that length of time is next April; six months away. The custody of Tom Clark – who is to bring him up – depends on the outcome of the trial and so has yet to be decided by the judge in the Family Division. Social Services have already said that Tom's future must be decided before his first birthday. Research shows that if the decision about a baby's long-term carers stretches beyond that time it can do permanent damage to the child. If Sally's trial is not going to begin until he is eighteen months old, Social Services will ask the Family Court to put Tom up for adoption by strangers. The parents cannot run that risk.

But what about the risk to Sally? If her experts do not have sufficient time to investigate and answer the charge of smothering, is there not an increased risk of her being convicted? Possibly not; the prosecution has been wrong-footed by Green's admission on Harry's eyes, and the sudden change to smothering has the prosecution experts 'on the ropes', contradicting one another. Surely no jury will convict, given such disarray amongst Sally's accusers! How could any jury find guilt beyond reasonable doubt? The prosecution now has to explain how they got the cause of death of both babies wrong the first time around.

The unknown quantity is the new statistic: that the chance of two cot deaths is 1:73 million.

Evidence can always be struck out by the judge in a criminal trial if its prejudicial effect outweighs its probative value – if the piece of evidence creates more prejudice in the minds of the jury than what it actually proves. I cannot think of a more clear-cut example of this well-known legal principle than 1:73 million. Mackey agrees with me. Bevan dismisses our concerns. In his opinion, the figure is too crazy for anybody to believe and the judge will be antagonised if he makes a flawed submission trying to keep it out. He dare not take that risk.

My promise to keep my own counsel gets lost. I rant at Mackey that that jury must not hear that the chance of two cot deaths is 1:73 million; that it is legally inadmissible. They will think it means that the odds that Sally did not kill her babies are 73 million to one. Sally has never claimed that either baby was a cot death, so the statistic is inadmissible, because it does not address *any* issue in the case! Bevan insists it is meaningless. Mackey agrees with me. But it seems, we do not know what we are talking about! I do know that any statistic is meaningless in isolation.

'What are the statistics for two murders in a family like Sally's?' I ask Mackey.

'I'm working on it with a statistician in Aberdeen,' he replies.

The only man I know who can provide the answer is Dennis Rosen, a professor at London University, who helped me with the science involved in my last book, *The Tesla Trinity*. With his brilliant brain and huge knowledge of a wide range of subjects, he is a true polymath. But Dennis cannot help: he died a month ago.

The arguments behind the scenes cease. The barristers have agreed that the trial will proceed.

The Trial

Sally enters the dock. She should not be surprised but is shocked that two Group 4 security guards take their places on either side of her. Nowhere is quite so lonely as a criminal dock. She has told all her friends to stay away, to save them the emotional trauma, so she is truly alone and can't even have Steve in the same room. The usher intones: 'All rise.'

Mr Justice Harrison enters, bewigged, in full-length purple and black gown with scarlet sash. Everybody bows to him. He returns the courtesy. Everybody sits. The clerk rises:

Clerk (to Sally:) Please stand.

She does so.

Clerk: Are you Sally Clark?
Sally: Yes.
Clerk: You are charged with the murder of . . .

Sally says she is not guilty. She has never felt so isolated, vulnerable and terrified. Can she keep her promise to herself, never to show it?

Hopefully, not. Juries need to see the vulnerability of the mother. It helps them think of her as innocent.

Sally and Steve may have familiarised themselves with the dimensions and furnishings and where the various people sit, but nothing has prepared

Sally for being the focus of everybody's attention. She is a very private person:

> 'I have never sought the limelight; never seen myself in a starring role; that is not me. I want to be an anonymous mother among many others, bringing up my son. Instead I am the "villain of this production". The starring role is only the first of the humiliations. Words can't describe the shame of being accused of killing babies, which goes against every mother's instinct, which attacks the core of what every woman is. It is unbearable. The fact that there are experienced doctors – Williams and Meadow – prepared to swear on oath that I have killed my beloved Christopher and Harry is not only beyond belief, it is more than my mind can cope with. I want to yell: "Stop this torture! I've done nothing but love my boys with all my heart! Why are you doing this!" But I know I can't do that and even if I did, it would have no effect except to embarrass everybody. I also know that I am innocent of causing any harm to either of my babies and that English justice does not convict innocent mothers.'

I take my place in the pew beside the dock and nod reassuringly at Sally. Beside me is Mandy Murphy, the law clerk from Mackey's office, whose job is to write down everything said at the trial – a handwritten account, available, instantly, to check what anybody has said. I will get to know her well during the trial and admire her skills, particularly in comforting Sally in times of stress and acting as liaison between Sally and Mackey, who is sometimes absent from court.

With a watching brief for Frank, I, too, will be writing everything down. It is good discipline; having to concentrate on writing it takes some of the emotion out of the anatomical details.

Tom's guardian *ad litem* – appointed to look after his interests by the Family Court judge – is in court, as are Sally's and Steve's separate solicitors for the family proceedings. Police officers, social workers and lawyers and clerks from the Crown Prosecution Service share the pews with us.

Jury selection is a truncated affair compared with what goes on in American courts, where a whole industry has developed trying to forecast what types of juror are most likely to say guilty or not guilty. The guiding principle for our juries is that they should be random. Defence and prosecution are allowed peremptory challenges, and for cause: if a barrister sees a relative on the jury he would be bound to say so and the judge would remove him. No challenges are exercised in this case.

Sally looks closely at each member of the jury as they are sworn in:

'I wonder who I can count on and who might not like me because I am "rich and successful". And so many of the men are so young! But I am not afraid of anything they can do. I know my innocence exudes from me and will be confirmed when they hear me tell my story; that innocence will be obvious.'

The historic grandeur of the courtroom and the splendour of the judge's robes, the wigs and gowns of counsel, the suits of everybody else, contrast starkly with the anoraks and T-shirts of the twelve people who shuffle into the jury box. Seven of the jury are men, most in their late teens or early twenties; one man and, perhaps, one woman is over forty. Three have difficulty reading the oath. They look as if they have just been beamed up to an alien planet by Scotty, in an episode of STAR TREK. *They will hear weeks of some of the most complicated medicine, all of it contested. Lawyers are used to reading strange material, on subjects they have not previously studied; they are trained to assimilate new information quickly; but this science is something else. There are obvious bits, but the use of so many unfamiliar words means that there is no way of telling if they are points for or against Sally. The jury has a zero chance of comprehending it.*

The law requires that, first, they decide the cause of death of Christopher and then the cause of death of Harry Clark. The chance of them getting at the truth is also close to nil: tossing a coin would be just as likely to reveal it. Then they must decide if Sally did it. They swear to give a true verdict – whatever that may mean! – according to the evidence. A true verdict is not the same thing as establishing the truth.

No sooner have the jury settled in their places than the judge asks them to take a break, while he hears more submissions from counsel.

Spencer wants the jury to be asked if any of them has suffered a cot death or recent infant death.

Mr Justice Harrison is in his late fifties, a well-built intelligent man with a courteous and considerate manner. He was appointed to the High Court Bench in 1993 after a successful career in planning law. This is not the obvious background for a judge in such an important case. But he has had regular training in criminal law and practice and has attended many courses on sentencing; all judges have to do this. He has presided over many criminal trials in the last six years. He gives me the impression that he will be fair but will stand no nonsense from anybody.

He rules Spencer's question improper. Spencer also wants the fact that Steve and Sally are solicitors to be kept secret from the jury; it's prejudicial –

That's rich coming from the man who wants to tell the jury about 1:73 million!

for it might predispose them to believe their evidence! A journalist intervenes to say that both have already been identified in the press as solicitors. The judge throws out that submission as well. He also orders that the press shall not make any mention of Sally's alcohol problem, nor can they make any reference to the fact that she has had another baby. Bevan submits that it is prejudicial because Tom is being brought up by a foster mother and is still alive, unlike his two brothers. The jury might draw the wrong inferences from that. Bevan wins the arguments.

The jury returns.

The press box is jammed as Robin Spencer QC rises to make his opening speech for the Crown, outlining the facts for the jury. His is the most newsworthy part of the trial. He will probably be quoted verbatim in every paper and on every newscast. When he sits, all journalists will leave court except for a 'stringer', who will be taking notes in the unlikely event that anything the public would be interested in happens. The next significant moment for the media may be what Sally says and then the verdict. Until then the national media interest will wither away. Allegations make headlines; defences don't. The press, of course, say that Sally denies the charges, but readers may gloss over that in the sensations of the allegations.

This is intrinsically unfair to the person accused. Admittedly, juries are told by the judge that they must not read or listen to anything about the case, except what they hear in court; but how many take that seriously? They will see news-stand posters; they will hear the news on the radio or television, even if they try to ignore it, and they will be influenced. And all they hear or see will be the prosecution side of the case. Many may not be able to resist reading the papers to see how 'their' case has been reported.

As she enters Chester Crown Court the next morning, Sally sees a jury member carrying a newpaper with '1: 73 million' prominent in a headline. Sally takes her place in the dock.

She listens to Spencer's opening speech to the jury in disbelief:

'So many of the phrases he uses are taken from what I said at the initial police interview; when I had chosen not to have a lawyer and was trying to be so honest and helpful to the police. How could my innocent and honest responses be interpreted as evidence supporting a murder charge? I am hurt; incredibly hurt. I am angry.

'What would he have said if I had demanded a lawyer? Unless you have been through my situation, it is difficult to appreciate that my way of thinking was that I had nothing to hide and therefore I should try to be as helpful as possible.'

The Prosecution Case

A murder trial is a bit like war: 90 per cent boredom, 10 per cent terror. Day three of the trial and the tedium – the boredom factor – is beginning to affect Sally. Although she is the focus of everything that is going on, she feels – as a baby must – helpless, dependent on others for everything; there is nothing she can do until she is put into a situation she knows about. That moment will not arrive for another three weeks, when, for the first time, Sally will know what she has to do: tell the jury what actually happened and why all these experts for the prosecution are speculating about cruelties of which she is incapable.

One of the first things Spencer says is that the chance of two cot deaths in the same family is 1:73 million. Sally is nonplussed:

'Nobody has ever called either of my boys a cot death. These numbers – however many noughts there are – cannot be relevant to my trial and have nothing to do with me.'

But that statistic is so large, such a wonderful and so easily understood soundbite, that – however many times it is destroyed by proper statisticians – I am sure it will become part of the lexicon of journalism, trotted out every time a parent suffers a second baby tragedy. All the lawyers in this case – the judge and myself included – must share the responsibility for the consequences that will follow, for countless other mothers and others, in the criminal and family courts here and abroad, whose prospect of proving their innocence will be blighted by this innumerate sensation. But the main legal responsibility is Spencer's. He is an experienced criminal lawyer – made one of Her Majesty's counsel, because of just that expertise; yet he has chosen – and it is his decision – to introduce it into the trial and the public domain.

He begins calling his witnesses.

Staff at the hospital where Christopher was taken tell of their attempts to resuscitate the baby, and Sally's reaction. Then comes the playing of the 999 tapes. Sally has to sit there, alone, isolated in the dock, without her husband even in earshot, listening as her beloved Christopher, and then her wonderfully feisty Harry, die again.

Sally's grief is plain for all to see:

'I never thought I would hear my own words played back to me. It is haunting and a dreadful shock. It is beyond belief. I am devastated, inconsolable. I try, as hard as I know how, to be my mother's daughter and not to show it.'

Two women on the jury are also in tears. There is silence in the court as the tapes end.

I am not writing. I glance at Sally. It seems kinder to look away. I want to help but know there is nothing I can do.

Consultant paediatrician Dr Jane Cowan testifies to Sally's genuine grief and pseudo-hysteria; she found nothing unusual in her behaviour.

The next witness, coroner's officer Christine Hears, was the first to be suspicious about Harry's death, because she remembered Christopher. She thought it unusual that Sally talked about how easily she conceived Harry so soon after Christopher's death.

Sally shakes her head:

'She makes it sound as if I was callous. That's not how I said it.'

The sensational parts of the story have already been highlighted; now it is time for the slow process of putting each of the building blocks of the case against Sally in place. There is a shorthand-writer, and audio-tape recording of everything, yet the judge still has to make a longhand note of the most important items of evidence, for his summing-up at the end of the trial. This slows everything down. The jury's boredom threshold is soon reached and they begin to nod.

Our adversarial system of justice requires that all the witnesses for the prosecution are heard first. Their counsel, Spencer, is not allowed to ask leading questions, those which suggest the answer required by the way they are put. Then defence counsel,

Bevan tests the truth of what the witness has said; he is allowed – in cross-examination – to ask leading questions.

Spencer now calls the medical evidence that Sally and Steve have studied but never fully understood:

> 'It meant reading things that are not only complicated but "not very nice somehow". It caused us great distress at times. Now I am glad I did it but have misgivings that if I am not careful in my reactions I may look more like a lawyer than a mother; but surely the jury will understand that.'

As the prosecution always goes first, all the worst aspects of a case are heard before the defendant's answers to them. What follows is the evidence of Home Office pathologist Williams. His findings are disturbing, and if true, would suggest guilt. But most, if not all, of them are dismissed by a combination of other experts, for the prosecution as well as the defence. When reading them, the words of Dr Sam Gullino, an eminent and forthright forensic pathologist, working full time for the state of Florida, who has never given evidence for the defence, should be borne in mind. They come from his report for the second Court of Appeal:

> *Throughout my review, I was horrified by the shoddy fashion in which these cases were evaluated. It was clear that sound medical principles were abandoned in favor of oversimplifications, over-interpretations, exclusion of relevant data and, in several instances, the imagining of non-existent findings.*

It is doubtful if any UK medical expert would make such an unequivocal criticism of professional colleagues.

Williams is a consultant histopathologist, an expert in the study of tissues in order to establish disease. He is also a consultant forensic pathologist for the Home Office, a bachelor of medicine and surgery from Liverpool and a fellow of the Royal College of Pathologists. He qualified in 1976 and has done 10,000 post-mortems on bodies of all ages.

This is an impressive list of qualifications, but how good he is at his job will now be tested when he is cross-examined. Bevan's task is daunting: if Williams is believed, Sally Clark is a liar and baby-killer. If Sally has told the truth about the deaths of Christopher and Harry, they were not killed by shaking or smothering or any other deliberate mechanism but by some unidentified natural cause. Bevan must not merely shake this witness; he must destroy his credibility if Sally is to be found not guilty. Only Bevan can do that. The stakes are almost as high for Spencer: unless he can show – by his examination-in-chief, and later by his repairing re-examination – that Williams is a thoroughly competent expert, in whose testimony the jury can have confidence, Sally will be acquitted. The art of examination-in-chief is to help the witness reveal himself and his expertise.

The untidy man who gave evidence at committal has been spruced up; he looks almost smart. He is certainly in a new suit, but there is still an air of untidiness and truculence about him.

Sally looks nervously at me. This is not going to be pleasant.

'I know what he is going to say, because I have read it so many times. It will be graphic and distressing. If I keep telling myself that I am not the monster being described, maybe I'll be able to hold myself together.'

Williams speaks from notes, of the fractured rib, the dislocated rib: they prove Harry was previously abused and beaten. Williams tells of the hypoxia – the brain's starvation of oxygen being a sign of asphyxia – the tears in the brain, the deluge of blood around the spine, the haemorrhages in the eyes. All of these findings confirm violent shaking.

Sally has seen him perform before, at committal:

'I cannot believe that a doctor – a home office pathologist – is doing this to me!'

Williams has a file of photographs taken of the body of Harry, mutilated by the autopsy process.

Sally looks, in dread, at that file. Mercifully, she is too far away to see them in detail – but she can't stop her imagination:

'I am forced to listen to a succession of tortures to which my beloved Harry was supposedly subjected; which could not have happened – because if they had, I would have known about them: Harry was with me almost every minute of his life. It is beyond understanding. But I can't run. I can't hide. I can do nothing to stop the jury hearing this litany of lies.'

Sally sits, and listens. Her head is down. The tears slowly flow. Is she even aware of them?

Without making any reference to Green's or Luther's findings, Williams says that Harry was shaken to death, but how will he explain changing the cause of Christopher's death from an infection of the lower lung to smothering?

Sally stifles a sob at Christopher's name.

Williams continues. He did not change the cause of Christopher's death because he found Harry had been shaken to death, but because of new research, brought to his attention by Green, of the significance of blood in the lungs as a marker for smothering.

Spencer sits, not exactly smug, but reasonably satisfied that he has done enough to persuade the jury that Williams knows what he is talking about and that both Christopher and Harry Clark were murdered.

In a sense Sally is relieved, but she knows this will be short-lived because Bevan will now have to go through everything again, trying to get Williams to admit that these things never happened; that he has misinterpreted what he saw or perhaps even never saw it at all – like the retinal haemorrhages. Will he succeed? Is he up to the task? Mackey assures me he will crucify Williams.

Williams' evidence – in chief, in cross-examination and in re-examination – takes up 168 pages of the transcript from which the following dialogue is taken. What follows is of course selective, but, to be fair to Williams, includes his most important allegations against Sally. The way Bevan tries to demonstrate that Williams is wrong, and his response, follows.

Bevan first establishes that Williams is not a paediatric pathologist: he is not an expert at doing autopsies on babies. But he says he has done post-mortems on hundreds of babies a few weeks old.

Bevan spends a long time laying the groundwork for the conclusion he tries to make Williams accept. Williams is no pushover. He is stubborn, aggressive, when he feels it will work, reluctant to give an inch. But I think Bevan has at last got him:

Bevan: The mechanism of shaking a baby, in a classical case, is of a baby shaken violently and its head rocks backwards and forwards, to use an ordinary expression; you cause brain damage?

Williams: Yes.

Bevan: And if you shake a baby violently causing it brain damage, in the typical case you also find, do you not, damage in the neck area, its neck at the top?

Williams: In the mechanism you're describing, yes.

Bevan: . . . Holding a baby by its chest and shaking? It is right, is it not, that there were no haemorrhages within the neck?

Williams: There are no haemorrhages in the neck, no.

Bevan: There was in fact no haemorrhage within the upper cervical cord, which is the top. That is right?

Williams: Yes.

Bevan: . . . the typical shaking case is where you find injuries, if shaken by the chest, and the head rocking backwards and forwards, brain injury, neck injury, injury to the muscles in the neck, haemorrhages within the neck, bleeding going down into the cord subdurally . . .

Williams: That is the classic in the mechanism you describe.

Bevan: And so, if, Dr Williams . . . if we exclude trauma to the brain . . . one: yes?

Williams: Yes.

Bevan: If we exclude . . . subdural haemorrhage damage to the brain, yes?

Williams: Yes.

Bevan: . . . if we exclude what I am going to term as diffuse axonal injury.

Williams: I would dispute that you can exclude it. It is not apparent in sections in less than two hours.

Bevan: I said if we exclude the tears.

Williams: No, you said diffuse axonal injury, which is a different condition.

Bevan: I will change that to no tears.

Williams: There are no . . . yes.

Bevan: So we have no trauma, no subdural haemorrhage, no tears, yes?

Williams: No tears.

Bevan: No trauma to the brain, yes?

Williams: I can't say that.

Bevan: All right. I'll leave that out. No subdural damage, no tears yes? If?

Williams: If no tears, yes.

Bevan: If no retinal haemorrhages?

Williams: Yes.

Bevan: If no haemorrhages within the neck muscles, yes?

Williams: Yes.

Bevan: Or upper cervical cord? If?

Williams: Yes.

Bevan: That begins to undermine, does it not, the opinion that this baby's death was caused by what I can only describe as a violent shaking. That is right, is it not?

This is the first part of the fight-back; the first opportunity there has been to put Sally's case. Sally knows this and is at last beginning to see why Mackey has such faith in Bevan. He is taking Williams apart; there is a grim satisfaction in it.

Williams: In the way you've described it. I am at a loss to explain the mechanism of shaking except that whatever mechanism has been used has resulted in thoracic and upper — well, no, lower spine haemorrhage

Bevan: Dr Williams . . . would you now demonstrate, to the jury . . . the shaking you have told us about . . .

Sally turns her head away. She cannot bear to look.

Williams: I don't . . .

Bevan: . . . over several days that has caused this child's death.

Williams: I've already dealt with this in chief; I do not know the mechanism that has occurred, I can only tell you the causation in that it is the hyperextension and flexion of the spine. There is no evidence from the examination of the child how the hands have been applied and how the effects that we find at post-mortem have been caused.

Sally can now look at Williams:

'What he is saying has to be invention; it never happened. Maybe, if I pretend it is happening to somebody else, I will be able to take it in.'

Bevan: I do not want to leave it. I want you to help us as best you can. You do not know, I understand that, but you are there, as an expert, and you can give an opinion. What, in your opinion, and I want you to demonstrate it, is the mechanics of the shaking that would have caused these injuries, so the jury know the position? Just help us with the mechanics of the shaking that are consistent with the injuries you found.

Williams: The mechanics of the situation is that this child in some way has been manipulated such that the spinal column has been over-extended and over-flexed, resulting in epidural haemorrhage.

After further questions Williams says: 'In some way the body of the child – if my arm's the back – '

At this point Williams begins his demonstration and this is too much for Sally.

'This is horror. I am incredulous. It never happened. Nobody did anything even remotely like what he is describing to my darling Harry. Why is he imagining such a terrible lie?'

Everybody watches, almost holding their breath, as the man demonstrates how Sally murdered her baby. And yet – however distressing and inhuman the demonstration – it is in Sally's vital interest that it happens, but that does not mean that it is right, that it is fair, that it is just.

Williams continues:

Williams: . . . has been flexed backwards and forwards and this has resulted in traction injuries within the spinal canal and this has caused the epidural haemorrhage.

Bevan: So it is not shaking as such?

Williams: It probably isn't the correct term but . . . a violent movement of the spine resulting in the injuries described.

Bevan: You used the expression whiplash . . . can you just demonstrate the whiplash you are dealing with.

Williams [*standing*]: Whiplash is a rapid flexion and extension of the spine . . .

Bevan: Imagine you are holding a baby . . . Now demonstrate.

Williams: I don't know where the child's been held, it could have been its head, it could have been held by the arms or the legs, there's no evidence as to how the child's been held . . .

Williams demonstrates again, this time as if holding the head of the baby, whipping its body backwards and forwards. It is obscene, revolting. The jury's attention is rapt: two women are in tears; a man has his head in his hands.

Bevan: In your years of experience, have you had a case of a person whereby the child's head alone has been held and then swung about . . . rock it from side to side or backwards and forwards . . . ?

Williams: I've said I don't know the mechanism. Yes, I've known cases where the head's been held.

Bevan: Just the head?

Williams: That was the evidence. I mean, one doesn't normally get a full version of the events . . . There were fingertip bruises to the head.

Bevan: . . . just the head being held? And the child being swung about? Is that what you are telling me?

Williams: I think that . . . yes, I think I've had several cases . . . some have more injuries than others . . . the assaults occur repeatedly over a period of time so that child has a number of injuries.

Bevan: Would you agree, Dr Williams, that the classic signs of shaking that I have underlined already, subdural haemorrhage, tears, retinal, etcetera, subdural cord are not present in this case?

Williams: This child does not show the full spectrum that one sees when the head is violently shaken.

Bevan: This child does not show the classical sign of death by shaking does it?

Williams: It doesn't show the features one expects to see in the head of a shaken baby where the head has been violently moved, no.

The cross-examination continues, dealing with old bleeding in Harry's eyes, which Williams agrees could be birth related, and other old bleeding which he acknowledges is found in many babies who have died naturally. He says he has never come across a shaken baby where bleeding around the cord begins as low down as in this case. He agrees that it is inescapable that, if a baby is shaken violently by the head, as he described, there would be injuries to the neck, and there are none in Harry Clark.

The cross-examination continues:

Bevan: There is no pathological evidence that this child was smothered to
   death?
Williams: No. There's no evidence of smothering.
Bevan: And that, no doubt, is the reason why, in your post-mortem report,
   there is no mention of smothering being the cause of death?
Williams: No. I don't think we've ever considered it.

The judge adjourns for lunch.

*Steve and Sally go off together, hand in hand. The only conclusion anybody seeing
them could draw is that theirs is a happy marriage – that's how it should be. But
why has all this happened to them? People as happy as they are don't do the things
the jury just heard described. And if there were any truth in the allegations of
shaking made by Williams, the health professionals would have been bound to see
some signs. Something is very wrong.*

Sally's reaction is different: 'I don't see the trial as a threat. It is just
something Steve and I have to live through to get Tom back.'
   After the lunch adjournment, Bevan goes on to deal with Harry's ribs:

Bevan: And you use these words: '. . . and possible old fracture of the right
   second rib'.
Williams: Yes.

Williams agrees that he took a section of the rib for analysis but that,
probably due to an oversight, he did not see the result for many weeks.

Bevan: Did you tell Wilmslow CID, at 3.25 on the day of the post-mortem,
   that the second rib, fractured, could be a birth injury?

Williams is not happy with the question.

Williams: Ageing of rib fractures is extremely difficult. Fractures can take
   up to eight weeks to repair, the child is eight weeks old, that is a remote
   possibility or it is at the end of the spectrum for healing.

Williams explains that callus is new bone formation, part of the healing
process. He agrees that the fracture did not show up on X-ray but explains

that this is not unusual. He never saw the fractured rib, only felt it. Nobody saw it. The fracture was nearly healed.

Bevan: . . . You estimate the age of the fracture at between six and eight weeks?

Williams: Within limitations of what is possible . . . there's an awful lot of factors that have to be taken into account.

Bevan: . . . Six to eight weeks would make this fracture occur when this baby had hardly been born. Not many days after birth?

Williams: The limit I've put on it is eight weeks, which is about the time of birth, yes.

Although it is his normal practice, he cannot remember if he photographed it. He has not seen such a photo.

A photograph of the section was later found and examined.

Bevan: It does not show any more than growing bone, does it?

Williams: Well, that's what a healing callus is.

Bevan now deals with the first rib, which was said to be dislocated.

Bevan: This is a fragile junction in a child?

Williams: Relatively, yes.

Bevan: Bone contains blood.

Williams: Yes.

Bevan: Bone is surrounded by tissues?

Williams: Yes.

Bevan: And tissues contain blood?

Williams: In blood vessels, yes.

Bevan: Was there haemorrhage at this site?

Williams: There were no visible haemorrhages at the site of the injury, no.

Bevan: This is not unimportant, is it? If, in life, a baby dislocates a rib there would be bleeding would there not?

Williams: Not necessarily.

Bevan: Are you saying that the bone would not discharge blood . . . ?

Williams: Yes.

Bevan: . . . that the cartilage, from which it has become separated would not itself bleed?

Williams: If there is no damage to the blood vessels there will be no bleeding. If the injury is an old one the blood will have been reabsorbed.
Bevan: Where is it mentioned in the post-mortem findings . . .
Williams: Because it's of unknown significance to me anyway. It's not an injury I've experienced previously, in children.

Bevan sits.

Re-examination is usually fairly brief, the occasion for opposing counsel to repair the damage done by cross-examination. Spencer is an able advocate but obsessive about detail. His re-examination takes up 26 pages of the transcript — it is two-thirds the length of his examination-in-chief. Why does the judge allow him to go over so much of the same territory yet again? The jury's reaction, save that of those who have paid attention, seems to be boredom — a good sign! Bevan has done a lot to damage Williams' credibility with the jury. Whether he has done enough to make them disregard his findings is much more difficult to judge.

So far the balance of advantage is with Sally. Under the English system, she does not have to prove her innocence: the prosecution has to make the jury sure of her guilt — that it is beyond reasonable doubt. The prosecution are nowhere near crossing that line yet, but the statistic is yet to come.

Williams, who conducted the post-mortems on both babies, is, in effect, the general practitioner of pathology. Now is the turn of the specialists. They will take each one of his most important findings and flesh them out.

As soon as the court business is finished each day, I call Frank on my mobile and bring him up to date. Sally and Steve run to the car, to drive to Tom, to spend as much time with him as they can:

'Foster mother Linda allows us two hours, every evening, Steve to bath him, me to feed him. Most of Linda's charges hardly see their parents at all. Tom is oblivious to all that is going on. This is good, not only for him but for Steve and me. I make another vow — not to read any newspaper.'

The next witness is Dr Christine Smith. Spencer does not need to do more than allow this experienced witness to make her own impression. She is grey-haired, in her late fifties, and has a quiet authority. There is no doubt that she is a master of her subject. The jury will be impressed.

She had a meeting with Professor David at which he formed the impression that Smith was very impressed with Green's evidence. He asked her if her opinion would change if it turned out that Harry did not have retinal haemorrhages? She said her opinions would essentially be unchanged. David was surprised at this reaction, so he probed further. Dr Smith said that having observed Sally at the committal hearing and her demeanour, it was quite clear she was guilty.

Bevan has to make serious inroads into Smith's testimony; her evidence, as it stands, backs up Williams.

Smith is a neuropathologist, with similar qualifications to Williams. Her speciality is the nervous system –the brain, spinal cord, nerves and muscle tissue. She has been specialising in this since the mid-1970s and was made a consultant in the mid-1980s. She sees many babies of this age every year – they are referred to her from all over the country, although she is based in Sheffield and often works with Green. She will give evidence only about Harry Clark, and specifically his brain, on referral by Green. Christopher's body was cremated after his death was certified as due to natural causes, so no second post-mortem could be conducted.

From the pattern and distribution of blood and macrophages – those are the 'sweeper' cells that mop up old blood – she estimates two episodes of bleeding. A baby does not bleed spontaneously unless there is some natural disease, of which, in Harry's case, there is no evidence, or it has been subjected to trauma. Unless it was caused at post-mortem, trauma – some form of direct or indirect injury – must therefore be the cause. She did not see any subdural haemorrhage or damage to the spinal cord. Like Dr Williams, she is unable to think of any mechanism by which this injury could have been caused. There was no evidence of natural or inherited disease anywhere in the body. To be consistent with the findings it must have been something that caused leakage of the blood vessels. Lack of oxygen could have caused this. She found no tears in the brain. There was some evidence of hypoxic change – lack of oxygen before death which can be caused by swelling of the brain, the heart stopping or disease of the cranial cavity. Swelling of the spinal cord can also cause it. Smith gives shaking as the likely cause of the fresh bleeding and retinal haemorrhages.

She understands that the prosecution no longer alleges retinal haemorrhages but says that she never regarded this as a classic case of a shaken baby.

What will the jury make of this? She keeps talking about injuries and trauma as being the only explanation for the findings, but then cannot explain how the injuries were inflicted. Surely an expert such as Smith – consulted by other doctors all over the UK – with so many years' experience, would be able, at least, have a theory? If not, what does it mean? Is the state of medical knowledge such that too many findings are still of unknown origin? If that is the case, how can speculative trauma, interpreted as murder, even be a commonsense possibility?

Bevan rises to cross-examine. His technique with Smith will have to be different from his approach to Williams. She is a respected, widely consulted expert. Williams, the generalist, was shown to be capable of mistakes; this doctor cannot be attacked in the same way. She has put some of Williams' findings firmly back into the arena of believability. Bevan faces a daunting task: he must make Smith change her opinions; an unlikely outcome. No matter how hard he has studied the subject, he will always be at the mercy of the expert whose lifetime's work he is about to challenge. The most he can hope for is to get her to admit that there is no certainty.

The cross-examination is lengthy. Bevan seems to be feeling his way in persuading Smith in the direction he needs. He takes each finding and attacks it, painstakingly, from every angle. Smith may be the expert in the subject, but Bevan is the master of his own craft of advocacy. In that sense it is a battle of equals, or at least of equivalent levels of skill. Bevan has done far better than could have been hoped as he comes to his summary:

Bevan: Is there any pathological evidence that Harry Clark was smothered to death?

The answer, after a certain amount of prevarication, is:

Smith: Nothing that specifically indicates that.
Bevan: We are left with epidural bleeding.
Smith: Yes.
Bevan: That on its own would not cause death?

Smith: No.

Bevan: We are left with no subdural haemorrhage to the spine?

Smith: Yes.

Bevan: No damage to the cervical part of the spine?

Smith: I have not examined the cervical cord.

Bevan: There was no evidence of cervical damage to the spine?

Again Smith prevaricates, but Bevan persists with the same question. She answers:

Smith: I have not seen any.

Bevan: We have the epidural bleeding which is in the lower part of the spine?

Smith: Yes.

Bevan: No injury to the neck muscles?

Smith: Yes.

Bevan: But what we do have is a child dying, no doubt, through lack of oxygen, ultimately.

Smith: Yes.

Bevan: The epidural bleeding would not itself cause death?

Smith: Yes.

Bevan: There is no evidence of traumatic injury to the brain?

Smith: No, but there is some evidence of damage within the brain, but yes . . .

Bevan: There is no evidence of injury to the brain, is there?

Smith: There are haemorrhages within the brain.

Bevan: But those have been explained by lack of oxygen?

Smith: They could equally well have been due to some traumatic disruption of the vessels.

Bevan: If I was determined to look on the black side . . .

Smith: I am merely pointing out the possibilities.

Bevan: I am trying to be fair. There is no evidence of traumatic injury to the brain?

Smith: I have seen no tears.

Bevan: You are in no position to totally exclude the possibility that this child did, in fact, die of natural causes?

She gives a long answer, reiterating the opinions she gave in answer to Spencer in the early part of cross-examination.

Bevan: The fractured rib could have been eight weeks old? It certainly did not cause death, did it?

Smith: No.

Bevan: Did you ever inform the prosecution that if there were no retinal haemorrhages you could not say shaking?

Smith: I cannot remember . . .

Bevan: Without the retinal haemorrhages one cannot say positively that this is a shaking case?

Smith: Yes.

Bevan: The truth is that this is an unexplained death.

Smith: There are pathological changes.

Bevan's patience runs out again:

Bevan: I want you to view this case as a pathologist, not as a detective, but as a pathologist . . . Not as a policeman or woman. You are here as a pathologist.

Smith: Yes.

The cross-examination on supposed damage to the brain continues and then:

Bevan: It is an unexplained death, Dr Smith, isn't it?

Smith: . . . I do not think you can say that it is totally unexplained. Perhaps we have failed to explain that . . . We have a child here with evidence of hypoxic damage to the brain. What is unexplained is how it received the damage.

Bevan: You cannot totally exclude that this child died in fact from natural causes?

Smith: I cannot exclude it . . . but there are features which suggest some insult to the child before death.

Bevan: It is an unexplained death, isn't it? That is the truth?

Smith: Yes, as . . .

The judge intervenes:

Judge: I want to make sure. You agree that it was an unexplained death?

Smith: Yes, but in total pathological terms.

Taking this expert from her position, in answer to questions from Spencer, of shoring up most of Williams' most suspicious findings to admitting that Harry Clark's is an unexplained death, is an example of the art of cross-examination at its best. John Mortimer, the renowned QC and writer, says that 95 per cent of cases are decided by the paperwork beforehand; the advocate can only affect the outcome in 5 per cent. This is one of the 5 per cent!

Spencer's re-examination occupies a mere 10 pages of the transcript. He does a good job of trying to retrieve the admissions extracted by Bevan, but is the jury impressed by Spencer or by what Bevan has done with this witness? They look at Sally – this is said to be a sign of approval. The intervention of the judge, at the very end probably swayed them in Sally's favour. He sits on high, everybody bows and defers to him; he is called my lord; he is the big boss. He is Mr Justice. And he is on nobody's side. His was the critical question, Smith's answer to which has put the verdict of guilty of the murder of Harry– the deliberate, premeditated killing proved to the point of certainty – right out of the reckoning.

Sally is not happy:

'I understand that words like unascertained and unexplained mean that there is reasonable doubt but that is not good enough for me. I am innocent and somebody ought to be saying this, over and over again, to every witness.'

Spencer's next witness is Michael Green, Professor of Forensic Pathology at Sheffield University since 1990.

If Green had not – at committal – described a 'pattern and distribution' of retinal haemorrhages in Harry Clark's eyes, he could not have told Williams that in his opinion Harry was probably shaken to death. If he had not told Williams there were retinal haemorrhages, would Williams ever have certified Harry's death as due to shaking? If Green had said there were none, surely Williams would have said: 'Show me under the microscope.' Green would have shown him what Luthert showed Green at the meeting at Moorfields three days before the trial. Williams would then have appreciated the difference between the retina and the choroid and the course of the trial might have been different. Would Williams have gone on to describe the other findings which other experts had such trouble confirming? Would the police have charged Sally with either murder? Would the Crown Prosecution Service have thought there was enough evidence to secure a conviction or that it was in the public interest to bring her to trial? The answer to all those questions must surely be no. Everything thrown at them by the police and prosecution, and the nightmares and torture Sally and Steve will now suffer, were, almost certainly, at this point, avoidable.

When Bevan gives Green his comeuppance, the jury will know that Sally must walk free from this ordeal.

Spencer begins his examination-in-chief. Green has similar qualifications to the other experts. He holds a diploma in child health, obstetrics and medical jurisprudence, which is at the interface of medicine and the law. He is in his sixties. He has an excellent manner and there is a glint of humour in his eyes. He is instantly likeable. The jury smile at him.

His particular interests are the abuse of babies, retinal haemorrhages in their eyes and babies' lungs.

After considering the slides given him by Williams, he has looked again at Christopher's original slides.

Green: The sections which were prepared in Sheffield . . . did not show anything like as many fresh red cells . . . and when I gave evidence at committal I relied on those sections. I have subsequently looked at the first lot . . . and confirm that they do show far more red cells . . . The sections prepared by Dr Williams showed lots of red cells and still show lots of red cells. The sections prepared in Sheffield . . . do not show the same large number of red cells and we are still seeking an explanation for this.

What Green is now admitting is that not only was he mistaken about the pattern and distribution of retinal haemorrhages in Harry Clark's eyes, he now says that evidence he gave which showed Christopher had not been smothered now – because of new information – turns out also to be wrong and that now there is plenty of evidence to support smothering.

According to Williams, Green is an authority on those two areas of medicine and he now admits to getting both wrong. When Christopher died, Williams did the post-mortem and certified death due to natural causes, a lung infection. He changed that to an unnatural death, smothering, only after Green confirmed that Harry had been shaken to death. Bevan will, surely, tell the jury that the reason Sally was charged with murder no longer exists. Green saying that baby Harry was not shaken effectively destroys Williams' reason for changing the cause of Christopher's death. Hence both charges – if there is any common sense, any justice – will be chucked out.

Does the prosecution calculate that the 1:73 million statistic will make the jury forget the disputes about many of the post-mortem findings? Surely, no jury could be certain about anything on this evidence.

Green then justifies his emphasis on blood in Christopher's lungs, by talking about research in New Zealand by Beecroft and Lockett which shows that old bleeding in the lungs is not diagnostic of but is a marker for smothering.

Green: . . . some sort of upper respiratory obstruction on at least one occasion in the baby's life . . . For example, a hand over the mouth, a piece of plastic over the mouth. Some form of smothering or suffocation. But it is a marker; no more than that. If the red cells are more than 10 per cent I am not saying that it is a smothering but the police need to ask more questions. In the case of Christopher it is 10 per cent plus.

He describes petechial haemorrhage – rupture of the tiny blood vessels caused by pressure in heart disease or by smothering – but says that none was found on Christopher's skin. He does not believe that the old blood in Christopher's lungs could be the result of his nosebleed at the Strand Palace Hotel one week earlier and has never come across a spontaneous nosebleed in a baby this age.

Spencer asks him about the bruises.

Green: I have known Dr Williams a long time . . . if he says something is a bruise I will accept his word.

Did Green also take Williams' word for the presence of retinal haemorrhages?

Spencer: Was there anything . . . to provide a natural explanation for Christopher's death? We know his actual cause of death was given as a lower respiratory tract infection. Do you now consider that a possibility?
Green: I do not think so.
Spencer: Can you think of any natural explanation for Christopher's death?
Green: I think it extremely likely that Christopher's death was other than natural . . . I would have given the formal cause of death as unascertained.

Green, in the cafeteria, during the mid-morning break, is heard to say to his companion: 'I'm beginning to wish I'd never got involved in this case.'

The judge then adjourns for lunch. Green will continue his evidence on Thursday morning.

Spencer's next witness is Professor Sir Roy Meadow.

At the committal hearing Meadow offered to supply the defence with details of the cases of smothering which Green had referred to him. Mackey wrote to Meadow for them. After several reminders, the Crown Prosecution Service wrote a letter to Mackey, dated 11 August 1999:

> With reference to your letter of 18 June 1999 enclosing a copy letter forwarded to Professor Sir Roy Meadow following his undertaking at the oral committal proceedings
>
>> Quote: 'I have material on which I have founded my evidence where pathologists have found no blood in the lungs. The cases extend back over a period of 20 years. So far as it is available, I am prepared to supply this information to the Defence.'
>
> It now seems that most of the raw material on which Sir Roy's paper was based has been destroyed . . .

Meadow has given evidence in hundreds of cases against mothers all over the world. He has disciples who give evidence based on his theories and papers. He has lectured judges on how to interpret the evidence of experts. The CPS now says that the data on which his most important paper on cot death is based have been destroyed.

His explanation seems to be that it is to preserve the confidentiality of the children involved. Cases involving children are occasionally reported in the press, usually on appeal. Anonymity is preserved by referring to cases, not by name but by an initial letter. It is an extraordinary thing to have happened, in a case full of unexpected surprises. Destroying the database of a key report means that nobody can ever check it. It not only shreds the data, but casts doubt on the study itself. The point of writing papers is so that the history of scientific development can be studied; that research is now lost.

Bevan will surely have a bonanza in cross-examination. How can Meadow explain what he did at committal, How will he answer the question: 'Why was your database destroyed? Was it with your knowledge? Is it just coincidence that you are now unable to supply the data you offered to the defence at Committal?' The answers should be interesting.

Meadow enters the witness box and swears on the New Testament of the Bible to tell the truth, the whole truth and nothing but the truth.

He is Emeritus Professor of Paediatrics and Childcare at Leeds University, Bachelor of Medicine and Surgery, Fellow of the Royal College of Physicians, Fellow of the Royal College of Paediatric and Child Health, with a diploma in obstetrics and gynaecology and a diploma in child health. He is a past chairman of the most important groups in the field and was for eight years editor of the *Archive of Disease in Childhood*, a prestigious European journal, and of the *ABC of Child Abuse*. His contribution to paediatrics was recognised by a knighthood in 1996. For twenty-five years he was a consultant at St James Hospital Leeds made famous, as Jimmy's, in a television series.

He has great charm and charisma; he is avuncular. He speaks with a slight Lancashire accent but with the sort of certainty and authority that will not be denied. He is a clever witness, reluctant to condemn the mothers he accuses, which makes his testimony powerful. No wonder so many judges set such store by his opinions. For Sally's case, he is the danger man; no member of the jury could doubt what this man says.

But first comes his examination-in-chief. Spencer asks him about Munchausen's Syndrome by Proxy:

Meadow: Yes. I discovered it about twenty years ago.
Spencer: There's no suggestion it is applicable in either of these cases?
Meadow: No.

In which case, why has the experienced lawyer Spencer introduced it and why doesn't Bevan object to it? If it has no relevance, it is inadmissible.

Meadow: A parent, usually the mother, invents false illness for her child, causing the child to have many medical procedures, and she sometimes harms the child by poisoning, smothering or injuring the child. It was taken up world wide.

Meadow then describes secret filming of mothers deliberately smothering or suffocating their children. It is not common practice but has been done many times in Britain, in America and in Europe when a child's symptoms warrant it and defy medical interpretation.

Meadow: Characteristically we would always intervene after 30 . . . 40 seconds. The baby would be on its back and the mother would put a hand over its mouth and nose, to block the airways. Sometimes she will use a pillow or a pad of material. Sometimes a mother has been recorded clutching a baby into their chest to smother . . . and if they have been asleep, after about ten seconds they start to wriggle and struggle quite hard, the child has to be restrained with an arm or hand . . . most people would think that to make a child unconscious the air would have to be cut off for probably at least a minute and to cause brain damage or death probably about three minutes, so it's a very upsetting thing actually to see and analyse.

The jury are looking at Sally. Are they trying to imagine her doing such a thing? Common sense says it is irresistible; in which case, as there is no suggestion of Munchausen in Sally, why is Bevan allowing such damaging images to be implanted in the jury's minds without objection? But if he did object, at this late stage, it could boomerang, drawing even more attention to the image.

Meadow describes the evolution of child abuse from the days when only obvious injury was acted upon, to hidden abuse, shaking and smothering. He refers to his paper published in January 1999 in the *Archive of Disease in Childhood*.

Meadow: There were 81 children who had been originally thought to have died of natural causes. The majority were described as Sudden Infant Death Syndrome. I have kept records of certain features of babies whose deaths I have investigated over a long period of time . . . to help paediatricians disentangle natural causes from unnatural or abuse causes.

Spencer: Were you struck by the time of day at which killings took place?

Meadow: The peak period . . . is between midnight and 11 a.m. The baby is put to sleep. The parents get up, often rather latish and to their tremendous sadness they find the baby dead at nine, ten in the morning in the cot and that's the normal circumstance of natural sudden death.

Spencer: So that would be the classic cot death?

Meadow: Yes . . .

It seems incredible, even laughable: a classic case of sudden infant death happens when the parents have a lie-in! Everybody seems to be taking this as profound scientific truth. What has happened to common sense!

Meadow [*continuing*]: Yes. For more than two-thirds of such babies, whereas the unnatural deaths, the commonest time for them to die was in the late afternoon/evening. Parents, when asleep, don't kill their children so it would have been surprising if the findings were otherwise. Child abuse is commonest at that time, they're often at their most annoying and parents are tired.

Spencer: Did you find it was not uncommon to find that a child had taken a feed normally two hours before being killed?

Meadow: In a natural death the baby was quite often a bit off colour the evening before, a bit snuffly but in these cases a large proportion were observed completely well . . . and then half an hour later suddenly found dead.

Spencer asks him what features are found in smothering.

Meadow: . . . a characteristic bruising of the face or body . . . sometimes fresh blood around the nose and mouth, little petechial haemorrhages into the soft tissues.

Spencer: Does immunisation have any role to play in either of these children?

Meadow: Immunisation is not a risk factor in sudden infant death. Research shows there is a slightly diminished chance of a baby dying within 48 hours, so completely discount immunisation as a cause of death.

Spencer: Are you aware that Dr Cowan noticed a difference between the explanation given by Sally Clark, compared to what she said to the ambulance men about where he [Christopher] was found. Can that difference be significant?

Meadow: They may be . . . the genuine event is recalled accurately and is repeated in a consistent way, whereas a story being made up often changes.

This is curious. It is a given, among lawyers and the police, that if ever defendants and their friends tell exactly the same story – getting the unimportant details right – it is probably the result of collusion and guilt rather than innocence. Those giving genuine accounts would usually make – sometimes glaring – mistakes about unimportant details. The BBC once conducted an experiment in the studio which proved that people's memories of what they see often deceive them. According to this world expert, Meadow, only guilty parents get the unimportant details wrong, the innocent behave – apparently by instinct – as the guilty do in other criminal cases.

Mr Justice Harrison obviously sees nothing remarkable about what Meadow has just said; nor apparently does Bevan. Spencer – as a very experienced criminal lawyer – may have his doubts, but he won't question evidence that will help him win his case.

Spencer asks him about Christopher's bruises:

Meadow: The worry here is the number of bruises and their distribution . . . I don't think there is anything specifically characteristic of smothering in these bruises. But it's non-accidental and could have been caused in the context of smothering, likely to have been close to death.

He then deals with the nick in the fraenulum, under the upper lip.

Meadow: Common sense says it could have been caused by the laryngoscope but such an injury has never been recorded. A torn fraenulum, in the absence of a satisfactory story, should be regarded as child abuse. It's a bit of dogmatic teaching.

The laryngoscope is an instrument introduced into the baby's mouth during resuscitation. There were several failed attempts to do this before they finally succeeded with Christopher.

Spencer asks him about Christopher's nosebleed.

Meadow: A spontaneous nosebleed in a baby should always be treated as an extreme emergency and the baby not treated in Accident and Emergency but immediately admitted to hospital for investigation.

What he says may well be true, but it does not sound true to me. But what do I know?

To Sally, he seems to be talking about a different baby:

'I don't understand how he can make up these things. I was there, practically every moment of both my boys' lives. If such things had happened I would know. Steve would know and with Harry, Lesley would know. What he says bears no relation to the truth.'

Spencer: As you know, Dr Williams originally said Christopher died of a respiratory tract infection. Did he, in your opinion?
Meadow: No. He did not.
Spencer: Can you think of any natural explanation for Christopher's death?
Meadow: No, I cannot.
Spencer: Can I now turn to Harry.

Meadow says that his inoculations, the afternoon of his death, would not have made Harry ill and would not have been a factor in his death.

It is interesting that such an experienced paediatrician should make such an unequivocal statement when Harry's death followed within five hours of his injections. Does he not know that Parliament passed the 1979 Vaccine Damage Payment Act, to compensate children killed or harmed by vaccination? And that it usually follows soon after immunisation?

Meadow says that Harry was already dead when the ambulance men arrived. The bleeding around and swelling of the spine suggest unusual trauma. Whatever caused the oxygen starvation referred to by Dr Smith would have been significant. Fractures do sometimes occur at birth but this would be an unusual one. If this was a fracture it would be significant . . .

Meadow: It's another evidence of injury or trauma for which there is no explanation. The other rib, if it was dislocated, would be uncommon but it would not be right to say that only abuse could cause it. Resuscitation does not usually cause fractures but I would be unable to exclude the remote possibility.

He said he would also regard the two petechial haemorrhages in the left eyelid as significant but that they are very small by definition and he would like to be certain they were there before calling them suspicious. He is not able to comment on Dr Williams' finding of haemorrhages at the back of Harry's eyes or that he had only previously seen them in cases of asphyxia. He has heard nothing in the evidence so far that is inconsistent with smothering. It is a possible cause of death.

Spencer: Can you find any natural explanation for Harry's death?
Meadow: No, I don't think so.

Next he is asked about the Confidential Enquiry into Sudden Deaths in Infants (CESDI), which is government sponsored and has recently examined over half a million live births in England and Wales from 1993, 1994 and 1995. Meadows is writing the preface. Eliminating factors such as smoking, the chance of one cot death is 1:8,543. Therefore, the chance of two cot deaths in a family like Sally's is 1:73 million, he says.

Sally is aware that Mackey and I are very worried about this evidence and believe that it is legally inadmissible:

> 'I am not angry. I'm not afraid it will convict me. Neither Steve nor I have ever claimed that either baby's was a cot death. We always said we did not know why they died. They know we pestered everybody who would listen to find out how our babies died. How can the judge allow Spencer to introduce it? He must know that we have never made such a claim.'

I don't think ordinary people who sit on juries understand how misleading statistics can be. They are simply numbers, bean-counting of how many things happened over a period of time, with no application to any one case, which may be affected by dozens of other factors. The idea that a statistic proves nothing in a particular case is too academic an argument for non-lawyers. They will see it as a serious scientific calculation of the odds against Sally being innocent. And the odds are so long that nobody would ever bet against them; hence no jury will acquit in the face of 73 million to one. That is my fear.

Meadow is asked about a study by Professor Emery of 57 infant deaths, where deliberate harm was suspected. Fifty-five per cent were found to be killings by the parents. Nine per cent – five children – were genuine SIDS and one family had a second SIDS. Counsel for the Crown continues:

Spencer: Does that paper in any way undermine the statistics in this very recent work?
Meadow: No, because the two things were addressing different issues.

Bevan rises to cross-examine Meadow. He puts his wooden podium in place and arranges his voluminous paperwork.

Will this eminent expert now be brought low?

Bevan begins by asking about Munchausen's Syndrome by Proxy and Meadow admits that fabricating an illness in a child is a form of abuse usually done by mothers to draw attention to themselves; they do not attempt to hide it. Child sex abuse is usually perpetrated by fathers or other males.

Bevan: It's a sad fact but babies up to a year old do suddenly stop breathing and die, inexplicably?
Meadow: No cause is found. That is correct. And in genuine SIDS cases they have appeared quite healthy the previous day.

Bevan asks him about Christopher's bruises, described by Williams as abraded, and he admits that scuffing of the skin would normally show up as it happened, but the police sergeant inspecting the body hours later saw no sign of it. Bevan then asks why Meadow would regard a spontaneous nosebleed, not due to abuse, as an emergency?

Meadow: Because of concern that there is a serious underlying disease. A particular liver disease causes blood not to clot.

Bevan then asks about the opinion of Professor Timothy David, the consultant paediatrician appointed by the Family Court to report on Tom's future, that Christopher may have been suffering idiopathic pulmonary haemosiderosis and asks if Meadow has discussed this with him.

Meadow: Well, it was a very one-sided discussion in that . . .
Bevan: What, he was talking and you were saying nothing?
Meadow: Exactly. I travelled across the Pennines to what was called an experts' meeting. I went there genuinely seeking to discuss issues and do things, and I've done that on many occasions, and I was as honest as I could be and expressed areas of concern and nothing was volunteered in return and I really felt that that was not what a meeting should be.

Is Meadow upset because his colleagues accepted his opinions without comment? What is wrong with that? Unless he is suggesting that they were not interested in his opinions; surely unlikely for such an eminent expert.

Bevan: Are you aware that Professor David is considering haemosiderosis as a possibility? Because of the abnormal results from blood analysis?

Meadow dismisses David's opinion, because of the unreliability of blood taken from a dead baby. Bevan asks him about the fractures and Meadow admits that he has never seen anything like them. Considerable force would be required, there is normally damage to surrounding ribs or tissue and there is none in Harry. He cannot explain them. They would be painful for the baby, who would be in discomfort and crying, particularly when picked up under the arms.

Meadow says that there can be cases where a baby has been smothered and there is no pathological evidence.

Bevan: On the subject of statistics you said there are 700,000 live births every year.
Meadow: About that in England and Wales.
Bevan: Mrs Clark falls into the category of 1:8,543 for a first cot death and if you multiply that by 8,543 you reach 1:73 million?
Meadow: Yes.

Bevan then refers to a report by the Care of Next Infant organisation.

Bevan: There were eight cot deaths out of 5,000?
Meadow: Yes.
Bevan: That's one in 214 times 214 is 46,000?
Meadow: The CONI Report has nothing like the standard of investigations and reporting factors in CESDI. There are no controls . . . It's not the same sort of scientific study at all.
Bevan: When Harry was born the chance of his being a cot death was the same as Christopher's? 1:8,543. Like tossing a coin? It's the same odds each time? Head or tails?
Meadow: That's why you take what's happened to all the children into account and the chance of two dying is very, very long odds indeed: 1:73 million.
Bevan: That's a double cot death every hundred years?

Again Sally is dying to shout: 'I never said they were cot deaths. How can you be talking about once every hundred years when all the doctors say "unascertained"? Nobody says they are cot deaths!'

Meadow: It's the chance of backing the long outsider at the Grand National. Let's say it's an 80 to 1 chance you back the winner last year and next year there's another horse at 80 to 1 and it is still 80 to 1. And you back it and it wins. To get to odds of 73 million to 1 you have to back that 80 to 1 chance, four years running. It's the same with these deaths.

Bevan: Have you heard the expression 'Lies, damned lies and statistics?'

Meadow: I don't like statistics but I am forced to accept their usefulness.

Bevan: You said in your report in May 1998, 'from the information available to me neither of these two deaths is likely to be due to natural causes'?

Bevan then refers to Professor Luthert's opinion which persuaded Green to change his evidence about retinal haemorrhage and points out that both now discounted shaking as a cause of Harry's death.

Bevan: You said then, 'Each death has the characteristics of unnatural causes which is enhanced by the fact that two deaths have occurred at about the same age in the same home.' Does that accurately reflect your opinion now?

Meadow: The further information I have received and evidence sadly increases the strength with which I feel that the two deaths are not natural.

And Bevan sits down.

Is that it? The end of cross-examination? He has not mentioned Meadow's extra-ordinary conduct at Committal or the shredding of his database. Was he worried that, in attacking such an authority on the subject, so admired by judges, he might do even greater damage to Sally's cause?

It is a matter of fine judgement, but so much damage has been done to Sally's chances of acquittal by the 1:73 million statistic that there could not have been that much more to lose, and there might be a great deal to gain, by really going for Meadow.

Spencer re-examines. Meadow dismisses the CONI Report as having no statistical value. Counsel asks him about the fact that the police officer found no marks on Christopher at 2 a.m. after he was declared dead at 10.40 p.m.

Meadow: . . . Police officers, when presented with a dead baby are immensely troubled, upset themselves, so it is common for things to be overlooked, and then there is the well-known phenomenon of recent bruises not being visible until later.

Is this a serious scientific observation? That police officers get too upset at the sight of a baby's body to be able to do the one thing they are specially trained to do — observe and record what they see?

He goes on to say that the nosebleed could have been the result of an earlier attempt, by Sally, to smother Christopher.

Sally cannot help feeling impressed by Meadow: 'If I didn't know I was innocent I would have believed me guilty.'

The judge releases Meadow. Spencer calls Dr Jean Keeling.

She is a consultant paediatric pathologist at the Royal Hospital for Sick Children in Edinburgh. She held a similar post at the Radcliffe Hospital, Oxford, from 1974 to 1989. She has performed several thousand autopsies on babies and written extensively about foetal and neonatal pathology. Professor J.E.M. Berry – who is to give evidence for Sally – is her co-author on a number of research papers. This is a seriously qualified doctor. The impression, as she takes the oath, is of a strong character, not likely to put up with foolish questioning.

She was first brought in to give evidence about Christopher's death: it is only in the last week that her opinion on Harry has been sought. She can find no natural explanation for the old or the new bleeding in Christopher's lungs. She does not think the bruises to his legs could have been caused by resuscitation after death and they are of great concern. She has never seen an injury to the fraenulum of a baby other than by abuse. She does not think it could have been caused by the laryngoscope. In her opinion, Christopher's is not a SIDS case. Asked if she can give a natural explanation for his death she replies:

I have given 'unascertained' as the cause of death, which means it may not have been natural.

Asked about Harry's inoculations on the day he died she replies:

The evidence suggests that babies who are immunised at the appropriate time are less likely to die of SIDS than those whose immunisation is neglected.

Asked about the fractured rib she says:

If he had a fracture, this was the result of an injury at least four weeks
   before death . . . The second dislocated rib is a most unusual injury. I
   was surprised there was no haemorrhage around it. It was very recent . . .
   A common cause for the finding of hypoxia would be the stopping of
   breathing, for any reason, some hours before death.

She can think of no explanation for the haemorrhage behind the eyes but
does not think it was caused at post-mortem. If the bleeding around the
spine was not caused at post-mortem and is not a common feature –
Professor Berry believes it is – she cannot account for it except by some
form of trauma, but it's not a shaking injury. She can think of no natural
explanation for the swollen cord. Asked about cause of Harry's death she
replies:

It was not a SIDS and I could not find a natural cause of death in the reports
   and material I looked at.

Keeling's cross-examination is postponed until the next morning.
   Steve and Sally rush off to Linda's house and their time with Tom. Sally
is:

'more angry than worried about the statistic. The trouble is I believe
   what Meadow said. I know it is not true. I know the numbers cannot
   apply to me. I know I am innocent, but the man is just so believable.
   I feel sure that Julian Bevan will tell the jury that it has absolutely
   no application to us because nobody is saying we had two cot deaths.
   The prosecution deny that they were cot deaths and so do we. All
   Julian has to do is tell that to the jury and that they must put it right
   out of their minds. As to the other evidence, surely the jury will
   recognise Williams' inconsistencies. I know his findings cannot exist
   because they were my boys and I was with them all the time. He was
   made to face mistakes so many times by Julian. Keeling is much
   more credible. I will wait and see what Julian makes of her in cross-
   examination.'

Spencer recalls Green to give his evidence about Harry. He gives a long explanation for his original finding of retinal haemorrhage in Harry's eyes, which led him to believe that Harry had probably been shaken to death. It was all to do with the way in which the slides were prepared. It sounds highly technical and convincing; that this is one of the most difficult things to diagnose and one of the easiest to get wrong.

Sally's reaction, again, is anger:

> 'This man is an expert on eyes. He has given evidence in hundreds of cases. He knows the routine. He must have known I would be charged with murder if he confirmed retinal haemorrhages – shaken to death. How could he get such a vital finding wrong? Professor Luthert says it is a simple matter; you look down the microscope at the slide of each eye and either the haemorrhages are there or they are not. I have gone through two years of hell mainly because of that incredible mistake. I can hardly bear to look at him.'

Spencer: Were you beginning to wonder whether you had seen what you noted in the first place?

Green: . . . also I was becoming concerned as to its significance. I saw reports from Dr Williams, Professor Berry, Dr Rushton and Professor Luthert. Williams, Rushton and Emery made reference to retinal haemorrhage but only in very small quantities. Luthert and Berry said they could see none at all. So there was this wide disparity of description which concerned me even more . . . I am now satisfied, bearing in mind the way those eyes had been prepared and cut downwards instead of across the top, like opening an egg at breakfast time, what I saw was post-mortem artefact.

This is quoted at such length so as not to be unfair. But Sally is a mother, a lawyer, charged with the most serious crimes; her life and family will be wrecked if she is wrongly convicted. For a world-renowned expert to get something simple so wrong is surely a very serious matter.

Green: I think in this case it could be discounted completely. I have never seen such symptoms before but I have only opened about 200 eyes; Luthert will have done far more and I'm afraid you'll have to ask his opinion.

He has seen bleeding inside and outside the dura of the spine in cases of non-accidental injury, but spinal bleeding in two handfuls of cases. It is definitely not a classic case of a shaken baby and the haemorrhage at the back of the eye is not an injury.

Green: I am concerned at the presence of any petechiae . . . Dr Williams on two occasions has shown me a slide which shows a healing fracture . . . a matter of great concern . . . There is no evidence of natural disease. Harry's death is not a SIDS. I believe that not ascertained is the appropriate diagnosis for both babies. I think Harry's death could well be not natural. I cannot be certain of this but there are abnormalities, which need explanation.

Junior counsel, John Kelsey Fry, rises to cross-examine. This is not unusual, because he is very experienced and about to become a QC himself, but it is so vital for the jury to understand that Green has made so many mistakes – on crucial issues that cast doubt, not only on his own credibility, but on that of the other experts, who have put their reputations on the line on the basis of his findings – that it is surprising that Bevan is not doing it himself.

Kelsey Fry: You are a forensic not a paediatric pathologist?
Green: That is right.
Kelsey Fry: But you have an interest in two facets of child deaths, the lungs and retinal haemorrhages?
Green: Yes . . . Babies' lungs and babies' eyes.

He admits that a number of features of a classic shaken baby death are absent.

Kelsey Fry: In the beginning you were told that there were three significant findings . . . Tears in the brain? Damage to the spinal cord? Subdural haemorrhage?
Green: Yes. I was relying on a conversation with Dr Williams.

There are questions about when he was told what, and then Kelsey Fry asks:

You were satisfied that you had seen intra-retinal haemorrhages?
Green: Yes.
Kelsey Fry: Were you in any doubt at committal about them?

Green: I relied on my memory and on this occasion my memory had . . .

Kelsey Fry: Let you down?

Green: . . . Haemorrhage is there but not as much as I remembered. At committal I said: 'The retinal haemorrhages in the case of Harry were definitely ante-mortem in origin.'

Kelsey Fry: Occasioned during life?

Green: Yes. I was relying on what I had seen the previous February and had had no opportunity to refresh my memory.

Kelsey Fry [*quoting*]: 'Had there been attachments present these might have been post-mortem artefacts, but the distribution and pattern of the haemorrhages which I saw could not have been produced after death?'

Green: I concede that I was in error.

Kelsey Fry: Still thinking they were significant, you said that the death of Harry could well have been unnatural?

Green: Yes.

Kelsey Fry: Based on that and the other findings.

Green: And a conversation I had with Dr Smith about hypoxic changes . . .

Kelsey Fry: By the Friday before the trial had you become concerned about the retinal haemorrhages?

Green: I knew Professor Berry said he could see none and also Professor Luthert.

Kelsey Fry: And that is why you wanted to explore all the slides?

Green: Yes . . .

Kelsey Fry . . . the upshot is that you now accept that one must discount haemorrhages in the eyes?

Green: I have to. Had the eyes been prepared in a different way . . .

And he gives a long explanation for his mistake, *which is complicated and difficult to understand.*

Kelsey Fry: Were there some macrophages?

Green: We are on a learning curve with eyes. Twenty per cent or more who have a rapid delivery have retinal haemorrhages . . .

Kelsey Fry: . . . If you readily accept that that may result from the birth process and therefore we cannot attach significance to it, why did you draw attention to it in the magistrates' Court without saying it may well come from birth?

Green: I was only told at the beginning of this month that Harry had had a rapid vaginal delivery.

Kelsey Fry: The rapid vaginal delivery was in the first paragraph of Dr Williams' post-mortem report!

Green: When Dr Williams came to see me I had not seen the report. I subsequently overlooked it.

Another finding, of some importance, being overlooked!

Kelsey Fry: . . . And you cannot exclude blood sites on the orbs of the eyes as post-mortem artefacts?

Green: . . . I cannot exclude it but perhaps Professor Luthert can expand on it . . .

Kelsey Fry: The eyes were accessed by Dr Williams punching through bone?

Green: I regard him as a gentle operator, not a clumsy one.

Kelsey Fry: He had to punch a bone to get the eyes out, and it is at precisely that area that the blood would drop?

Sally feels revulsion:

'I want to be sick. I know I am crying and I shouldn't be, but this is too much for any mum to bear. Don't they know what it is like for me, as they make me live through the brutal mutilation of the baby I loved so much? For me, Ferkin Features is still alive and they are doing these terrible things to the baby to whom I gave birth, who was and is an extension of my body. Please stop!'

The 'culprit' is not Kelsey Fry: Green and Williams having made their diagnoses, Kelsey Fry has no option, in Sally's best interest, but to destroy them if he can – in all their harrowing details.

Green then launches into another long-winded explanation using chicken-pox blebs as an analogy which neither the judge nor I understand.

Kelsey Fry: Have you ever seen it before?

Green: In living patients, yes; but not at post-mortem.

Kelsey Fry: Or seen it referred to in medical literature anywhere?

Green: Not in standard textbooks.

Kelsey Fry: If Professor Luthert is right in saying there was a fragment of bone there, the only sensible origin would be the puncturing of the orbital bone?

Green: I think that has to be the case.

There is then further examination of blood around the spine.

Kelsey Fry: In those circumstances is it fair to link it with trauma?

Green: I think it has to be regarded as a serious possibility.

Kelsey Fry: Can you think of how trauma occasioned that injury?

Green: It would be uninformed speculation to try . . .

Experts claim that a finding is due to trauma and then say that the reason they cannot think how such trauma was inflicted is because it has never been recorded. But Green and other experts spend their lives interpreting what they see. Is it right – is it fair – that if experts can't say how a finding was caused, the defendant still has to come up with an explanation or leave the jury believing the worst?

Evidence that a finding is due to trauma should not be admissible unless the expert claiming it can say how it was inflicted. However many difficulties that may make for the experts, it is as nothing compared to the prejudice to the defendant of saying: 'this was trauma but we can't figure out how it was inflicted'. They seem to say: 'Trust me, I'm the expert. I know what she probably did, but don't ask me how. I'm not that much of an expert!'

Kelsey Fry: You know Professor Berry?

Green: He is Professor of Paediatric Pathology at Bristol.

Kelsey Fry: In his report he says that a finding of . . . red cells surrounding the spinal cord is a common occurrence and does not indicate shaking? You accept his experience in such matters?

Green: Yes.

Kelsey Fry: Bearing that and everything else that has changed in mind, what view do you now hold as to Harry's death?

Green says that Berry had not seen everything and was talking about something else in his statement. Kelsey Fry does not accept that and then asks:

Since you originally said 'could well be unnatural', what can you now say in respect of Harry?

Green does not say that it has shaken his confidence in his original opinion, which purely from a commonsense view, would seem to be surprising. Instead he refers back to all his 'great concerns'. Green lectures that up to 40 per cent of cot deaths are murder. He teaches pathologists to think dirty at post-mortem. He is a man with strong views on the subject of sudden infant death.

Kelsey Fry: You still say Harry's death was unascertained?
Green: That is the view I have held all the way through.

The next subject is Christopher.

Kelsey Fry: At page 114 of your statement did you say 'The lungs from Christopher showed no evidence of recent significant haemorrhage'?
Green: Yes.
Kelsey Fry: And you repeated that at committal?
Green: Yes.
Kelsey Fry: Professor, this is a murder case. Someone of your experience would obviously take the utmost care in a case which is so dependent on the medical evidence?
Green: Indeed.
Kelsey Fry: As you knew, from the outset, that there was significant haemorrhage how did you come to make a statement saying the opposite?

Green is embarrassed and struggling to answer. He gives a further explanation involving the slides.

Green: . . . the committal proceedings were from time to time confusing . . .
Kelsey Fry: With respect, you had already put it in your witness statement.
Green: But I also had a file which contradicted it.
Kelsey Fry: Is it a case of your memory letting you down?
Green: Yes.
Kelsey Fry: Do you think that you have really exercised the utmost care throughout this case?
Green: I have tried to.

And then he goes on for another eleven lines of the transcript to justify his contradictions.

Kelsey Fry: You said in your report: 'There is nothing in the pathological findings to show that asphyxia is the cause of death. There are suspicious findings, the mouth and bruises, but no more than that.' And you were not able to observe those findings. You are dependent on Dr Williams?

Green: I know Dr Williams and place reliance on his description. The proper diagnosis would be 'not ascertained', drawing attention to those matters.

Kelsey Fry has done a great job on Green. Bevan could not have done better. It was skilful and must have persuaded the jury that they should not rely on any of Green's evidence.

Sally's reaction is disgust:

'Going to such lengths to save face at my expense, the expense of an innocent mum, is despicable.'

What follows should have a 'health warning'. It is not so much a mainstream legal opinion, as a practical reaction to what appears to be obvious injustice in the legal process.

I believe at this point that this trial should not be allowed to continue in the light of Green's performance. No defendant should be put through the hell of a murder trial on the basis of such medical contradictions. Spencer and the Crown Prosecution Service knew the full extent of Green's mistakes about eyes, about the lungs; they knew that Williams' findings were contradicted by a raft of highly qualified experts and that his findings of retinal haemorrhages in Harry were bogus; they knew about Meadow's incredible denials of evidence he had given at committal just a couple of hours earlier; they know he failed to supply details of cases he cited as damning Sally. How could a prosecutor allow the case to go ahead? How, in the light of it, can Spencer continue to seek to convict Sally Clark? The prosecution team know she has always denied harming her babies. They know that her husband and father and nanny proclaim her innocence. They know there is no direct evidence that she ever had harmed or ever would harm a baby and that all experts – except Williams and Meadow, over whose testimony a large cloud of doubt has formed – say the cause of both babies' deaths is unascertained. They know that all the healthcare professionals who attended Sally had nothing but the highest regard for her as a loving and caring mother.

Do those considerations not demand a re-think about allowing the case to go any further?

Dr Keeling is recalled for cross-examination. Bevan's is another fine example of that art. It occupies 27 pages of the transcript and deals with all the findings that have been canvassed with other experts. Ultimately, on Christopher, he asks:

> In your report you said: 'The presence of the unusual circumstances of death, the pathological findings and the absence of a natural cause of death means the possibility of non-natural death should be considered.'
> *Keeling*: Yes.
> *Bevan*: And no doubt you still hold the same view?
> *Keeling*: I do.
> *Bevan*: In Harry's case would you say unascertained?
> *Keeling*: I would say unascertained.

Sally recalls the hours and days she and Steve spent studying all the medical reports:

> 'If even one of those medical findings actually exists, it must mean that at some place and some time, either Steve or I, or maybe both of us, did something, accidentally, that injured our boys. The truth is that everybody who handled Christopher and Harry, including his parents, treated them with such care and love that we cannot come up with a single incident that could account for harm coming to either of them.'

Bevan could not have got any more out of this witness. The jury seems not particularly impressed.

Spencer then recalls Williams to reinforce his opinions on the ribs and on the swelling of the spinal cord. Nothing new comes out, but Williams has a chance to try to justify his findings. In my opinion he does not succeed.

That is the end of the case for the prosecution.

Now is the time when the defence could make a submission to the judge that there is no case to answer and ask him to throw it out. But would that succeed? Two expert witnesses support murder: Williams, still saying that Christopher was smothered to death and that Harry was smothered and/or shaken; and Meadow, who still says neither death was natural. And there are the other suspicious findings that call for an answer by Sally and her medical team.

It is Friday night. What about the trial so far. the good and the bad? It is for the prosecution to prove that Christopher and Harry were murdered. and their case is overflowing with reasonable doubts. The worry is 1:73 million. If Bevan is wrong about that, Sally is in trouble; trouble as bad as it gets.

Sally and Steve have the weekend to contemplate what the following week will bring. They know that the most important part of the case begins on Monday: her evidence and Steve's. Her fate is now in her own hands:

> 'If I can convince the jury of my innocence – I know it's not up to me to prove anything, the prosecution have to prove me guilty – but I am thinking beyond that to the reality of what the jury has heard. That reality is that I have to defend myself. I have to make them see the real me; the person who is incapable of the terrible things so-called experts have said I've done. I know that what I say, how I behave, how I react to that man Spencer, will be the difference between returning to my family and normal life or spending the rest of my days in jail. And for two murders that never happened. But if the prejudice of Meadow's infamous statistic, and the relentless weeks of excoriatingly negative press coverage, put everything else out of their minds, my life is over.'

It cannot be said too often that an English criminal trial is not a search for objective truth. It is a game in which the player with the strongest hand will probably win. Is 1:73 million a trump card?

The Defence Case

The roles of counsel are now reversed. Bevan will now put each of his witnesses into the box and examine them in chief, being careful not to ask leading questions; Spencer will then cross-examine – asking as many leading questions as he likes – to test the truth of what they say.

Traditionally, the first witness for the defence is the defendant. This case is no exception. Sally walks from the dock to the witness box and takes the oath.

She has been dressed throughout in her normal working clothes – a business suit.

Sally's Evidence

She is nervous:

'What makes me so, is appearing in public, taking the stand, being in the spotlight and having to lay bare, to strangers, the most intimate details of my family and personal life.

'In spite of the setback at every turn of my case, every forecast that I would not be charged, not be committed, I still believe that, as I am innocent of any wrongdoing, I am safe. All I have to do is tell the truth; the system will protect me. I know I have to live through this nightmare, but that is all it is. Being convicted of the murder of my adored babies is simply an impossibility.'

Bevan rises. He smiles at Sally. By this time she knows him reasonably well. He is forbidding because of his eminence in the law, of his aristocratic aura, that 'Eton, Christ Church and the Guards' attitude, and because of his formidable grasp of the facts and the medicine. In spite of his often-stuttered delivery, he exudes confidence. Sally has no doubt that she is in the best of hands.

She does not know what to feel.

'I convince myself that this is my chance to show who I am, the sort of person I am. I know the first bit is the easy part. Bevan is on my side. He will make it as painless as he can. The danger man is Spencer. Will he make me suffer?'

She reads the oath from the card in a quiet, careful voice. The judge invites her to sit if she wishes. She takes a deep breath.

Bevan begins with the formalities: who she is, when she married; easy questions to make her familiar with the intimidating environment. Then:

Bevan: When you discovered you were pregnant with Christopher, what was your reaction?

Sally: I was shocked, but completely delighted. I was shocked it happened so quickly after we decided to have a baby, but delighted it happened so quickly.

Bevan: After he was born did you take him to the office?

Sally: I wanted to show him off. He was just so perfect.

Sally describes the nosebleed at the Strand Palace Hotel; returning from a shopping trip with Elizabeth Cox and both of them hearing Steve's explanation.

Sally produces the invitation to Christopher's christening in Salisbury and describes preparations for Christmas; how Steve had always dreamed of having presents from his son and how she was making that dream come true with the many she had bought him from Christopher.

She tells of the night he died; of him being in the bouncy chair with her when she had a bath, the doctor having told her the steam would help deal with the baby's sniffle. She then breast-fed him; he fed normally, probably about eight o'clock.

Bevan: Did you then put him in the Moses basket?

Sally: Yes, that's correct. We had a bit of a play. I cuddled him, things like that on the bed. I sat on the bed watching television with him beside me in the Moses basket. I went downstairs – I don't remember looking at him – and pottered around. Back upstairs I put my mug of tea down and he was just this dusty grey colour. I pulled back the cover and knew something was wrong. I don't think I picked him up. I dialled 999.

She tells how she picked him up and went downstairs and then could not find the key to let in the ambulance men. Christopher was floppy, limp.

Sally: I'm saying 'I'm locked in. I'm locked in, please help me, my baby's dying' . . . I was just screaming.

Bevan: Do you remember what Dr Cowan said about the bouncy chair? When you have been told now, that Christopher is dead?

Sally: I was completely hysterical . . . I was telling her about the events of the evening . . . I was getting hysterical about the breast-feeding . . .

Bevan: Are you able to recount accurately what you said to Dr Cowan?

Sally: No.

Bevan: Have you ever done anything untoward towards that child?

Sally: Absolutely not.

Bevan: Did you kill your own child?

Sally: No, I didn't. I loved him.

Bevan asks her about Harry.

Sally: We decided that having another baby might ease the pain of having lost Christopher . . .

Bevan: He was born on 29th November that year?

Sally: Yes, he was.

Sally describes going on to the CONI programme and her relations with the health visitors, keeping the weight chart, plotting everything from bowel movements to anybody who came to the house who smoked. She described learning how to put the apnoea alarm on Harry and hiring nanny Lesley Kerrigan as a home help.

Bevan: Have you any idea how Harry may have fractured a rib in the early weeks of his life?

Sally: Absolutely not.

Bevan: If you picked him up would he yelp? Show some signs of pain?

Sally: Absolutely not. No.

Bevan: You had lost Christopher. How much attention did you devote to Harry?

Sally: I tried not to be paranoid but I was watching him all the time. We didn't go out much in case he caught the same virus that killed Christopher.

Bevan asks her to read the letter she wrote —as if from Harry – to Frank and Rosemary.

Sally [*reading*]: 'Dear Grandma and Grandpa. I thought I would write you a little note to say thank you for all your help last weekend. I know it made Mummy's day to come home to a nice tidy house, you know how she is about things like that. She kept saying over and over again how much she appreciated all you'd done. Well, it's nice to be here at last, although the midwives now believe that my original due date was in fact correct and that I am here early. I'm beginning to get hungry now and need lots of meals. Mummy seems very pleased today and I have put on weight. Daddy has already let me watch my first football match with him, which was good fun, although Mummy kept reminding him to watch his language and shouting now that I'm here. Mummy and Daddy seem pretty pleased I'm here and I'm healthy and cute, in fact I'm getting a bit fed up with Mummy looking at me with goo-goo eyes and talking to me in a silly voice. The days are a bit boring and I'm not into cookery programmes or soap operas yet, so I tend to sleep and look angelic. Night time is far more exciting, I tend to keep awake and make lots of noise so that Mummy and Daddy stay awake as well. Anyway I must go now. Hope to see you soon. Lots of love. Harry.'

This is painfully difficult for Sally. What do the jury make of her? Do the women identify and perhaps sympathise? Are the men – the younger ones – sceptical?

Bevan now returns to the apnoea alarm.

Bevan: On 26th November you asked for a replacement bleeper?
Sally: Yes, I did. It had been going off more than it should, the connection seemed to be Okay . . .

Bevan then asks her to read another letter, this time to Frank and Rosemary, the other grandparents, as if from Harry. After thanks for presents she writes, and Sally reads:

'I fear I've caused a fair bit of disruption in the Clark household . . . I like to sleep and look angelic most of the day but at night, I prefer to stay awake and keep Mummy and Daddy awake with me . . . The Health Visitor assured Mummy that I will sleep for longer intervals once I've caught up on myself, given that I was quite tiny at birth . . . lots of love Harry.'

Sally then describes Harry's inoculations at 4.20 p.m. on 26th January and the replacement of the monitor.
Bevan asks if she remembers what time Steve got home.

Sally: I now know he came back about 5.30 p.m.
Bevan: So you can check through the taxi notes?

Sally: That's how I know. I breast-fed him about 7.30. He appeared to feed. I was on the bed upstairs. Steve was with me. Steve played with him for a bit . . . we chatted . . . the thing I remember distinctly was that Steve put him in his little bouncy chair, his side of the bed. Steve went downstairs. At about nine o'clock. To make his bottle . . . I looked over at Harry . . . His head was down like that . . .

Sally demonstrates with just her head falling forward.

Sally: I could see this part of his head. This was different . . . it just wasn't right.

Bevan: What was your reaction?

Sally: Panic. Complete panic. I screeched out, we'd had some resuscitation training . . . I'd not been able to do it because it brought back too many memories of Christopher . . .

Later she is asked:

Bevan: At the hospital you were told that Harry had died at twenty to eleven that night?

Sally: That's right.

Bevan: Do you remember having a conversation with Mrs Hearst, the coroner's officer, the next day?

Sally: It was quite a long conversation . . . She expressed her condolences . . . I kept saying 'Why me? Why has this happened?' and she said they would do all they could to find out why Harry died . . . I said it seemed so unfair that we could have children so easily and yet something like this happens, when so many of our friends can't have children at all . . . I used the word genetic four or five times . . . She said 'I need an authority for your medical records . . . I want you to draw me a family tree, with any children who have died in infancy . . . '

Bevan [*later*]: What was your reaction to losing two children?

Sally: Complete disbelief. I couldn't believe it, that it could have happened twice, and you know, we were just meant to have children and I loved them so much, I couldn't believe it had happened a second time.

If members of the jury believe that the chances of two cot deaths were 1:73 million, will they be able to believe Sally is telling the truth? That is why prejudice is so dangerous, why it can lead to miscarriages of justice and why it is inadmissible in any court of law, unless what it proves is greater than the prejudice it creates, in the minds of the jury.

Bevan: I'm going to ask you a very stark question, Mrs Clark. Did you murder both your children?

Although everybody knows what she is going to say, it does not stop the goose pimples rising.

Sally: No, I did not.

Her examination-in-chief has taken an hour and a quarter.

After a short adjournment Mr Justice Harrison reads out a question from the jury:

Judge: 'Please could we have a detailed description of the locks and bolts on both the front and side doors?'

Sally's answer occupies three pages of the transcript. She describes the keys and Bevan asks her to produce them. Her handbag is still in the dock. It is handed to an usher, who takes it to Sally. By one of the strangest of the many coincidences of the case, Sally cannot find her keys. The same thing happened the night Christopher died. But eventually she does. She is very embarrassed.

It is uncanny corroboration of what happened that night at Hope Cottage.

Then she describes how the keys work and the mysteries of her handbag.

Bevan sits.

Spencer rises to cross-examine.

If he is to win this case he has to break Sally. If it takes a verbal rack to do it, he may use it. He will not be gentle with her; there will be no sympathy. He wants the jury to see this woman as a cold-blooded serial baby-killer.

His first question is bang on target:

Spencer: Mrs Clark, motherhood didn't come naturally to you, did it?

The shock, the hurt of the question goes so deep, Sally can hardly breathe; the lie that it implies is cruelty. There is visible pain in Sally's eyes. If she is a serial baby-killer it may be justified; if she is not . . . Sally blurts out her answer, fighting back tears.

Sally: Yes.
Spencer: You found it a real shock to the system.

Sally is beginning to get the drift. She decides to give as good as she gets, to do battle with Spencer. Would a 'helpless mum' attitude not give her a better chance with this jury?

Sally: Shocked but delighted.
Spencer: You hadn't wanted to have children so soon?
Sally: In an ideal world, that's correct.
Spencer: You and your husband differed as to when you should start a family.
Sally: We never differed. No.
Spencer: You didn't have much by way of family support in Wilmslow?
Sally: My mother died some years ago . . . Family, no.

He emphasises what long hours Steve worked and his time away from her on sports.

Spencer: Did you find it disconcerting when you began to get larger . . . your looks were going . . .
Sally: I think I complained at various times that I couldn't get into suits but I was working into maternity wear. All mothers do that.
Spencer: It was very tiring, demanding, after Christopher was born? Steve didn't get any paternity leave . . .
Sally: He had two weeks off . . .
Spencer: Both these babies were found about 9.30 in the evening. After a long and tiring day?
Sally: Not particularly long and tiring, no. I was getting tired of an evening with Harry, yes. He was more demanding than Christopher.

There are pages of questions that seem to me to be leading nowhere about times and places where things happened. Then:

Spencer: At the Strand Palace Hotel, was your husband there all the time, before you went out shopping?

Sally: Yes.

Spencer: Did you do something to Christopher? Did you try to smother him?

Sally: No I didn't.

Spencer: He was perfectly all right, was he?

Sally: I had no cause for concern.

Spencer: No problem with his nose?

Sally: He had a snuffle and large bogies . . .

Spencer: You're not suggesting that Christopher would somehow pick his own nose?

Sally: He used to spend a lot of time with his finger up his nose. I mentioned it to Doctor Levitt . . .

Spencer: You will remember Professor Meadow's evidence . . . Did you make some traumatic contact with Christopher's nose?

Sally: No I didn't.

Spencer: Trying to smother him?

Sally: No I didn't.

Spencer asks many questions about the details of the nosebleed, trying to trip Sally up in contradictions, but gets nowhere. He moves on to the night Christopher died.

Spencer: Are you absolutely sure that you found Christopher in his Moses' basket?

Sally: One hundred per cent sure, yes . . . I remember Dr Cowan's evidence talking about the Moses basket.

Spencer: It's not something you would get mixed up about, is it?

Sally: She didn't ask me that question but about the events of the evening and I said he'd been in his bouncy chair. She didn't ask me where I found him.

Spencer: Did you put him in his bouncy chair after his feed or not?

Sally: I can't remember. When he died, I found him in his Moses basket. On his back.

Spencer: When the police challenged you that Christopher was found in his bouncy chair, you must have been bursting to answer?

Sally: Yes, but Mr Mackey advised me to say nothing to any question. I'd been bursting to answer the question on many occasions over the last eighteen months, but I was told to say no comment, or to say nothing . . .

There are pages of questions, trying to elicit contradictions from Sally, on where Christopher died and then about the keys, but Spencer gets no admissions.

Spencer: Somehow he got bruises to his legs and arm.
Sally: I didn't see any bruises.
Spencer: You're not aware of anything that could have caused bruises on Christopher?
Sally: Absolutely not.
Spencer: You smothered Christopher, didn't you?
Sally: No I did not.
Spencer: And he put up quite a struggle?

Sally is very upset by this and cannot stop the tears.

Sally: I did not smother my baby, I loved him.
Spencer: And that's how he got those bruises and the injury to his mouth.
Sally: I didn't see any bruises. I didn't see any injury to his mouth. I did nothing to harm him in any way. I loved him so much.

Will Spencer press home his advantage in the hope that she will become even more upset and break down completely and then confess? – a theory of advocacy that sometimes works. The problem with it is that if the defendant is innocent, pressing home the advantage may antagonise the jury because of its cruelty. Sometimes it is rewarded with a 'confession' which may be true, or maybe said to stop the 'torture'; but that's not a risk with Sally. Spencer backs off. He changes the subject: to Harry.

Spencer: Harry was a different character from Christopher? He tended to cry more . . . He would play you up at night?

Sally smiles as she says:

Sally: Oh yes, he did. Yes.

Sally cannot help smiling. That's what always happened whenever she or Steve saw, picked up or spoke about Ferkin Features: he provoked smiles. 'He was just that sort of lovable baby.'

Spencer: . . . Despite having help in the day you were very, very tired by the evening?

Sally: I was still tired, yes.

Spencer: He was 'spirited', in the nicest possible way, a 'little devil'?

Sally: A little character, yes.

Spencer: You called him 'a little bugger'. To your husband?

Sally: Not in front of the baby.

Spencer: You were concerned because your husband was going to Glasgow the next day.

Sally: He had been out late but this was the first night away since Harry was born. I was apprehensive . . . that he might be upset by the jabs. I didn't want to be on my own with him if he was distressed . . . I wasn't having anybody to stay overnight.

Spencer: You walked home from the clinic?

Sally: I got home about twenty past five and Steve was there within a quarter of an hour.

Spencer: Are you sure about that?

Sally: Absolutely. Sure with hindsight, because we checked the taxi records for him getting home that evening, and he got in about twenty-five or twenty to six. It was only when you're piecing these things together that you can recall these things.

Spencer makes her look at notes of her police interview.

Spencer [*quoting*]: 'Question: What time did Steve get in? (A) I think it was about 7, 7.15. I'm sorry I can't really remember precisely. All I know is I'd had a bath and that I was . . . (Q) You'd had a bath by the time Steve got in? (A) Yes.'

Spencer: Now is that right?

Sally: I was completely wrong there. I was mistaken . . . and to some of the events of that evening.

Spencer: You must have turned the events of the evening over in your mind endlessly . . .

Sally: What he looked like when I found him, but not the events of the evening, no. Since I was arrested I've thought about it nearly every day, but not prior to then.

Spencer: When did you have your bath?

Sally: After Steve got in. I can't remember what time . . .

Spencer: With Harry with you in the bathroom?

Sally: I don't think so. I think he was with Steve. There are two or three instances where I got muddled up with Christopher. What this interview doesn't show is that I was in tears for most of it . . . All I can remember is . . . he was in his pram . . . I got him out, it was parked by the door and Steve came home about a quarter of an hour later. I was on my own with Harry until then.

Spencer: Do you remember having tea?

Sally: It was a normal evening . . .

Spencer: Between the time he was fed and your husband getting home who was Harry with?

Sally: With Stephen and I.

Spencer: Together all the time?

Sally: Most of the time . . . Steve could not move because of his leg in plaster . . . I'm talking about a typical evening . . . we would be upstairs . . . Steve would put on his civvy clothes . . . We would go down to the kitchen together . . . I would carry Harry.

Spencer: I'm asking about that last night. It must be very vivid in your mind.

Sally: The sight of him in that chair.

Spencer: Are you saying he was always in your joint company during that period or may you have been alone with him some of the time?

Sally: I may have been alone with him some of the time.

Spencer: After he was fed . . .

Sally: I gave him to Steve . . . we had him on the bed together and then Steve put him in his bouncy chair and then went to make his bottle.

Spencer: And within three, or . . . five minutes – that was all the time it took him to hobble downstairs?

Sally: Yes.

Spencer: Do you remember telling Ann McDougal, the health visitor, that Harry was alongside the bed in his crib?

Sally: I think she's mistaken. I think she's muddled the two babies.

Spencer [*quoting McDougal's statement to police*]: 'And then Mrs Clark glanced at the baby and he appeared to be sleeping. After a while she looked again and she felt the need to prod him and realised there was no response and screamed for Mr Clark.'

Sally: I can't recall that conversation.

Spencer: It's not what you told the jury happened?

Sally: I looked over at Harry, his head was down and I got out of bed and ran around the bed, picked him out of his bouncy chair.

Spencer [*quoting the her statement to police*]: 'So you had to go like that to see him' – meaning to lean across to see him?

Sally: I certainly demonstrated it to police.

Spencer [*quoting Detective Cantello's statement*]: 'You said before that when you saw his head had flopped you panicked straight away. That's because yeah, because he was just, it was like his whole body, I was going to say.' Police Officer: 'Yes, so his shoulders had fallen down as well? (A) Yeah. (Q) Did you know straight away that something was wrong? (A) Yeah, because even when he slept in his bouncy chair he always used to just put his head to one side and he was upright, just wasn't putting his head down, he was right forward.' Your words, Mrs Clark?

Sally: Yes.

Spencer: It couldn't have happened like that, in that chair, could it?

Sally: His head was forward, he'd flopped, flopped down, like that.

Spencer: It can't have happened like that . . . with his whole body slumping forward, shoulders as well, could he?

Sally: His head was flopped right forward.

Spencer: Somehow you had implanted in your mind an image of Harry in a strange and unusual position?

Sally: 'Cause I could see that part.

Spencer: Bent in some way?

Sally: He wasn't bent, his head was bent . . . just from his neck.

Spencer: How did Harry get damage to his brain some hours before he died?

Sally: I've no idea. I didn't harm him in any way at all, I loved him.

Spencer: Damage consistent with smothering him? Before your husband came home that night?

Sally: No, I didn't.

Spencer: And when your husband was downstairs, you did something else to Harry?

Sally: I didn't get out of bed except when I saw his head flop forward.

Spencer: Who took Harry out of his bed?

Sally: I did.

Spencer: Have you any doubt about that?

Sally: Yes . . . whether I actually took him out and just picked him up and put him back in, I can't remember.

Spencer: You had to do something before your husband went away the next day?

Sally: I don't understand.
Spencer: Kill Harry!

Sally bursts again into tears.

Sally: Absolutely not, no. Absolutely not. He was so precious.
Spencer: You caused some injury to his back and you have this image of how he looked after you had done it?
Sally: I loved him to bits and I didn't harm him in any way.
Spencer: And you smothered him as well, at the end?
Sally: I didn't harm my baby in any way at all.
Spencer: The truth is that, for whatever reason, you did kill both your babies?
Sally: I loved both of them in their own little ways more than anything, together with my husband.
Spencer: While you were at the end of your tether?
Sally: Never at the end of my tether. Harry was too precious for that.
Spencer: Thank you.

It could have been worse.

And he sits. Bevan rises and asks a number of questions in re-examination.

Bevan: Did you discuss with your husband that you were so tired that you needed more help in the house?
Sally: No, because I didn't feel I needed it.

Because Sally has been criticised for not answering some police questions, Bevan quotes Mackey's recorded statement at her interview:

Bevan: 'Can I just say to you' – that is to the police officers – 'this high-lights the difficulty of seeking to advise you in the absence of disclosure of reports. I suggest that you make no comment about the observations that the officer just put to you. None whatsoever.' Yes?
Sally: Yes.
Bevan: It has been suggested that you killed Christopher because he interfered with your career?
Sally: I had another baby because I wanted another so much and my career could take second place.

Bevan is about to call his next witness, Steve, when the judge asks Sally about the position Harry was in, in the bouncy chair, at the end. Bevan sits, looking warily at Harrison.

Judge: Why did you say . . . to the police . . . about Harry . . . 'it was like his whole body' if it was only his head?

Sally: I think what I was trying to say was it just wasn't right, his whole body wasn't right, but I wasn't trying to say that his whole body was flopped forward. It just . . . it wasn't right.

Judge [*quoting a further passage from the police interview*]: 'And then the officer said: "Yes, so his shoulders had fallen down as well," and you said "Yes."'

Sally: Yes.

Judge: If his shoulders had fallen down as well, then it wasn't just his head going down, was it?

Sally: No . . . I . . . it was his head down like that but his whole body was not forward, it was just sagged and his head was like this . . . limp I guess is what I'm trying to say.

Judge: So rather than he was right forward, his head was right forward?

Sally: That's correct, yes.

Sally is greatly relieved to be out of the witness box, out of the line of fire. She is pleased that she did not get angry or drawn on any of the more hurtful remarks that were made:

> 'Spencer must genuinely believe I am guilty. I think I did as well as could be expected, given the shock to my system of Spencer's opening question.'

Is she right?

As Bevan walks out of court with Mackey he says: 'If that wasn't a lady telling nothing but the truth I've never seen one!'

Mackey: Right!

Is this wishful thinking by Bevan? The exchange with the judge is worrying. Juries take notice of questions from the judge, and a baby of eight weeks does not have strong enough back muscles to pull his shoulders off a reclining bouncy chair. Will the jury think back to Meadow saying that the parents of natural deaths recall unimportant details accurately, but killers make mistakes about them? Hopefully not.

But there is a more compelling argument: if two experienced and intelligent lawyers, like Sally and Steve, had colluded to murder their babies, would they not have got their stories straight? Will the jury work that one out?

Steve's Evidence

Bevan: Call Stephen Clark.

The usher fetches him. It is nerve-racking but he is not charged with a crime. The CPS wanted to charge him jointly with Sally, but he was absent from Hope Cottage the whole of the day on which Christopher died and the police were unable to break his alibi. So he is a witness for the defence, and a vital one. All he has to do is to tell the truth and he will get through it unscathed, and so make certain his wife is found not guilty.

This is an emotional moment for Sally:

'My darling Steve has not been allowed in court for all that has gone before this. We have been deliberately kept apart, at the worst time of our lives, by rules that seem to us to be cruel and unforgivable. As he walks into court, my love for him wells up. I register the fact that he looks smart; he looks composed. But I can still see, underneath it, his vulnerability. I love him so much.'

Stephen Clark speaks in a firm, strong voice:

'I swear by Almighty God, that the evidence I will give will be the truth, the whole truth and nothing but the truth.'

The words are so routine that some witnesses seem able to forget them the moment a lie is necessary. What I know of Steve tells me that he will take the oath literally and seriously and – although he does not believe in God – he would rather lose his right arm than lie. I have quoted the words of the oath in full because things will develop during the course of his evidence which will enable Spencer to allege that Steve has lied, and lied again, to save his wife.

Bevan asks the usual preliminary questions, and then about having a baby.

Steve: We'd waited a while before seriously trying because Sally had changed careers and she needed time to settle in . . . We talked about it long and hard . . . she was thirty-two at the time and we thought it was probably about time to start trying; about the end of 1995.

Bevan: By early 1996 she was pregnant. What was her reaction?

Steve: Delighted . . . Slightly shocked at how quickly . . .

Bevan: And when Christopher was born did she appear devoted?

Steve: Absolutely devoted, she loved him.

Steve describes the journey to London and the nosebleed at the Strand Palace Hotel.

Steve: Blood was running out of his nose . . . both nostrils, into his mouth . . . he was in his car seat, leaning back, so it was going into his mouth and he was swallowing it . . . obviously in difficulty breathing . . . so I ran into the bathroom and splashed his nose and mouth with water . . . That seemed to help his breathing. I rang reception . . . Two men arrived quickly . . .But by this time he was a lot better. No more blood from his nose . . . Breathing normally. They gave me the name of a doctor . . . I rang him . . . He said it probably wasn't necessary to bring him into the surgery, but I could if I was worried. I decided to wait until Sally got back.

Bevan: And did he seem all right?

Steve: After a very terrifying few minutes . . . no problems.

He told Sally and her friend when they came back. And told other friends as well.

Steve recounts the plans for Christopher's christening in Salisbury.

He tells of the night Christopher died; of being at the party. He describes the unusual locks on both doors. The front door is always locked and everybody uses the back door. But Sally, who is frequently upstairs with Christopher, keeps that locked when Steve is not there.

Bevan asks about the decision to have another baby.

Steve: We thought it would be part of the healing process. And honour Christopher's memory if we could have a brother or sister for him.

He describes the accident and having his leg in plaster and the hiring of Lesley Kerrigan and the birth of Harry.

Because of Williams' evidence about a fractured rib, Bevan asks him:

Bevan: Did you at times lift up and play with your baby son?
Steve: Yes, I did.
Bevan: Did you ever get any indication, in the first four weeks of his life, that he was in discomfort or pain when you picked him up?
Steve: None whatsoever.

He describes trouble with the apnoea alarm going off two or three times a day, and says that the problems began almost as soon as they had the alarm.

Bevan asks about the firm's arrangements with the taxi company.

Steve: I think there's an account.
Bevan: Do the taxi firm keep records?
Steve: My firm does, I don't know if they do.
Bevan: Your firm keeps a record of someone like yourself booking a taxi?
Steve: Destination, whose account is to be charged.
Bevan: What about times?
Steve: The time it is booked . . . the time they rang . . . I'm sure you could have booked for a particular time . . . In my case it was usually as soon as possible . . .
Bevan: Just out of interest, does your firm have a record of you booking a taxi for 26th January? [the night Harry died]
Steve: The record shows that a taxi was booked at that time, but I was getting a taxi to the airport . . . I was going to Glasgow, the record shows that booking. At the same time they booked a taxi to take me home. It's not clear from the record about the first taxi, but I know that the lady who works on reception who booked it for me . . .

Spencer rises:

Spencer: I'm sorry to interrupt but . . . I don't know if this evidence is going to be produced, this documentary evidence . . .
Bevan: I don't know if it is going to be necessary or not, I am just interested in the time you arrived home, whether there's a record supporting it. That's all.

Steve gave the records to Mackey the previous July.

Steve: The lady who booked the taxi for me . . .

Bevan: Give me a moment, Mr Clark . . . I don't want my learned friend to
    be upset. You can only give admissible evidence. Do you understand?

Steve: Yes. The taxi in my . . .

Bevan: There is a record in your office in relation to booking a taxi?

Steve: Yes.

*What the defence team do not know is that the police have already checked with
Addleshaws, and been told there is no taxi record. Spencer may, understandably,
think Steve is about to produce a forgery.*

Kelsey Fry does not understand what Spencer is so uptight about. He beckons
to Mackey and asks him to check with the taxi firm. Mackey leaves the court.

Bevan: What precisely it says, I suppose one has to look at the record?

Steve: Yes.

Bevan: What time did you arrive home that night?

Steve: It must have been between five thirty p.m. and about quarter to six.

Bevan: And how do you know that? Is it pure memory or have you been
    assisted by any record?

Steve: I've been assisted by the recollection of the lady who booked the taxi
    for me.

Bevan: You are not allowed to say what the lady told you . . . What is her name?

Steve: Helen.

Bevan: I'm sure we can supply a description if the prosecution want to
    chase her up and see her.

Bevan is treating this lightly. Steve also seems relaxed; so far as he is concerned, he is giving evidence of unimportant technicalities on which nothing
now turns because he has had independent written confirmation from a
trusted company employee who had booked his taxi home at 4.48 p.m.

Steve: Yes.

Spencer rises, interrupting again.

Spencer: These are important matters . . . There is a proper way of dealing with them . . . If there are documents we should have been shown them before this point was taken. We have now had, through the back door as it were . . . some hearsay evidence . . .

Bevan: My lord . . . if I can get the record I will . . .

Spencer sits.

Judge: What Mr Spencer has said is correct and it is up to you to take such steps.

This is a judicial rebuke.

Bevan: I did not know until this moment that there was a record, my lord . . . I am just trying to establish, through you, Mr Clark . . . your recollection is about quarter to six?

Steve: Yes. It can't have been later than that, it would have been between 5.30 and quarter to six.

Bevan: Can we produce the records from your office?

Steve: I think I've already provided it to my solicitor.

Bevan: Good. Then I shall show it to my friend for the prosecution . . . Now you are going away on a business meeting the following day?

Steve: Correct.

Bevan: Can you give a summary of what happened when you got home?

Steve: I can't remember the detail because it was a perfectly unremarkable, normal evening, but I can tell you what our routine was and it would have followed something like the routine, because if it hadn't I would have remembered. I would have gone upstairs, got changed out of my work clothes, because I was still on crutches. I couldn't wear jeans; I would put on my dressing-gown. I would have then sat on the bed, the most comfortable place to be with that injury, with Harry, cuddling him, talking to Sally and Harry about what happened during the day for me and for them. Depending on how Harry was, he may have had a feed. If he didn't want it I would have given him a bath, which would involve taking all his clothes off, washing him, changing his nappy, putting cream on him, dressing him again and then he would have had a feed. He would have gone to sleep after his feed and at that point we would probably have had something to eat,

in the kitchen or bedroom. We would then have watched television
sitting on the bed.

Bevan: Where were you physically when you became aware of anything
wrong at all?

Steve: In the kitchen, making a bottle.

Bevan: And immediately before?

Steve: In the bedroom with Sally and Harry. He'd just been on the breast,
whether he was taking or not I do not know, sometimes he just used it
for comfort . . . Sally handed him to me. He'd fallen asleep. He gave me
a funny sort of wiggle to say 'I was happy there, why have you moved
me?' I would normally have winded him after a feed but because he was
asleep I didn't, I don't think. I then put him in the bouncy chair, which
was on my side of the bed, and strapped him in.

Bevan: What was the time gap?

Steve: It wasn't more than a few minutes . . . I'd started making a bottle
when Sally screamed.

Steve then describes his attempts at resuscitation and relives what is heard
on the 999 tape; and Harry's death. Bevan takes him to the following day
and Sally's telephone call with the coroner's officer, Mrs Hearst.

Steve: We wanted her to do as much . . . whatever investigations . . . to try
to discover why Harry died. Having lost Christopher we were concerned
there may be a problem with me or Sally . . . something genetic.

Later Bevan asks:

Did your wife, at any time, appear . . . too tired to cope?

Steve: We were both tired because Harry was – compared to Christopher –
quite a demanding baby, but she was never too tired to cope.

That is the end of Bevan's examination-in-chief. Spencer's cross-examination is postponed until the next morning.

Judge: You must not talk to your wife about the evidence at all overnight,
you realise that I'm sure.

Steve: Yes, my lord.

The judge's warning to Steve is correct in law and practically ridiculous. They will share a car ride to look after Tom and then go home. They are in the middle of the most important events of their lives and they're forbidden to talk about them. These are, probably, the only two people in the country whose code of honesty is so unbelievable that, having made such a promise, they will keep it!

And they do! Neither Sally nor Steve will take any risks whatever:

'We are too scared to go against what the judge said. We both know that neither of us harmed our two boys. We know we are up against a formidable system that is trying very hard to prove me guilty. Our only way of fighting it is to play it straight down the line; never to waver an inch either side of that line. However unlike a man and his wife in bed together at the most crucial time of their lives it may seem, that's how we played it. Some may think we are crazy; others may not believe it. Neither of us said a word to the other about it!'

If Steve's evidence is allowed to stand, unaltered, Spencer's case is in trouble. Steve is an impressive witness. He stands really upright; a no-nonsense man and yet with a reasonable, non-didactic manner. He is rather formal – he 'wears his qualification on his sleeve' but he is likeable and believable. Spencer must destroy that impression.

The next morning, Steve resumes his place in the witness box. Spencer asks Steve to look at his statement to the police.

Spencer: You say at the top there: 'I can't remember what time I got home from work but it would probably have been between five and six I suppose, as I'd always been coming home, possibly earlier. Again I can't remember really what happened really, up until about nine o'clock. We'd have had tea, we were both upstairs . . . At about nine o'clock Sally fed him . . . '

And he carries on with the description of what happened.

Spencer: This is what I'm coming to because your wife has told the jury . . . that it was only a matter of four minutes or so after you left the room . . . that she found Harry dead . . .
Steve: It can't have been more than three or four minutes . . .

Spencer: But that was 9.27, the phone call . . . It was first thing you do isn't it?

Steve: It would have been within a minute or two.

Spencer: So if the phone call was made at 9.27 she can't have found Harry more than three or four minutes before that . . .

Steve: We are guessing really, aren't we . . . that it was round about nine o'clock.

Spencer's suspicions are building.

Eventually he says:

So are you telling this jury that from the moment you got home Harry was constantly in your presence?

Steve: Yes. I was on crutches . . .

There are many more questions, seeking to trip Steve up on minute details. Spencer gets no satisfaction.

Spencer: You are aware that it may be important as to how long she was alone with Harry at home that evening before you got back?

He is referring to the evidence of hypoxia, which, if it existed, could be the result of repeated attempts at smothering earlier in the evening.

Steve: Yes. I'm aware of that.

Spencer then refers him to an internal office memo to Steve from Helen Knowles.

Spencer: Does it say this? 'I have been requested by Suzanne McLaughlin, who received a telephone call from Stephen Clark this morning, to provide confirmation that I booked a taxi for Stephen Clark from 100 Barbirolli Square to 39 South Oak Lane at 16.55 on 26th January 1998. My role was to book the taxi. I did not see if it was occupied.'

What date did this message pass?

Steve: This was yesterday, but there was an earlier note which is more accurate, but this was rushed through yesterday because of all the issues on the point.

After a load more questions in similar vein, Spencer goes to an earlier
document dated 20th July 1998, from Helen Knowles.

Spencer: Just read it out . . .

Steve: 'Steve: to confirm a taxi was booked on 26/1/98 at 16.48 from
   Barbirolli Square to 39 South Oak Lane . . . NB: This was a note to
   Sally's solicitor, see attached sheet.' Helen booked it at the same time
   she had booked me a taxi to the airport for the following morning.

Spencer: So Helen was not telling you that in her note to you, but in the note
   to your wife's solicitor?

Steve: She's saying she booked a taxi for me at 16.48, i.e. the same time as
   she booked me the taxi to the airport, she did them both together. I said
   to her 'That's not what I actually want, I want to know if it is possible
   for you to say whether you booked me a taxi to go home on the evening
   of 26th and what time?' And my note is the result of that phone call to
   her. She then did an e-mail to confirm it.

Spencer: I don't know if you are aware that the police have been in touch with
   your firm asking if there were any records in relation to the booking of the
   taxi . . . and were told that there were not. No one told you about that?

Steve: No, they didn't.

Spencer: The document in front of you is an extract from a book kept by
   your office . . . Do you know why the booking of a taxi to take you home
   would not be in the book?

Steve: No, I don't.

There are many more questions along the same lines then:

Spencer: Do you remember what time you got home that night?

Steve: No I don't, but I do remember it was shortly after Sally got home.

Spencer: Because she told you 'I've just got home . . . ?'

Steve: Yes. She'd been delayed at the Health Centre and then bought
   Calpol . . .

More questions then:

Spencer: Are you trying to put as much distance as possible between the
   possibility of your wife being left alone with this child?

Steve: No. I'm telling the truth.

Spencer: Although you have a very hazy recollection . . . ?

Steve: . . . hazy apart from two things that were different that evening . . . the events around nine o'clock and getting home very shortly after Sally, because that was unusual. Normally she'd be in the house. I'd ring her from the office to say I'd booked a taxi . . .

Spencer asks how Steve resuscitated Harry and asks him to look at the post-mortem photographs of Harry's mutilated body:

Spencer: . . . in particular the third photograph . . . Yes?

Steve looks at the photographs and gags.

For Sally, Spencer has just crossed a line:

'I have always tried to see things from his point of view, in order to be fair to the man, believing that he was only trying to do a difficult job. What he is doing is unforgivable and unnecessary. I find myself now hating the big man in the fine silk gown.'

Bevan [*standing*]: I am sorry, I think this is particularly distressing, whether it is utterly necessary to show the father his dead child, whether it is entirely necessary . . .

Spencer: My lord there is a good reason for it.

Judge: If you feel it is necessary for your case, then you have got to do it. I have to leave that judgement to you.

Spencer: Perhaps I can deal with it another way . . .

Spencer is trying to eliminate any possibility that Steve could have fractured Harry's rib when using two fingers to stab his chest during resuscitation.

Steve, in his usual obsession with accuracy, describes compressing Harry's chest away from the site of the supposed fracture, when he could so easily have lied to help his wife.

Spencer challenges Steve on how Harry was found in the bouncy chair. Steve says Sally told him his head was flopped forward.

Spencer then tries to prove that the nosebleed in London never happened. Every aspect is explored, again, and again and again. The implication is that

Steve is lying about every piece of evidence; about calling for help with the nosebleed; that he is lying about talking to the doctor.

But Sally told her GP when they got back to Wilmslow from London. How could it not be true? What is Spencer's point?

Steve is accused of lying about Christopher and Harry to protect his wife. There are many more pages of cross-examination. Spencer is beyond persistent. In one sense his performance is superb: the CPS will be delighted! He leaves no stone unturned, no suspicious nuance unexplored. At the end, I feel Steve has come out of it comparatively unmarked.

The jury then pass a question to the judge, who reads it. It is passed to counsel, who both shrug. The Clerk of the Court then reads it to Steve:

Clerk: What makes you think that the false alarms of the baby monitor were not mini attacks of not breathing?
Judge: You may answer.
Steve: They told us it was a bad electrical contact.

That should augur well for Steve, and therefore for Sally. The jury are, at the very least, open-minded about what happened to Harry.

Trouble

Wednesday, 27 October 1999, may prove to be the worst day of Steve's life. It may make the difference between freedom – a not guilty verdict – and the rest of her life in prison for Sally. While Mackey has been out of court, Steve has answered everything Spencer could throw at him and his evidence looks solid; it has greatly improved Sally's chances. If the prosecution had anything with which to ambush Steve, Spencer would have used it by now. Sally's prospects are – 73 million to one apart – getting better.

Mackey has made his phone call to the taxi firm. He then bought three packs of cigarettes – Bevan and Kelsey Fry also smoke – and went to see them in the retiring room. They are relaxed, smiling, congratulating themselves on a good day's work, and saying that Steve has come through unscathed. Mackey hands each of them a pack of cigarettes, lights them all up, and then drops his bombshell.

A few minutes later, Mackey takes me by the elbow.

Mackey [*sotto voce*]: We have a problem. The taxi collected Steve from his
    office at 7.40 p.m. When Helen Knowles, the receptionist, answered
    Steve's e-mail asking her to check the time of his taxi, she had only
    looked at the bookings up until 7 p.m. on 26 January. She had forgotten
    that taxis booked after that time were recorded the following day.
    When she saw the call booked at 4.48 for Glasgow, her memory played
    her false; told her she had booked to take Steve home at the same time.
    She got it wrong. Without realising it, she gave Steve false information.

I ask him what he is going to do.

Mackey: I'm not a bent solicitor.

*What is said to a lawyer, in the course of a court case, and anything he discovers,
is confidential, and he cannot divulge it. But there are exceptions to this rule and
this, unfortunately, is one of them. A solicitor is forbidden to put forward evidence
he knows to be untrue. If he does so, he may commit a crime himself and will be in
serious professional trouble.*

Steve, originally, could not remember what time he got home. He later
tells me: 'It wasn't important until July 1999, when Sally was charged. I
then checked and obtained what I thought was unassailable proof of the
time I left the office, from Helen Knowles in Reception. I told the jury –
based on what she told me – that I must have got home at 5.30.'

*That is untrue because the taxi records now show that he got home two hours later.
During those two hours, Sally was alone with Harry and had the opportunity to
smother him repeatedly. Steve has denied that could have happened because he was there
all the time, and he wasn't. This was an agonising decision for Mackey. In the most
important case of his career he had it in his power to keep quiet about this and maybe
secure the acquittal he is convinced Sally deserves. This is the stuff of ambush, but do
the prosecution know? No. Spencer might have thought there was a forgery, he would
never have imagined the truth, surely If he had, he would have nailed Steve by now.*

I ask him what happens now.
    'I've told Bevan. He'll tell Spencer. They'll both tell the judge, who will
decide what is to be done about it. Meanwhile keep your mouth firmly
shut. Not a word to Steve or Sally,' he says.

The judge sends the jury out for a break and holds a conference with counsel and solicitors in his chambers. Spencer insists that this is proof of Steve's perjury and that he, Spencer, should be permitted to face him with it, without warning. Bevan reminds the judge that it is the defence which has unearthed this new information – if the police had discovered it, Spencer might be entitled to ambush Steve with it, but not when it is the defence who have discovered and disclosed it.

Bevan wins the argument: more confirmation of this QC's skill. It may seem a small victory, but at least Steve will be given time to think about it before he is recalled. Spencer, now armed with ammunition, could destroy Sally's chances of being acquitted. The judge orders that nobody can help Steve, prepare him, advise him how to deal with this terrible turn of events.

Bevan is in the robing room on his own. Steve is in the room beside him, also on his own. Bevan has just told him what will happen.

I ask Bevan if I can have a word with Steve. I want to say something to help the poor man.

Bevan says: 'As if this was not already the most difficult case I have ever . . . You can say nothing. Leave him alone.'

I disobey even that. I put my head round Steve's door, possibly at some risk to my own status as a solicitor, as I say: 'Just tell the truth, Steve.'

As with so many developments in this case, Sally and Steve seem to have so little control. None of what has happened or what follows is the fault of either of them. I can think of nothing more either of them could have done, to prevent what happened or to avoid the evidential disaster that will now follow. Nobody else knows what has happened; nor will they know until it is revealed, exactly as the judge prescribes, in court. I can't tell my wife, Jane, in my regular mobile calls, except that something bad has happened, bad for Steve, and he is in isolation until he is recalled. The jury does not know what is afoot: merely that they have been sent on another coffee break. I can't tell Frank, which in a way is a mercy, because he will recognise, immediately, the dire consequences that may follow from this incredible cock-up. That's what it is. Nobody could invent such a convoluted conspiracy, knowing that turning a page in the Reception Book or making a call to the taxi firm would unmask it.

Steve is left in that room, on his own, for about three hours while Professor Berry is called to give evidence.

Berry

J.E.M. Berry is probably the leading UK paediatric pathologist, a highly talented and respected doctor with many papers and books to his credit. He is a joint author, with Professor Peter Fleming, of the CESDI Report. He is most frequently a witness for the prosecution. That he is, in this case, appearing for the defence should tell the jury something. He is a tall, spare figure of a man with grey hair and a very upright stance. He is professorial in a businesslike, not academic, way. He is formal, precise and usually firm in his opinions. I have spoken to him a few times in the court corridors and have been impressed with his knowledge and unassuming authority.

Bevan begins his examination-in-chief. Berry's major interest is the unexplained death of infants. First Bevan deals with Christopher.

Berry: I found moderate haemorrhage in the air spaces in the lungs, it is similar to what I have found in 190 cases of genuine SIDS. It is not possible to distinguish accidental or deliberate suffocation by blood in the lungs. What I found in this baby is not diagnostic of suffocation. There is old blood. I do not think a normal nosebleed would cause it but this was not a normal nosebleed. I think it must be associated.

He is asked about the bruises.

Berry: There are all sorts of marks on this body, the vast majority due to post-mortem changes. I looked for microscopic slides, to prove it one way or the other, but there were none. I cannot place much weight on what are called bruises which I think are abrasions. Such marks do occur after death. The photographs do not help . . . Abrasions before death would have been visible. I am not convinced these are bruises.

What about the fraenulum?

Berry: The photo does not help. Normally it is a worrying finding but I am not convinced that this is what it was. Williams dismissed it originally. I would have thought it impossible for a Home Office pathologist to do that if it was a genuine torn fraenulum. I looked for a slide, to prove it or not, and there was none. The laryngoscope could have done it . . . I see no cause of death. I would say unascertained . . . I cannot find out why or how he might have died of natural disease . . . This post-mortem was done, as are many, not sufficiently thoroughly to document symptoms that might have indicated the cause of death.

This is a serious criticism of the decision to continue to prosecute the murder charges against Sally. Berry's statement has been with the prosecution for months. They know who he is, that he is usually a prosecution expert. His is not an opinion that can be bought.

Berry puts no weight at all on the finding of haemorrhages in the epidural space of Harry; it is found in the majority of cot deaths. Despite Williams' claim of a swollen cord Berry cannot confirm it because there is, in the photographs, clear space – a gap down beside the spine.

Berry: There was no damage to the spinal cord. I can confirm that.

This is a most significant statement – a flat contradiction of Williams. Most experts use circumlocutions to avoid embarrassing professional colleagues.

Berry: Recent haemorrhages in the brain are quite common.

Bevan asks him about hypoxia.

Berry: I cannot put weight on this quite subtle finding, particularly in the absence of a clinical episode in the child's history. I leave the jury with the choice of my opinion or that of the neuropathologist. The damage to the neurons is at least two hours old. Petechial haemorrhages are worrying but one or two do not point strongly to suffocation. I give the cause of death as unascertained.

He is asked about the fracture and dislocation of the ribs.

Berry: None is shown in the X-ray. If they found a possible fracture it should have been re-broken and it wasn't. The photo shows new bone formation, not a fracture. I cannot say it came from the rib or that the rib was fractured. It is in a well-protected area. If there had been a dislocation in life I would have expected to find haemorrhage . . . it must have been post-mortem.

Spencer's cross-examination of Berry is postponed until the next day because of a prior commitment.

If they did not know it before, the jury must now realise that there are serious questions about Williams' analysis. Spencer must know that crossing the line of certainty is becoming more remote by the hour.

Luthert

The next defence expert is Professor Phillip Luthert, one of Europe's leading experts on eyes. He works at Moorfields Eye Hospital in London, the centre for excellence. He is a tall, rather thin, modest and laconic man whose intelligence and good humour are palpable. I know, instinctively, and I suspect Spencer does too, that if this man is to be challenged, the preparation must be good.

Luthert: I was supplied with incomplete slides and told there were retinal haemorrhages. I could find none whatsoever. On the Friday before the trial I met with Professor Green and we looked at all the slides together. There was blood next to the retina but none in it. Green agreed with that. He also agreed that blood in front had got there post-mortem. It has no significance whatsoever. The blood on the surface of the eye is not associated with any particular disease and could have got there during the removal of the eyes. Blood at the back of the eye accumulated after death.

Spencer cross-examines.

Luthert: There is no reason to believe that there was any pre-mortem blood in Harry's eyes. The surface is like blotting paper . . . There was no blood at all in the retina . . .

Williams disagrees with both Luthert and Green and still maintains that there were retinal haemorrhages in Harry's eyes.

Luthert: . . . there is no pathological significance in anything found in Harry's eyes. Blood in the retina is typical of shaking. There was none here. I am not aware of any warning about finding blood on the surface of the eyes. I have never seen it. I referred it to a colleague who immediately said 'post-mortem blood'. It is pure speculation where that blood came from.

Spencer persists.

Luthert: I cannot totally exclude the possibility of an association with suffocation but it has never figured anywhere in medical literature.

Re-examined by Bevan he says that there is no reason whatever to suspect suffocation from these haemorrhages.

Luthert: I would expect to find more than this in cases of strangulation.

Whitwell

Bevan calls Dr Helen Whitwell, a neuropathologist currently working in New Zealand but who is Professor of Forensic Pathology designate at Sheffield, to succeed Green.

The contrast with Green could not be greater. Whitwell is much younger, dark-haired, a handsome woman. There is no arrogance, just a quiet command of her subject. This should be interesting.

She talks about Harry.

Whitwell: There is early hypoxic damage too difficult to time in an area vulnerable to hypoxia. The shrinkage of the neurons is due to lack of oxygen. Minimum time for showing in adults about two hours. The result of Dr Smith's tests means that it is impossible to identify any injury that caused it, and that is a surprise. I would have expected a more positive result if the hypoxia was genuine . . . There is no evidence of traumatic injuries . . . Other haemorrhages are related to birth. Fresh blood in the epidural space is not what one sees in shaking injuries . . . This case has no features of shaking.

That, too, is unequivocal: another contradiction of Williams.

Whitwell: There are no subdural haemorrhages, there is no damage to the spine or brain. My cause of death is 'unascertained'. It could be natural, it could be unnatural. If the cord was swollen there would be damage to the cord, and there was none.

Another strike against Williams.

Cross-examined by Spencer, Whitwell admits that the hypoxic damage could have been caused at about 5.30 the day Harry died. She would never diagnose trauma on hypoxic damage alone. Small haemorrhages in the brain are not diagnostic of any mechanism and may well be quite normal. She admits that haemorrhages and petechiae are consistent with smothering.

Whitwell: The bleeding around the spine is artefactual. I don't know how it was caused. It could be something you just see at post-mortem. I could not say it is more marked than normal . . . If there is a swollen cord it is difficult to explain other than by injury.

Re-examined by Bevan she says that it is simply not possible to say that this baby was smothered.

Whitwell: I simply don't know why he died. In thirteen or fourteen years I have never seen these findings in association with shaking deaths. There is no pathological evidence that this baby was smothered.

The looks on the faces of the jury suggest that they were impressed by Whitwell. Certainty of guilt is becoming even more remote, medically.

But as Helen Whitwell takes her place in the bench below me she leans back and whispers to me: 'I could kick myself. There was not that much hypoxia. It was not significant.'

The Taxi

The time has come to deal with the new evidence from the taxi company. Sally has no idea what has happened:

'I look down at Julian, Kelsey Fry, Mike and John Batt and all I see are glum faces. I have been kicking my heels in the cell below, not knowing what is going on in my trial. I am supposed to be the accused person and I am being kept in the dark about something so important. I am worried sick and nobody will tell me what it is about. I soon find out when Spencer reads an agreed statement to the jury telling them the basic facts. They all sit up and take notice. I can barely believe it. After all the trouble we took . . . all the hours we spent going over the sequence of events, that I originally thought he got home later and then the e-mails from the office "proving" me wrong. But they were the ones who got it wrong. I was right all along. Surely the jury will see that!'

At last something has happened to engage the jury's attention. Are they thinking that, with any luck, there will now be some real drama injected into this incomprehensible tangle of medicine and the law?

Bevan calls Helen Knowles, from Steve's office. She is a long-time and trusted receptionist at Addleshaws. She is in her forties and there is an air of quiet competence about her. She has, quite unknowingly, created a serious problem. When Steve called her – in July 1998, only a few days after Sally had been charged – about the taxi time he did not mention why it was needed, or that it had anything to do with Sally's trial. She thought it was something routine and relied on her memory, which told her that she had booked his taxi home at the same time as the one to the airport for the following morning. Steve called her twice more, because there was no specific reference on the taxi page to the ride home and Sally's recollection was that he was back later, but each time Helen gave the same information. If the taxi book system recorded everything that happened on the day it happened, this mistake could not have arisen.

Almost everybody touched by the strange events of this case has forgotten important facts, but that is how memory often misleads. Such a taxi record system is not an aide-mémoire!

Helen Knowles is troubled and anxious about her mistake; her embarrassment and regret are obvious. She confirms the information about how taxi records are kept and the e-mails and memos with Steve; that reception is manned from 8 a.m. to 7 p.m. and taxis ordered after 7 p.m. are entered in the log for the following day.

Cross-examined by Spencer:

Knowles: I looked at the book; there was an entry not long before 5 p.m. I assumed I had booked both taxis at the same time . . . Steve did not tell me his enquiry was to do with this murder trial. I assumed the taxi would have come soon after the call was made . . . I did not speak to him again until 25th October – two days ago. Suzanne needed confirmation of taxi bookings on 26 January 1998. I said I would e-mail Steve, which I did . . . I don't remember if Steve mentioned the time concerned. Yesterday, I called the taxi firm. They said: 'At the request of the defence the archives were researched and there was a record of a taxi going from office to home on 26 January 1998 at 7.29 p.m.'

Stephen Clark is then called back into the witness box.

The Judge looks at him sternly as he says: 'There is no need to be re-sworn. You are still on oath.'

Steve: Yes, my lord.

What has happened is so unusual that the judge has ordered that nobody except Steve can be forewarned, and that includes the person in the dock. There could be no opportunity for Sally and Steve to collude in making up a story to deal with it. Yet again, the person whose fate – maybe for the rest of her life – is being decided can do nothing to help herself. Mackey looks worried sick; as do Bevan and Kelsey Fry.

Spencer now has something rare in an advocate's life: hard evidence that an opposition witness has given evidence that was untrue, and in detail. If Spencer does his job well, the jury will believe that Sally's husband has lied to save her from a murder conviction. Moments like these don't come much sweeter in an advocate's career. The fact that nearly everything else points to Sally's innocence is irrelevant in this adversarial system. This is Spencer's chance to ensure Sally's conviction.

Spencer: When you gave evidence yesterday you were absolutely certain that on 26 January you arrived home only a few minutes after your wife got back from the clinic . . .

Steve: Well, I said that, based on the information about the taxi, I must have got home . . .

Spencer: Mr Clark . . .

Steve: . . . about that time.

Spencer: Can you just answer yes or no to the question . . .

Sally feels desperately sorry for Steve. She wants to do something . . . anything to help him. But she can't.

Steve: Yes.

Spencer: You said, 'I am telling you the truth. I'm very hazy apart from two things that at about nine o'clock there was the episode with the wiggling and that I got home soon after her'. Sure about?

Steve: It was very hazy that evening, yes.

Spencer: You told the jury that you got a taxi about five o'clock, arriving home at 5.30 to 5.45?

Sally is consumed with worry; surely the jury will realise it was the e-mails and memos that caused all this misunderstanding!

Steve: That's what I said, based on the note from . . .

Spencer: Can you just agree to that evidence?

Steve: I'm sorry, Mr Spencer.

How does anybody behave when they have been caught out in so many 'errors'? Steve is doing his best to tell the literal truth as he knows it. But circumstances have conspired to make him look a liar.

Spencer: You also said that your wife told you she had just got home . . .

Steve: Yes.

Spencer: . . . And that the clinic was a good mile from home and it would have taken her 15 to 20 minutes?

Steve: Yes.

Spencer then introduces a map which proves that Hope Cottage is no more than half a mile from the clinic.

I do not understand Spencer's change of tack. He has Steve in double trouble on the time he got home. By concentrating on whether the clinic is a mile or half a mile from home he appears to be dissipating the impact of Steve's 'lie' on the jury.

Spencer: Another example of your bending the truth?

Steve: I was trying to give you an estimate of how long it would have taken Sally to get home, pushing a pram . . .

Spencer: Do you now accept that your taxi was not even booked until 7.29
   p.m.?

Sally's thoughts are in turmoil again. She knows Steve has got the distance
from the clinic wrong and she remembers telling the police she thought he
got home about 7.30 and then changed it when the e-mail came in from
the office. 'What a terrible mess!'

Steve: No. I don't accept that.

Spencer: Before you came into court the jury was told there was agreed new
   evidence as follows: 'At 7.29 p.m. on the Monday a cab was despatched
   to Addleshaws, 100 Barbirolli Square. The fare is shown as Stephen
   Clark and he was going to Wilmslow. The fare was £17. Because of the
   plotting system of taxis in Manchester Town Centre, it is more than
   likely that the cab would have picked up the fare within 10 minutes of
   being despatched . . .'

Sally has a panic attack. She thinks of all she has said in answer to questions
about time. She is so worried – not about herself and the effect it might
have on the jury, but for her husband. For the first time she realises a little
of what Steve has been feeling over the previous eighteen months, about
her arrest, charge and trial. She wants to shout out 'Say what you like about
me but do not accuse a man of such incredible integrity, of deliberately
lying in court.'

Steve: I was told that there was a taxi record, but not what it said . . . I was
   aware there was a conflict between information I was given by Addleshaws
   and that.

Spencer: You were not home until after eight?

Steve: It would have been about then.

Sally shuts her eyes against the implications of this.

Spencer: Do you dispute the taxi record?

Steve: My thinking has been influenced by what I was told by Addleshaws . . .

Spencer then tries to prove that Steve misled Helen Knowles.

Spencer: You asked her to confirm five o'clock.

Steve: I said, 'There is an entry at 16.48 for the taxi the next morning. What about the taxi to get home? I booked it at the same time.' I said, 'It's not in the book, can you drop me a note to confirm because I need to know,' and then she sent me the e-mail.

Spencer: You were very late home that night?

Steve: Yes . . . If I did that, yes.

Spencer: That was very unusual?

Steve: Not really. I had been out late before while Harry was alive.

Spencer: It made that Monday unusual?

Steve : Not particularly.

Spencer: Are you really saying that in your police statement . . . that within a month of Harry's death that you had forgotten the strange feature that you were very late home?

Steve: I don't think it particularly strange and yes, I am. I had. I don't remember last month sometimes. I have a very busy business life and it was a very traumatic event.

Spencer: How did your wife greet you? 'Late again?'

Steve: Absolutely not. She was used to my being late.

Spencer: Your wife would have been alone with Harry for two . . . two and a half hours . . .

Sally suddenly realises where this is going and fear grips her.

Steve tries to evade the question, but Spencer won't let him.

Steve: Something like that.

Spencer: You appreciated the importance of your wife not being alone with Harry that night . . .

Steve: That's not true.

Spencer: You have known throughout that you got home much later than you ever told the police?

Sally wants to yell at them:

'You've no idea how much time we spent trying to work out the time he got home. My own recollection was that it was about 7.30, as I told the police. Steve – however hard he racked his brain – just could not remember.'

Steve: No I haven't.

Spencer: And that this was an important part of the night's events.

Steve: No, that's not true.

Spencer: You don't know what your wife did to Harry before you got home?

Steve: No, I don't, but he was perfectly all right when I got home.

Spencer: What had you done to check before you saw the police?

Steve: We had long conversations and came to the conclusion we could not remember. Neither of us could remember what we did that evening. We racked our memories but it was a perfectly normal evening. There was nothing wrong with Harry. The routine was the routine.

After more and more questions seeking to discredit Steve about other details . . .

Spencer: You have deliberately deceived this jury about these times, have you not?

Steve: No, I have not.

Spencer: To shorten the time your wife was alone with Harry.

Steve: Absolutely not.

Spencer: During which injury could be inflicted?

Steve: Absolutely not.

Spencer draws the parallels between the importance of time in the nosebleed incident and Harry's death sequence.

Spencer: The details of that incident involve the same questions . . . a time when your wife was alone with the baby, Christopher in that case. You understand the importance . . .

Steve: I understand the importance.

Spencer: Not much turned on whether she was left alone with Christopher, at that stage?

Steve: She was often alone with him. It only became an issue when we were both charged with murdering Christopher . . .

Spencer: If you have been prepared to lie about Harry, you would be prepared to lie about the nosebleed incident?

Steve: I did not lie. I am a solicitor. I try to uphold the best practices of honesty and integrity. What I said about Harry was based on information

I did not know when I got home. Once I had that information I stopped thinking about it because it seemed settled .

Spencer: Conveniently settled.

Steve: Not by me. She gave that note of her own free will . . .

Spencer: You knew on the night Harry died that you got home late?

Steve: That's not true.

Spencer: And the day after . . .

Steve: I don't recall that . . .

Spencer: You have known for months that the allegation is that your wife suffocated Christopher . . . because of old bleeding in the lungs? That's why you've put in all the detail about the nosebleed.

Steve: It was only when Professor David asked me because he had a possible medical explanation . . .

Spencer: Quite recently?

Steve: Yes.

Steve tries to get out of answering questions about old bleeding in the lungs, saying he is not a doctor.

Spencer: You are a solicitor giving evidence on oath. Are you saying you did not realise that it was alleged that your wife had suffocated Christopher?

Steve: I knew there was an allegation.

Spencer: And you hoped for an innocent explanation?

Steve: I knew she could not have done it.

Spencer: You're not a doctor. How did you know?

Steve: I knew my wife could not have done that to our little boy.

Spencer: You've told the same truth about the nosebleed as you told yesterday about the time you got home.

Steve: That was based on information I believed . . .

Spencer: Are you telling the jury that that had gone from your memory within a matter of days?

Steve: I don't remember what happened up until the time Sally handed me Harry.

Spencer: You were prepared to lie to cover up for your wife, weren't you?

Steve: No, that's not true.

Spencer: You lied because you were concerned about what really happened? And if you lied about that you are quite capable of lying about other things.

Every time Spencer accuses Steve of lying, Sally feels the pain. She closes her eyes and prays for it to stop.

Steve: I'm a solicitor and I'm giving evidence on oath. I have not lied. I've told you what I remember to the best of my recollection.

Spencer: You did not want to believe that your wife could have killed your two babies but deceived you as well?

Steve: I know she could not have done that. I've been with her for over twelve years . . . She has never even raised a little finger to anyone or anything. She loved those boys with all her heart and would never have done anything to hurt them . . . I made the enquiries about the taxi . . . I could simply have come here and said I didn't know.

Spencer: Thank you, Mr Clark.

Sally cannot understand what the fuss is about:

'If I were sitting on the jury, I would be asking myself: "What do these lawyers think they are doing?" It must, surely, be obvious to everybody that this was a mistake. The idea that Steve would even consider trying to make a receptionist at the office fabricate such a story is beyond comprehension. The reality is that, until Harry died, that night, nothing out of the ordinary happened. There was no reason for either of us to remember what time Steve got home. It never occurred to either of us that the time he got home could have any significance, be it 5.30 or 7.30. It was not until Mike produced the taxi record and explained exactly what interpretation Spencer was trying to put on it – that Steve deliberately tried to make out he was home early so that there was no time in which I could repeatedly try to smother Harry – that we realised what was at stake. I did not attempt to smother my boy and Steve would never believe that I had. So each of us just told the truth, as we remembered it and – yet again – the system gave Spencer the chance to turn what to us were innocent mistakes into conspiracies to avoid convictions for murder. I am certain the jury will see that it was a simple mistake; possibly hard to believe, but it is Spencer's sinister interpretation that more surely stretches credulity.

'I know this makes it look as if both Steve and I lied to the jury . . . If only we had thought to tell everybody, more clearly, that we really could not remember; that what we were doing was making a reconstruction of what must have happened, based on what the taxi records showed . . .'

Sally steals a glance at the jury. Nobody is looking at her.

Bevan begins his damage limitation exercise in re-examination. He quotes from Steve's interview with the police in which he says:

'. . . I can't really remember what happened until about nine o'clock . . .' Even on 23rd February you said you could not remember what time you got home from work?

Steve: Yes.

Bevan: You made your call to Helen Knowles from your office. Had you ever looked at the taxi book?

Steve: No.

Bevan: Why were you making enquiries of Helen at all?

Steve: We were trying to piece together what might have happened . . . I'd checked my diary and there was nothing in there . . . I was not driving because of the crutches . . . So I checked about a taxi.

Bevan: Did you know on 20th July that scientists had discovered hypoxic damage?

Steve: I don't think so.

Bevan: Dr Smith's statement is dated 31st July . . .

Steve: I think she was the first person to mention it . . .

Bevan: You may not know this but the committal papers, containing all such information, were not served on the defence until 21st August . . . in relation to hypoxic damage. It relates to an injury caused before death.

Steve: I've heard it used, yes.

Bevan: Before 21st August did you have any knowledge of previous or prior injury to Harry before he died?

Steve: No.

Bevan: You told the police very early on that you had gone home by taxi. It is not beyond the wit of police to have checked on that?

Steve: I would have thought so.

Bevan: The notes of times you supplied contained the name of the taxi firm?

Steve: I didn't know that.

Bevan: Did it never cross your mind to make a phone call to the taxi company?

Steve: No.

Bevan: It is suggested that you deliberately lied to conceal your wife's guilt, to give her an alibi. Before setting out on such a course of such deliberate lying, did you check with the taxi firm as to whether they had a record of it?

Steve: I took Helen's word for it.

Bevan: You have been asked about the nosebleed. What did you know then about macrophages?

Steve: I think when the committal papers were first circulated . . .

Bevan: In August of last year?

Steve: Yes.

Bevan: Thank you, Mr Clark.

Sally is now worried that she might be recalled and subjected to the same routine by Spencer. She does not know if she could cope with that.

We wait. Spencer does not ask for her recall.

My personal involvement in the case makes it difficult for me, as a lawyer, to look at it objectively; that is in every lawyer's basic training. The analogy usually given is that a surgeon could not operate on his wife or daughter, but that is not the same. Before this case, I had not had personal experience of the reason for the rule. Now I know why it is there, and that obectivity is vital in the interests of the client. I was inclined towards Sally's innocence from day one, but what really convinced me was that the prosecution had to rely on experts contradicting each other on the only reasons to think her babies had been murdered; even to the unheard-of extent of changing the cause of death of both babies. I could not believe that a jury would convict on that.

I wanted to hold my breath throughout Steve's evidence: I was willing him to come out of it without damage to Sally's chances. When the taxi records were produced, Steve held his wife's life in his hands. He is going through self-torture: 'What happened was my fault.' 'Why didn't I simply ring the taxi firm instead of relying on Helen?' 'Why didn't Mackey do it earlier?' Simple answer: 'There was no reason to do so: I believed Helen's e-mail, not because it was convenient, in that it helped prove Sally's innocence, but because I had absolutely no reason to doubt her word.'

Has Steve done enough to persuade the jury of the truth – that he reconstructed what must have happened from information that was wrong and then told it as if it was what he remembered? I do not think he lied. I think he believed what he was saying when he was saying it; that it turned out to be untrue does not make him a liar. But do the jury see it like that?

At last, that court day ends, as the judge adjourns for the night. Sally leaves the dock and goes to Steve and puts her arms round him:

'It's all right; you have nothing to reproach yourself with,' she tells him.

Steve will not have it. 'It is my fault. If only I had phoned the taxi firm . . . '

Sally does her best to comfort him but at the moment he is beyond consolation.

Steve is an old-fashioned man – he believes that it is the job of the husband to protect his wife in every way; that is what men are for. The arrest and charging of his wife was bad enough, but there was nothing Steve could do about that; he suffered the humiliation of his male helplessness, telling himself that it was outside his control. Now, something very much within his control has gone terribly wrong and it is his fault. It is his memory that has let him down. Why? Why? Why could he not remember? He tried hard enough. Why had he not simply accepted what Sally first said, about 7.30? Because he is an obsessive about detail – he cannot bear to get little things wrong; that is the way he is made. That is why he took the trouble to check with Helen. Why did he not double-check with the taxi company?

'Because it never occurred to me that Helen could be wrong,' Steve muses. 'She is one of the most reliable people in the office. I am a partner, as such, her employer. I have never known her get an answer wrong about anything before and had no reason to doubt her then. I did not set up the damned system that bookings after 7 p.m. are entered on the following day. Now my shortcomings as a man – as a husband – have been demonstrated in open court for everybody to see and hear! If Sally is – God forbid – convicted, it will be my fault!'

Sally knows her man well:

'I know exactly what is going through his mind. I tell him it is not his fault. I try every way to give him solace, but know it will not work. Perhaps giving Tom his bath when we get to Linda's will take his mind off it for a while.'

Berry's Cross-examination

Spencer must have been reading Sally's mind as he asks Berry if either baby's was a SIDS death – a cot death. Berry says no.

'Unascertained' is used when there is no cause of death found at autopsy but here he believes there are suspicious findings. He agrees there are matters of concern in both cases. Some cot deaths have happened soon after a feed. Two cot deaths in the same family is very unusual.

Professor Peter Fleming, the main author of the CESDI Report, has told him that Meadow did not properly use the 1:73 million statistic. He did not take into account that there may be familial factors which predispose a mother to another SIDS death. It is theoretical, not the result of observation. Previous studies showed that the risk of a second death was 1:200. $8,500 \times 8,500$ does not reflect the true risk.

Is there no more robust rebuttal of the 1:73 million statistic than that? I wonder what members of the jury are thinking about it.

Spencer asks about hypoxia. Berry disagrees with Whitwell that there was hypoxia. He says he often sees the same features at post-mortem where there is no suspicion. He does not attach the same weight to the finding. He has seen many more brains than either Whitwell or Smith. Haemorrhages in the brain are seen in many deaths.

Spencer presses him on the fracture. Berry insists it was not there; there was no fine dust on the slide. It was not possible to say, from the slides, that it was a fracture or that the bits of bone came from a rib. If it was a fracture, it was at least four weeks old and he would be concerned. Dislocation from CPR (resuscitation) is unusual:

Berry: Two petechial haemorrhages 'don't make a summer'! They are unusual in SIDS but are not significant . . . I have never known a case where so many apparent findings have turned to dust on critical examination.

That is the most significant thing said by any expert so far. Coming from such an eminent paediatric pathologist, this dismissal of Williams' findings, which form the foundation of this murder trial, puts paid to any chance of certainty of guilt. Are the jury of the same mind? They don't seem to be impressed.

Spencer asks about the fresh bleeding in the spine. Berry says it often arises naturally. He does not know why it is not more marked. Old bleeding is frequently found and has no significance. A nosebleed – very unusual in a baby of Christopher's age – could be caused by trauma. Old blood in the lungs is consistent with suffocation.

Spencer challenges him about the bruises.

Berry: I would expect a competent pathologist to recognise them, but they were not borne out on examination.

Spencer: What about the torn fraenulum?

Berry: It is inconceivable that an experienced forensic pathologist would give a cause of death without taking into account a torn fraenulum. It could have happened during the autopsy or CPR. If there was pre-mortem bruising I would do tests that were not done here. If all Williams' findings were actually present I would give asphyxia as the cause of death.

The women on the jury seem to be impressed with Berry. The older man in the front row has made copious notes throughout Berry's evidence. He has just made another.

Rushton

Dr Ian Rushton is the next witness called by Bevan. He has thirty-six years' experience as a paediatric pathologist and has written over a hundred papers: he is an academic as well as a highly skilled practitioner. He is a largish man, who is no tailor's dummy. He gives an impression not unlike that made by Meadow: likeable, avuncular; an expert who knows his subject.

He says that the nosebleed would account for the old blood in Christopher's lungs. Even a small amount would show up. It need not make a baby ill. He draws no conclusion from the new blood. It is consistent with smothering but does not mean it must have been caused by it. He has diagnosed bruises with the naked eye that turned out not to be bruises when under the microscope. There is no evidence for the 'small bruise slight slit' in the fraenulum; CPR could cause it.

The old blood in Harry is birth-related, the fresh blood is a common finding in SIDS. He has seen similar hypoxic changes in SIDS cases: it is not indicative of any injury.

Rushton: I have looked at several thousand brains and I conclude that this child did not suffer a significant period of hypoxia in the immediate past.

It was difficult to say whether two petechial haemorrhages have any significance. He could not confirm a swollen cord. If it was there he would expect to find other damage but there was none, and no injury to the neck or para-spinal muscles, and no subdural haemorrhage.

Rushton: I cannot think of any injury to account for this combination of symptoms.

Fresh blood was partially, if not totally, created at post-mortem.

Rushton: I would give the cause of death as 'unascertained', but there are areas of great concern. That is why it is not a SIDS.

Spencer's cross-examination takes on the familiar pattern of trying to shore up Williams' findings, but without much success.

On re-examination, Rushton says that he cannot see how the inside of the spine can be injured without injuring the outside.

The judge releases him.

Sally is disappointed:

'. . . With Berry, Rushton and Whitwell. I know, as a lawyer, that "unascertained" is enough to tell a jury there is reasonable doubt. But as a mother, reasonable doubt is not enough. I want answers to how my babies died. Not perhaps or maybe. I will always be grateful that they formed opinions that support my innocence. I thank them for their dedication and – I suspect – their belief in me. But I want more. I'm innocent!'

David

Bevan tells the judge that he proposes to call Professor Timothy David, but that he is not an expert instructed by the defence. He hands in the 300-page report David wrote on the instructions of the Family Division.

Judge: You don't expect me to read this?
Bevan: No, my lord, but it may be needed for reference purposes.

Professor Timothy David is dark, of medium build with an air about him that makes you want to confide in him. Clearly, he is a man with a compassionate obsession with children's health. He is a consultant paediatrician at Booth Hall Children's Hospital, Manchester, with twenty-eight years' experience.

He is the most impressive of all the experts. This is not because he is on Sally's side – he is on nobody's side – his role is competely independent. He is the paediatrician advising the Family Court on Tom's future. His has been the most painstaking research into every aspect of the deaths of both babies. But how will he stand up to Spencer's cross-examination?

Sally regards this man very highly:

> 'He is the only expert who actually came to see us and to question us in great detail. I knew that if we told him the truth, he would not distort it. I know there is a disagreement among my lawyers about him; because he has not been instructed by Mackey we cannot rely on him to be on our side. It is another and usually absolute rule of advocacy, that you never call a witness to support your own case unless you know exactly what he will say and that it will help your case. Neither Steve nor I hesitate for a moment in wanting him called. I am surprised that the judge does not want to read his 300-page report. It is the most comprehensive and independent overview of the deaths of our two boys. Whatever he says – good or bad – I know I will believe him. Whatever his conclusions, I will abide by them.'

He is dismissive of Christopher's bruises as sinister because a violent grip leaves a pattern and there is none, and nobody else saw them. He says that bruises do, rarely, develop after death. If they were bruises, it would be extremely unusual for them not to be visible to a police officer three and a half hours after death. Abrasions almost certainly excluded the possibility that they were inflicted during life. Many babies look bruised at death and are not.

David: I know cases where a coroner has been called and the sections revealed no bruises. Unless CPR is very vigorous so that it makes the blood reach the capillaries, it is useless, and that might account for the [injury to the] fraenulum.

He admits that blood deteriorates quickly after death and contamination is caused by resuscitation fluids, but having excluded all possible causes of contamination or deterioration he is left with some very unusual results from the blood analyses. The sodium levels alone show that there was something wrong with Christopher when he died.

As to the nosebleed:

David: One blow to the face could do it. Sally might have done something before she went shopping, it's not plausible but it fits. That leaves some sort of disease, uncommon in babies of this age. Picking the nose is not a likely cause. Bleeding from both nostrils is not a normal nosebleed. I think the blood came from the lungs. Idiopathic pulmonary haemosiderosis is a very rare disease indeed, but it would account for the symptoms I found.

This ought to be the seminal moment in the trial. A respected and unquestionably independent expert has come up with a possible natural cause of death for Christopher, something no other witness in the case has been able to do. The trouble is that none of Sally's experts give it credence, mainly because it is so rare and blood taken after death can be so unreliable. But is it as rare as a mother murdering her two babies? Even the fact that David is certain that Christopher was seriously ill, because of sodium levels, is brushed aside by other experts. What do the jury make of this? Insofar as I can judge, it does not impress them. Maybe they think it is just another piece of incomprehensible medical jargon.

Bevan asks him about Harry.

David: It was presented as Shaken Baby Syndrome, but most of Williams' initial findings were shown not to be there. There is no evidence of Shaken Baby Syndrome. As to the blood at the surface of the eye, even if it is not a post-mortem artefact, there is no evidence that it is due to abuse. Even if the fracture of the rib existed – which seems to be in considerable doubt – it could not have caused Harry's death.

Spencer rises to have his go. He charges straight in with the point about the fractured rib.

Spencer: Would you agree with me that it is evidence of abuse?
David: If it existed, that would account for it.

Spencer knows this expert carries probably more authority than all the others because he has been appointed by the Court – the Family Division judge – and not by either prosecution or defence. It is important therefore to discredit him.

Spencer makes a valiant attempt, but David is much tougher under cross-examination than I expected. It is not often that a witness exudes such confidence. He will not be shaken even by counsel as good as Spencer. The professor might even give some answers that will damage Spencer's case. Will Spencer go for him? If he does there is a good chance that the more Professor David says, the more it will improve Sally's chances with the jury. Spencer is too clever to fall for that, and soon sits down.

During the course of David's evidence the jury submit a written question, asking if there were tests on Harry's blood, as there were on Christopher's. They want to know if there is any possibility that Harry, too, suffered from a rare disease, like Christopher, but the questions relate specifically to blood tests.

These questions and their consequences demonstrate, to politicians and others who want to reduce access to jury trials, that juries can sometimes discern truths that evade all the knowledgeable lawyers and experts involved in a case. The jury members have no medical knowledge, the experts they have heard must have baffled them with their jargon, but while getting only an overall impression of what the medical picture is, something has become apparent to those sitting on that jury that has eluded the highly paid and distinguished experts.

The jury could not know that theirs are the most important questions in the Sally Clark case, a real 'smoke signal' to the 'fire' that is the microbiology report, given to Williams shortly after he did the post-mortem on Harry, which he put in his file and which has so far been kept secret from the defence: the one that showed a lethal bacterium in eight sites in Harry's body. Will Williams choose this obvious opportunity to reveal the report, or will he still keep it secret? If he keeps it quiet and those results are later made public, he may be in serious trouble. Will he recognise that danger?

The jury take a break and Spencer goes into a huddle with Williams. Spencer tells the judge that the answer to the question about tests on Harry's blood is no. The judge asks him if he will tell the jury himself. Spencer says he prefers to call Williams to deal with it.

The jury returns. The judge explains that Dr Williams will answer their questions.

Williams Recalled

Williams returns to the witness box.

Judge: You are still on oath.

Williams: Yes, my lord.

Spencer: . . . Having heard what Professor David gave in evidence do you wish to revise that you would not set any store by Harry's blood tests?

Williams: No. I stick to my opinion. The chemistry of blood is so unreliable after death as to be of no diagnostic value.

There is more in the same vein then:

Spencer: Can I turn to the blood sampling on Harry . . . ?

Williams: There is no recorded sample taken during resuscitation or immediately after that which was subject to chemical analysis.

Spencer: In the notes there is a reference to C & S?

Williams: . . . We have a fixed protocol for SIDS. A sample of heart blood is taken for blood culture to establish if the child was suffering from septicemia.

Spencer: So the initials stand for?

Williams: Culture and Sensitivity.

That is a direct reference to the microbiology tests.

Spencer: Was a blood sample taken at post-mortem?

Williams: It is always taken . . . It was submitted for toxicological examination and some of it would have been sent for viral studies.

Spencer: To see if there was some viral infection?

Williams: Yes.

What Williams says may be the literal truth but he has been asked questions that should have made him think about the microbiology results. 'Culture and Sensitivity' refers to the swabs he took from eight sites on Harry's body and submitted for microbiological and other tests. The report contains evidence that some pathologists would say was infection, and that in one site, the spinal fluid, Harry's immune defence had already created polymorphs to fight that infection. The jury wants to know if there is any possibility of disease in Harry, similar to the haemosiderosis which Professor David suggested might be the cause of Christopher's death. The microbiology results answer that question affirmatively and yet Williams does not reveal it. Why?

As Bevan rises to cross-examine, he does not know about the report. This case has been pored over by some of the best brains in medicine and they have not uncovered what Williams has not disclosed. How could that happen? Very simply: most microbiology tests are negative. If they had been positive, the other experts would have assumed that a Home Office pathologist would disclose them; he disclosed the results of microbiology in Christopher, which were positive but not significant. That, alone, would have confirmed, to the other experts, that there was nothing of note in Harry's microbiology.

Bevan: I have only one question of you, Dr Williams. No doubt you
    provided these two reports to the prosecution?
Williams: Yes.

The jury has been told, by one expert or another, on thirty-nine occasions that there is no evidence of natural disease in Harry. Every time it was untrue, but none of them knew what Williams had not revealed about microbiology.

Some procedural matters are dealt with, but that is the end of the evidence. All that remains are the closing speeches: first of Spencer, then of Bevan – his will be the last piece of advocacy the jury members hear, followed by the judge's summing-up.

Sally reflects that the defining moment of the trial was probably Meadow's statistic:

'At the time he said it, I was not particularly bothered, because if you are innocent, you know there cannot be evidence that proves you are guilty. Now, with hindsight, as decision time approaches . . . I am not so sure. The defence never said these were cot deaths! I console myself with the thought that doctor after doctor said "unascertained", which means "we do not know why these babies died". How could any jury, faced with so many "don't knows", find that Christopher and Harry, beyond reasonable doubt, were murdered?'

Sally still does not admit to herself the possibility that she will be convicted, that she will be sentenced to imprisonment for life. It is beyond her imagination.

Closing Speech for the Prosecution

Spencer begins reasonably enough with a summary of the possible verdicts: murder or manslaughter, meaning assault with the intention of causing grievous bodily harm leading to death. He dissects the medical evidence, putting the best prosecution interpretation he can on the many mistakes, inconsistencies and contradictions of his experts. He has a remarkable command of the complexities of the science. He paints Sally as a baby-murderer whose motives for killing her babies were that she resented the interference with her career, she hated being fat and ugly and she couldn't get into her clothes; with Steve away having a good time, she snapped and smothered Christopher to death. It was the same story with Harry but her motivation was set out in her own pen, in the letters to the grandparents.

Spencer: They were not the fun pretended by the defendant, but real expressions of the tiredness, anger and frustration that the baby brought into her life; faced with her husband flying away from her and her fractious baby – leaving her, just as he did, at the critical time with the firstborn . . .

Sally sobs:

'I can see myself now, sitting at my desk, writing that letter, Harry in his bouncy chair beside me, gurgling away. I cannot imagine a happier moment in his short life. Spencer is a monster to distort the reality in this way!'

Spencer: . . . Again she snapped and shook Harry or twisted him or smothered him too, to death. The inconsistencies in both her story and her husband's could not be the result of the traumas of their deaths for the simple reason that everybody knows where they were the day Kennedy died and so it is unthinkable that parents do not remember accurately the details of their own children's deaths.

One of Spencer's final comments is that he accepts that Christopher had a nosebleed!

Is he admitting, at long last, that Steve told nothing but the truth about something?

Closing Speech for the Defence

Mackey comes over and tells me that I am about to hear the best 'close' I have ever heard. 'Trust me,' he says. 'I know how good this man can be. There's nobody to touch him.'

I do trust Mike Mackey. I believe him. I relax; at least Spencer's diatribe is over and that might have been worse. Now the tables will be turned. Bevan will make the jury see Sally Clark's innocence. By the time Bevan has finished with them, they will have no doubts.

Bevan's opening words to the jury are:

Members of the jury, this is a very worrying case. There is suspicion but no certainty.

I want to yell out 'No!' I am shocked at these words. A cold shudder goes up and down my spine. I dread the impression they will make on the men and women who have to decide Sally's guilt or innocence. To me, he seems to be throwing down the gauntlet, daring the jury to convict: 'OK she may have done it, but because there's not enough certainty, you've got to let her off!' As an intellectual argument it has considerable force, but is that the way to persuade this jury? Mackey tells me later that he thinks I am mad to react in this way: 'It is not only the perfect way to put this to the jury, it is the only approach any advocate could use in such a difficult case.'

Steve's reaction is the same as mine but not Sally's:

'I would have preferred him to be more aggressive, less equivocal; more positive about my innocence, instead of concentrating on the uncertainty.

But it does nothing to shake my belief in Julian Bevan. I could not be more certain that I am in the best of possible hands. That is not the reaction of me as a lawyer, but me as a mum, fighting for her life – her future. I believe in Julian, totally and completely. I do not believe there is a better advocate to plead my cause anywhere.'

I have made closing speeches in magistrates' courts and at courts-martial, but I have never done one in a murder trial before a jury. So Mackey's experience and Bevan's outnumbers mine by a factor of thousands, but – for what it is worth – I would have lambasted the prosecution; said the case should never have been brought. Its only justification was Green's belief that Harry had been shaken to death. When that dreadful mistake was exposed, the case should have been abandoned and Sally's innocence recognised.

I still my anger to concentrate on the rest of his speech. To my relief, it is good.

In fact it is a *tour de force*, demolishing, piece by piece, every bit of the medical evidence, highlighting every expert, both for the prosecution and the defence, who destroyed one Williams finding after another. He holds up to ridicule the so-called motives for murder in a grown, highly intelligent woman. If she didn't want babies there is a simpler solution than killing them: why go through nine months' gestation only to murder them? Don't have them in the first place. He deals with Steve's mistake over the taxi very cleverly:

Bevan: In my submission it could only have come about by errors. It could not have been done by design, because, if he had lied, the records would never have seen the light of day. It would be wholly wrong to cast this man as a liar. It defies human nature; it defies common sense.

He is equally clever about the day Kennedy died.

Bevan: Do you remember the death of Diana? But do you remember, now, what you were doing four hours before you heard it?

He makes a valiant attempt to destroy Meadow's statistic, but I think its damaging impact is still there. Emphasising that the chance of a second death is 1:214 does not even sound plausible against the sombre skill and certainty with which Meadow pronounced 1:73 million.

However, Bevan has done a wonderful job. He has convinced me. I am beginning to feel he may have the jury on his side, that he may have made them forget his opening words. I am waiting for his punch line: the last words they will carry into the jury room; the best sound bite of innocence.

Bevan: Members of the jury . . . there is suspicion in this case but there is no certainty.

I cannot believe he has repeated that sentence! And I experience the same cold dread.

As we wait for the judge to get his thoughts in order before he begins his summing-up, I tell myself I am an idiot to have such forebodings. I persuade myself that if the jury were to retire at that moment they would concentrate on the contradictions in the prosecution medical evidence, and those are the only opinions that say murder. Surely, at least enough people on the jury will opt for Sally's innocence to make it a 'hung' jury? Could ten people really vote guilty? I do not think so.

As Bevan and his junior leave the court, Kelsey Fry holds out his hand to Bevan and says: 'Julian, that was brilliant. You've done it!'

The Judge's Summing-up

Before they retire to debate their verdict, there is now the judge's summing-up. He could go either way. He could sum up for an acquittal or for a guilty verdict. He is not supposed to do either. His job is to tell the jury what the law is and then review the evidence. He should tell them that his own opinions are irrelevant. But a judge as experienced as this man could, if he wanted, indicate which way he is thinking, and that would have a big impact. He has given the impression, throughout the trial, that he is a reasonable, intelligent and fair man. It is impossible to tell whether he thinks Sally is guilty or not. He would probably agree with Bevan, that there is suspicion but no certainty. He can be expected to sum up impartially, dropping the babies firmly in the jury's lap, without giving them a clue what he thinks.

Mr Justice Harrison: . . . Members of the jury . . . it is very important that you put out of your minds any feelings of emotion, whether it be anger, distress, sympathy . . . because it may prejudice your minds. You should approach your decision unemotionally and dispassionately and have regard only to the evidence you have heard . . .

He tells them they can rely on good circumstantial evidence but not on pure speculation.

Judge: . . . The defendant does not have to prove her innocence, the burden of doing that is on the prosecution. That means you must be sure of guilt. If after considering all the evidence on one count you are sure the defendant is guilty you must return a verdict of guilty. If you are not sure, the verdict must be not guilty. If you found she was guilty of murdering Christopher, it does not follow that she must have murdered Harry. You must consider the evidence on that quite separately . . . If you are sure that she deliberately killed one child you must then consider if she intended to kill him or cause him serious bodily harm, if so you should convict. If you conclude that she did not intend serious harm then your verdict should be guilty of manslaughter.

He reminds them of the similarities. He then takes the medical findings in turn and reviews what each expert had to say about them and does so fairly. He tells them they may think there is suspicion but no certainty!

The Judge has obviously has been impressed by Bevan's words to the jury.

The next day the judge continues the summing-up. He tells the jury he will not send them out to consider their verdict until Monday.

He turns to the case of Harry and the fact that Lesley Kerrigan, the Clark's nanny, had never seen any signs of abuse in Harry. He reviews all of Williams' findings and what the other experts had to say about them. He lets Green off lightly on his mistake on retinal haemorrhages, accepting his explanation that it was an understandable error because of the unusual way the slides had been prepared.

He deals with Meadow's evidence in detail:

Judge: His figures were derived from a very thorough research study . . . the probability of one cot death is 1:8,543 and the probability of two is 1:73 million live births. That means there is a chance of two SIDS in the same family happening once every hundred years. In addition to that, in these two cases, there are the features which are suspicious in any event.

He reviews the statistical evidence against that and then says:

> I should, I think, sound a note of caution about the statistics. However compelling you may find those statistics, we do not convict people in these courts on statistics. It would be a terrible day if that were so. If there is one cot death in a family it does not mean there cannot be another. Statistics are part of the evidence . . . no more than that. It may be a part of the evidence to which you attach some significance . . . but it is necessary for you to have regard to the individual circumstances . . .

Will they hear those words as giving them permission to convict on the statistic if that is what they really want to do? I believe, as a lawyer, that the direction is wrong in law; I believe that the judge was wrong, in law, to allow the statistic to be admitted in evidence. A judge has not only the right, but the obligation to intervene to stop inadmissible – over-prejudicial – evidence being presented to the jury. In layman's language, the statistic puts the odds against Sally's innocence at five times the chance of any member of that jury winning the lottery. Would any jury understand that this is the very calculation they must not make.

The judge deals with the police evidence quite objectively.

His summary of the defence case begins with Sally's evidence.

Judge: . . . You should take her good character into account in two ways. Firstly she has given evidence and her good character supports her credibility, and secondly it means that she is less likely to commit these crimes. How much weight you give to those two matters is entirely up to you.

He summarises Steve's evidence, reminding the jury that, since he gave evidence, the defence has now admitted that Steve knew, on 9th April, of the allegations that Harry had been shaken earlier on the night he died.

Judge: Do you really think he would have forgotten that he had got home late that evening when his son died only about an hour or so later, or do you think he genuinely may not have remembered and was relying on what Mrs Knowles told him? If he did know what time he got home and lied about it, would he have risked the possibility of the taxi records being checked? These are questions for you . . . Finally he told you that he supported his wife throughout this terrible ordeal . . . He denied covering up for her, saying that if he thought she had done anything to them he would not have supported her or stayed with her.

He reviews all the defence medical evidence. I cannot help thinking that his summing-up might have had a different tone if he had read David's report.

It is Sunday, 7 November 1999. I am at home, in Surrey. I have two adult daughters, Gina and Joanna. On my weekends, they have been observing my reaction to the trial with 'increasing concern', they tell me. They suggest that my wife, Jane, should come with me to Chester, to be with me when the verdicts come in, and on the way home. They do not tell me that they have a premonition that Sally will be found guilty. (Their insights have a nasty habit of coming true.) I accept Jane's offer with alacrity; driving on a long journey, with her beside me, is one of the joys in our marriage. Jane's company makes that drive to Chester a pleasure and, for a few hours, takes some of the anxiety way from my imagination of what the morrow holds.

On Monday morning, we leave the car at our hotel and go by taxi to the Crown Court. Jane gives Sally a hug as we wait.

Mr Justice Harrison continues his review of the defence medical experts. He then deals with the closing speeches. He recalls that Spencer said:

'The probability of two SIDS deaths within the same family, namely 1:73 million, are even longer odds if you take into account the old and fresh injuries, and the seven similarities between the two deaths.'

He quotes Bevan as accepting that this is a very worrying case because there are some unusual and suspicious features, but he submits, correctly, that you cannot convict on mere suspicion.

Judge: You must be sure she has killed both her children. The question is not whether the findings are consistent with smothering but whether the prosecution has proved that the child was smothered.

He reminds the jury that Bevan attacked Dr Christine Smith, saying that she was not independent, objective or fair and was on a mission to assist the prosecution at all costs.

Judge: That is a serious allegation to make against a professional witness and you will have to consider it. The defendant's neuropathologist agreed with her that there was hypoxic damage to the brain of Harry. Berry and Rushton disagreed . . . If the defendant had wanted to kill her child, why, it was asked, had she first inflicted gratuitous violence on the child and then smothered him? Why not simply smother him?

The judge tells the jury eighteen times that there is no natural disease in Harry; but the judge did not know what Williams had kept secret, he did not know that what he told the jury eighteen times was untrue.

After a few more remarks about the necessity for separate verdicts in each case and for unanimity, he sends the jury out: to take a vote as to whether the prosecution has satisfied them, beyond reasonable doubt, that Sally Clark is guilty of murder as defined in law.

We all rise as the judge departs.

The Verdict

Now comes what may be a long wait. Bevan says to Mackey: 'I have to go back to London now, but I think this one is all right.'

He thinks he has persuaded the jury to acquit Sally, and that gives me confidence. With all his experience of murder and other trials, he should be able to judge which way a jury will jump. Mackey is not so sure.

Sally and Steve are in a room with Mackey, Kelsey Fry, occasionally Bevan and Sally's friend Alison. Sally feels apprehensive but not fearful.

Everybody is called back into court, but it is a false alarm. The jury has not reached a verdict and is sent away for the night.

Sally's bail is renewed. She and Steve go to see Tom; then home. Neither sleep much but there is nothing to say that can help. They are numb with fatigue and dread. Sally is still convinced that as she has done nothing, no murders have been committed in her family, she cannot be found guilty. So what the hell are the jury talking about? What are they taking so long over?

Unusually, the Press Association issues a warning to journalists: 'Be careful with this one; she's going to be acquitted!'

It is now Tuesday. Bevan is still in London. Kelsey Fry is now Sally's only advocate.

The judge calls the jury back in. They tell him they have not reached a unanimous verdict. He tells them they are now at liberty to try to reach a majority verdict, but at least ten of them must agree.

Sally and Steve join Jane and me in the cafeteria. Sally asks: 'What is their problem? I didn't do it. Can't they see that?'

The tension gets to all of us. We drink our coffee and wait.

At last the jury returns.

Mackey tells Sally that, just as a precaution, she should take off all her jewellery:

'I don't want to do it, but I know I must. I give it to Alison. It is the first time I have ever taken off my engagement ring.'

I ask Jane to wait outside the courtroom. I don't know why I do that.

The judge comes in first, then the jury file into their places. Two women are in tears. The older man in the front row, who made so many notes, has his head in his hands. The foreman rises. It turns out to be one of the younger men. I was certain it would be the older man. Does that mean the youngsters have held sway? The security guards close in on Sally.

Clerk: Are at least ten of you agreed on your verdict? Please answer only yes or no.

Foreman: Yes, we are.

Clerk: On count one do you find the defendant guilty or not guilty?

Foreman: Guilty.

Clerk: On the second count, do you find the defendant guilty or not guilty?

Foreman: Guilty.

It is ten to two in each case.

Sally goes numb:

'It must be a dream. It is not happening to me. I am on the outside looking in on somebody else's life. I look across at Steve. He is waving his arms in despair at the jury. One of the jury is crying, head in hands. When I left Hope Cottage that morning, I was utterly convinced I would be acquitted; that I would be coming home tonight with Steve. I did not say any goodbyes or prepare myself for the worst. We were both totally unprepared for this verdict. Prison was nowhere in our vocabulary. Neither of us had the slightest notion that last night was the last night of my freedom.'

Sally's look cries out to me. I try to look strong, comforting, reassuring. I don't think I do a good job. She turns to look for Steve, finds him. His arms are still in the air. He mouths 'I love you.' He takes off his Armistice Day poppy and grinds it under his heel. Steve is disgusted:

'This is not the country I love . . . grew up in. I was brought up to believe in British justice. This is not justice. It is a mockery of it. How could they have reached those verdicts on the evidence? How? I blame the prosecution and their experts for going at it so hard, when there were massive holes in their medical evidence: not only at trial but at committal. They knew they were presenting mistakes, changes of causes of death. This case should never have been taken further when these things became clear. Full marks to Spencer: he has turned a hopeless case into a conviction. It is a victory for injustice. Condemning a loving and caring family . . . a mother who never could harm anybody, let alone her own babies, to purgatory on unbelievably flawed evidence. I feel anger and despair in equal measures. The prosecution has done a great job.'

A cynical and famous criminal prosecutor once said that the satisfaction of convicting the guilty is only eclipsed by the thrill of convicting the truly innocent.

Steve does not know what to do:

'My honest, law-abiding family has just been crushed by the machinery of the State. Once they decided to charge Sally, nobody would press the stop button, admits that they were wrong when Williams' findings 'turned to dust' as Professor Berry put it. Maybe they were just doing their jobs but the exposure of every mistake seemed to spur them on with greater determination to convict Sally, and there was nothing I could do to stop it. I am used to being in control of my life, normally able to make things happen through hard work, persuasion or sheer determination. But I have felt totally impotent through this whole process – unable to protect my family, to prevent the destruction of our lives.'

Spencer rises, hesitant, and yet he must know that things will now take their inexorable course.

Spencer: My lord, now that the jury has returned its verdict, may I presume that your order against reference to Mrs Clark's alcohol problem is now no longer in force?
Judge: I think that must be right.
Spencer: Thank you, my lord. I think it right that the full facts of the case be made known now and I take this opportunity to make clear that it would have formed part of the prosecution's case that alcohol played a part and that it was so serious that Mrs Clark was treated for it at the Priory.

Why does Spencer do this? He knows that there was no evidence of alcohol when the babies died. The papers will use it as the reason Sally killed her babies. He is a very clever man. He will know that. Was that his objective in asking for the restriction to be lifted? Insurance against the inevitable appeal? It is often said that to win in the Court of Appeal, you have first to win in the court of public opinion.

Journalists are busy writing. Spencer sits. The judge looks at Kelsey Fry.

Judge: Do you wish to address me on anything, Mr Kelsey Fry.
Kelsey Fry: No, my lord.

There is chaos in the press box as reporters rush for telephones.

Judge: Mrs Clark . . . you will be remanded in custody for a date to be set for your sentencing. Take her down.

The Group 4 security officers take Sally by the arm and guide her down the stairs to the cells below.

'A woman from Court Legal Services asks me if I understand the nature of my conviction. She tells me it has probably not sunk in yet, because I am showing no sign of emotion.'

I see two women on the jury in tears; are they the ones who voted not guilty? But what happened to make the man put his head in his hands? Was he persuaded, possibly against his better judgement, to go along with the other nine? We shall never know. But that's what it looks like. I realise I will have to call Frank, before he hears it on the radio.

I leave quickly and tell Jane, but she already knows. I pick up my mobile.

Me: Frank . . . it's me. It's not good news. Guilty, I'm afraid.
Frank: On both?
Me: Yes. I'm so sorry . . .
Frank: Really? Well . . . thanks for being there . . . I think I'd better get off . . .

My wife comes to me. We hold each other. I have kept my cool this far – and others' spirits up – by telling myself that it would all be over in a matter of days, and I could return to a normal life. But my situation is as nothing compared to Sally's and Steve's.

Mackey and Kelsey Fry see Sally in the cells. She is too distraught to take in what they say about immediately lodging an appeal. They explain that there will be a separate hearing for sentencing, that there will be psychiatric reports. They tell her that there is only one sentence and it is mandatory: life imprisonment. She must prepare herself for that, but she will never serve it; this conviction cannot stand up on appeal.

Steve goes to the cells. He can see Sally but she is behind a glass screen. He cannot even touch her! They are both utterly spent. Until now they thought they had trouble, but could never have envisaged it ending this way. Sally is thinking of Steve:

'All I can think of is that I have to be strong for Steve, because he looks so distraught and pitiful. I make him promise he will go and see Tom this evening. I tell him he must not miss a single visit with our son. I know, somehow, that this is the right thing to do. And Steve does it.'

Tomorrow is not just 'another day' for Sally Clark. It is the first of many days, months and years of misery, fear and separation.

Serving Time

Thursday, 11 November 1999

Sally is left in a cell underneath the Crown Court for two hours waiting for Group 4 to take her to prison:

'I am given leggings, a jumper, prison-issue nightie and knickers and taken to the hospital wing, not because I am ill but because it is the only place where they can guarantee my safety. It is staffed not by prison officers, but entirely by nurses. I am given an initial assessment by one of them, then by a doctor.

'My cell confirms all my worst fears: it is tired, dirty and stark. I sit on the bed and sob.'

Steve is driven back to Hope Cottage by their friend Alison. He looks round his family home, knowing he should make dozens of phone calls to family and friends before they hear it on the News. He realises he should start dialling. The calls to Tom's grandparents will be the worst. Eventually he goes to bed, the one he shared with his lovely wife only a few short hours ago. Now he is sleeping cold and alone. And where is she? Is she alright? Where will she be sleeping, if at all, tonight, and for however many nights, before they are together again. Steve knows it may be years:

'I try to send my thoughts to my darling Sally; thoughts of love and support. It tears me apart to think of her in a stark prison.'

He undresses and knows he will not sleep a wink. A moment later he is unconscious, the sleep of utter exhaustion.

The girl in the next cell keeps Sally awake all night:

'banging her head against the door, screaming for help. I feel as if I am in an asylum. To my surprise, some prisoners on this unit treat me well – the tendency to rally round one's own – but all of them have mental and psychiatric problems. I feel isolated and worry about my own sanity; might I, too, start 'rocking'? My heart goes out to them.

'Next morning, I am allowed a Reception visit with Steve. He is grey with anguish and pain. He has put together a bag of what I shall need, not knowing that I will not be allowed a hair dryer, curling tongs, CD player or mobile phone.'

Sally is on the hospital wing:

'My safety is paramount, therefore only rarely will I leave the wing, when they can spare the manpower to give me escorts: every time I am shouted at and verbally abused. Sleeping at night becomes even more difficult as more people find out where I am. At night, they shout abuse out of their windows and discuss me in unpleasant terms. That said, I feel safe there.

'The only act of physical violence takes place when a girl comes into my room and asks what I am in for. I tell her and she bashes a plastic mug into my face. It is empty, so I am not scalded, but I have a bruise under my eye for days. I report the incident but it was not witnessed by any member of staff. No action is taken against her. A few days later, the girl apologises for having been 'so judgemental'! She had been to church since she did it and God told her to say sorry. I was touched at first, but then realised that, while the incident took place behind closed doors, the apology is in full view of nursing staff and other inmates and the girl herself is coming up for parole.

'The verbal abuse continues, unabated, throughout my two months at Styal. I am in a prison within a prison. I spend most of my time in my cell, writing letters and reading. I do venture into the association room to watch television. The other inmates seem to spend all their time in front of the set; it's a bit like a nursing home. The conditioning and control soon take effect. One morning, I watch a repeat of an episode of *Coronation Street* and as it finishes I assume it is bedtime and make for my cell. Am I going mad? It is the lack of control, the humiliation and loss of dignity that hits me most. I am struggling to cope, emotionally and physically, but never once do I contemplate suicide. I resolve to keep fighting – for Steve, for Tom, for family and friends.

'Twice-monthly visits with Steve keep me going. But the goodbyes tear me apart. I am also buoyed by the deluge of letters of support that arrive on a daily basis; complete strangers somehow sense that my conviction is wrong. I know I am innocent but how could anybody else, who read the press coverage, sense the injustice and make such a great leap of faith?

'The most difficult times are missing Tom's first birthday – 29 November – although Linda and a social worker are allowed to bring him to see me for two hours on that day, and Christmas 1999.'

Steve knows all about Sally's love of Christmas but the only visit he is allowed is on Christmas Eve. Sally has to miss lunch to see him. The prison authorities are considerate in arranging for visits when other prisoners are nor around – for Sally's own safety. They even bring her lunch. Steve is not impressed with a cold cheese pasty:

'As I leave her abysmal lunch, I can taste my tears. I try to pull myself together and make a resolution that this is something I will never accept. Whatever it takes, however much money or time or effort, nothing will stop me getting her out.'

Sally has always had a childlike and fairytale approach to Christmas:

'The Day itself is a particularly bad one to be separated from Steve and Tom. I feel a special sense of isolation and bleakness in my cell as midnight strikes the Millennium, listening to the fireworks and festivities in the outside world, wondering what the New Year holds for me. I am kept going by the reassuring talk and plans of my legal team for my appeal.'

Sally is visited in her cell by the Lifer Governor:

'He tells me that, given the nature of my convictions, and that I am a solicitor and the daughter of a police officer, I will always have to watch my back. If I do not face up to my crimes and admit my guilt, my chances of ever getting parole are negligible.'

Is there a qualitative difference between this approved prison policy and forcing a confession out of a prisoner in a Saudi Arabian cell? That Middle Eastern country denies it happens; our authorities order it to happen, but justify it on the grounds that, unless the prisoner shows remorse, she may re-offend. The cause and effect are the same: State-sponsored torture, leading – most probably – to false confessions.

Sally has a robust answer for the Governor:

'I look at myself every morning in the mirror, knowing I never told a lie in court. Why should I begin to lie now?'

The other aspect of prison life that troubles Sally is the official attitude to appeals:

'Many people claim they are innocent when they are not and most of their chances at appeal are negligible. But I guess this is their way of keeping their hopes of freedom alive, and I understand that staff are often dismissive. But when one really is innocent, such an official reaction is so distressing and disheartening. I hate being told to "get real" and face up to a lengthy prison sentence.'

Steve must now sell the house to pay back the bank the money he has borrowed for Sally's defence, or part of it. They still owe Mackey £100,000.

Addleshaws in Manchester, the firm for which they both work, is a great support to Steve throughout, in many ways, and gives him all the leave he needs to cope with the trial and the fight for custody of Tom, following Sally's conviction.

My wife Jane and I fly to Florida to spend Thanksgiving with our son Charles and his family. The phone rings as soon as we get to our hotel.

Margarette Driscoll is writing a piece for the *Sunday Times*. She has been briefed extensively by Mackey, but still spends time with me, checking background.

A few days later, the family and grandchildren arrive. When the kids are in the swimming pool, our daughter-in-law breaks her news: she has breast cancer. A biopsy revealed a tumour and it's aggressive. But the oncologists are very hopeful. Although the tumour was one inch in diameter, they have caught it early and it should respond to chemotherapy. It is a shock. Susan always seemed such a vibrant person with such an appetite for life. Jane and I tell each other that as Susan is a nurse they must have told her the full seriousness of her situation and she will be OK. Susan has three children: Derek is ten and six feet tall, a natural sportsman; Lizzy is nearly nine, a freckled beauty with a delicious character – she will drive many men to distraction; Janie is five, a real blonde, the image of her grandmother, on Jane's side, with many of her formidable characteristics.

We have two weeks at the beach, in the sun and the pool, spoiling our grandchildren.

After the initial assessment at Styal, Sally will spend the first stage of a life sentence either at Bullwood Hall, in Essex, or at Durham.

'I am informed I am to go to Bullwood Hall in Essex, tomorrow morning. But the sale of the house has not yet gone through and Steve has not found anywhere to live down south. The prospect of being so far away from him and Tom fills me with dread. I feel safe here, at Styal, despite all its problems. What will it be like at a new prison? I ask to phone Steve. This is denied, on security grounds. Once there, I will be allowed to call him.

'The move in January is hard to bear. Steve not even knowing it is happening makes it so much worse. I am transferred in a people carrier, with prison officers. One other inmate is being moved out of Styal, for bullying and fighting. Luckily she does not have a clue who I am; she spends the journey telling me what she would do to that "Sally Clark nonce" if she could get her hands on her.

'Reception staff at Bullwood Hall are kind and sympathetic. It is a welcome surprise but it adds to my anguish and emotion. I am allowed my phone call to tell Steve. He asks if I am OK. I lie.

'There is aggression and tension in the air as I walk into the dining room. Another lifer has been detailed to point me in the right direction. I take my meal and sit down. It soon becomes clear that I am in somebody else's place. I think they must be expecting trouble because there are a lot of officers on duty. I suffer no abuse. I am still shaking and cannot hold the cutlery properly.

'When we get back to the wing I follow a girl into her cell, but others are already there, for a meeting. They get up and leave. I go back to my own cell.

'A little while later my cell door opens. A tall, heavily built and intimidating woman looks down at me: "You sat in my place at dinner. You will not do so again! You are not welcome at my table or on my wing. There is a code of ethics, even amongst women in jail, and the lowest of the low are people like you – women who harm children. I do not intend to do anything physical to you myself, provided you keep out of my way."

'Annie – not her real name – turns and slams my cell door shut.

'I sob myself to sleep. I know there is a locked door between me and everybody else, but I am still rather surprised to wake up in the morning and find that I have not been killed in the night. If I had known half of what other mothers like me had been through on their first nights, I would not have slept at all.

'My first impression on getting to the wing is that I am in the set of the TV series *Porridge*. It seems that an officer has leaked news of my arrival, so I am expected. Staff, in the main, are non-judgmental, but I am told to watch my back. They say that they will not tolerate bullying or intimidation, and yet one woman with a similar conviction has been continuously bullied, beaten up and intimidated. I am given two options: I can be escorted everywhere, which will draw even more attention to me, or I can go it alone, and staff will keep an eye on me from afar. I choose the latter. Being taken to my cell feels like the longest walk of my life.

'I spend the first days and weeks at Bullwood Hall keeping my head down, scuttling around, and fearing for my safety. I am given a job in the laundry, known to be a safe environment. I go to and from work outside normal times, for my own protection. Going to the dining room is fairly pointless, because it is such an ordeal, running the gauntlet of abuse. I lose my appetite, and a lot of weight.

'I work extremely hard in the laundry and win the respect of other prisoners there. They thought I would regard such work as beneath me and shun the dirty jobs, but I get on with it, although I find it physically challenging. I am glad to be out of my cell, having something to do to keep my mind off my situation; and it is not in my nature to be lazy.

'I decide, from the start, that I will not proclaim my innocence or thrust my injustice down other people's throats. I try to keep my own counsel, to respect the wishes of others and smile at the few who make the effort to chat to me. I am still getting abuse from inmates on other wings, but on my own, I begin to get a warmer vibe.

'But abuse can be only a moment away. One day in the dining room, a woman from another wing throws a tray of food at me. Most of it hits my neighbour, but I get gravy and vegetables in my hair and on my face. Instinct tells me not to flee the room in tears, so I sit there, getting on with my meal. I score a lot of points for that! The thrower claims it was an accident.

'The lifer wing becomes a safe haven – it is rather like Styal. I am not naïve enough to think that it is all down to me. It is more to do with support from an unexpected source. Susie W. is the leader of the wing – her word goes! Several weeks into my time there, she comes into my cell:

' "I've been watching you from afar," she says. "As a mother, I hate baby-killers, so I can't understand why my spirit has taken to you. Are you prepared to tell me your story?"

'From that moment onwards, my life there changes. The mood on the lifer wing alters from tolerance to acceptance, and is to become, eventually, belief and support. With that wing on my side, aggression from the other wings subsides. There is still sporadic abuse but now, when it happens, a lifer will leap to my defence, sometimes physically.

'I make three friends on the wing: Susie W., Susie B. and Tracy A.; they become essential to my daily existence. It amazes me that there are three such genuinely compassionate people in such a place. Even though I am becoming stronger mentally and emotionally each day, I am physically unable to take care of myself when faced with aggression or violence; and I am not streetwise, in comparison to other inmates. It would have been easy to walk into all sorts of trouble without realising it.

'It is my separation from Steve and Tom that tests my emotions and endurance and causes me the greatest upset, rather than my day-to-day existence around the prison.

'It becomes more bearable when we are moved out of the dirty wing into a purpose-built block. The accommodation is more like bedrooms than cells. There are no bars on the windows and we have a shower, basin and toilet *en suite*.'

Kelsey Fry and Mackey are stunned by Sally's guilty verdict. Getting to know her made both of them 'know', instinctively, that she was an unlikely candidate for baby murder. Apart from the emotional shock of the verdicts, there is the incomprehension that any jury could have thought that there was evidence, to the point of certainty, that even one murder had been committed. Bevan is similarly shaken. This is a case to which he has probably given greater commitment than to any other.

My observation during the four weeks of the trial was that Bevan believed in Sally, and she picked up on that. Lawyers must be objective; getting emotionally involved clouds professional judgement and can be dangerous for the client. But an innocent client needs to know that her lawyer believes in her; it gives her the confidence to face the cruelties of the criminal justice system. I do not believe that his belief in Sally clouded Bevan's objectivity.

Bevan has described this as the most difficult case of his career. I do not doubt that. Non-lawyers do not understand the awesome responsibility of defending somebody in court: their fate is in your hands. When the charge is murder it is worse, much worse. Capital punishment was abolished in 1963 but a life sentence can still mean your client's life is over. Once the trial begins, every decision has to be made against the clock, weighing competing interests – in this case – of Sally, of Steve and their son. 1:73 million was sprung on Bevan five days before the trial began. Things like that often happen. The prosecution could have introduced the statistic out of worry about the many medical inconsistencies. Williams had changed the cause of death of Christopher from natural causes to smothering, having said, at committal, that there was no evidence of it. Green made two crucial mistakes: on the eyes of Harry and the lungs of Christopher. It must have seemed to the prosecution that their case was in trouble. Would any jury interpret those mistakes as anything other than reasonable doubts? In which case, why not pursue that to its logical conclusion and offer no further evidence? Let the case be stopped? When Meadow plucked the statistic from the draft CESDI Report, did that change everything?

Was it seen as a case-saver to Spencer? It was a nightmare on top of nightmares for Bevan. He was already dealing with the change of Harry's death from shaking to smothering, trying to come to terms with what his experts – all of them – had to say about it; what it meant for the tactics of the case. And there was the fear that Tom might be put up for adoption.

Guilty verdicts do not enhance defence lawyers' reputations. This is the most important and high-profile case of Mackey's career; it is a case he thought he had won. Mackey's wife, Christine, tells me he has invested more of his professional and emotional capital in Sally Clark than in any other client.

Jane and I set off home from Chester in silence, each preoccupied with thoughts of what Sally must be going through. After a few miles, Jane says we need fuel. The visit to that filling station is unforgettable; not because it is in any way memorable, but because it isn't. Doing something as ordinary as putting petrol in a car is something Sally may never be able to do again.

It dawns on me that I can no longer be a spectator. Whether anybody likes it or not, I will now have to become actively involved. I do not know how; I do not even know what I am qualified to do, but I do know that I was in the wrong place at the wrong time, and now is too late to pull out.

Sally's conviction is something I cannot live with. However long it takes, whatever else I have to give up, however much it costs me, financially and emotionally, I will not rest until Sally walks free. No, that does not make me some sort of hero; it is the inevitable consequence of being a lawyer. I am not alone in this. It is exactly the same for Mackey and for Frank – and particularly for Steve – as well as for others caught up in this bad verdict. Whenever a lawyer steps into the path of a miscarriage of justice the result is the same; it takes over his or her life.

The appeal will not be easy. The Court of Criminal Appeal is in business to uphold the law, to maintain sound convictions and so to keep the guilty behind bars. Discharging the burden of proving that Sally's verdict is not only wrong but unsafe will be difficult. That court has the reputation of sometimes making up its mind in advance and then finding the necessary legal arguments to back it up. But that should not be a worry: every lawyer I talk to tells me they can't believe she has been convicted.

One ground of appeal cannot be denied, in law, and should quash her conviction: 1:73 million! I 'know' it convicted her. I 'know' that the jury did the same sums I did and worked out that if the chance of her being innocent was five times their chances of winning the lottery, she must be guilty.

That night, I thank the Almighty that Sally has one ground of appeal that no bench of appeal judges could reject. If Mr Justice Harrison had considered it inadmissible he could have stopped it going to the jury. Three judges of appeal will not get it wrong.

Mackey, Bevan and Kelsey Fry will put together the grounds of appeal. That will require hours and days of work and complete dedication to getting it right this time. They are the best. This is their exclusive area of expertise. The gauntlet has been publicly thrown at their feet. They will pick it up. Spencer will come second, next time. I will beaver away on my own, hacking my way into the medicine and law relating to cot deaths, to see what comes up.

Mackey says that Channel 4 wishes to make a *Rough Justice* type programme about Sally. They have offered £100,000 for research into cot deaths and the thrust will be miscarriage of justice. It will be made by an independent company, Just TV, and the presenter will be David Jessel. What could be better! I meet John Ashton, their researcher, at home at the end of December and brief him on all I know, including my diagnosis that Green's description of non-existent haemorrhages in Harry's eyes was the trigger for Sally's arrest. In my opinion she should have been freed the moment Green confessed his mistake. I go to Salisbury, where Jessel is interviewing Steve for the programme.

When I worked in television, it was with the drama department; documentaries are virgin territory. This is the expertise of others. I co-operate fully, but only when asked, and I get to know David Jessel: he believes Sally has been wrongly convicted. He promises to let me see a rough cut of the programme in advance.

It arrives the day before transmission. Apparently, Channel 4 has changed its mind; there is no £100,000 and it will not be an investigation of a miscarriage, but an even-handed documentary, giving equal weight to both prosecution and defence. That is not what happened at

Chester Crown Court. In spite of the verdict, the prosecution case was in tatters at the end; only the statistic saved the day for it. I do not like the programme as it stands. Frank, Steve and others have seen it. The family is very worried, but Jessel and his producer are editing the programme and a row is in progress with Channel 4. I have watched the rough cut again and again, and have identified the most damaging parts. Eventually I speak to Jessel and give him a 'must-have' list of things to be changed or omitted, if the programme is to be a true mirror of what happened. All Jessell will say is that he will do his best.

The programme goes out. My family watches it with me. They think it's fine. Frank calls me. 'I suppose it could have been worse,' he says.

Friends divide fairly evenly: my show business friends love Frank because he cried on television; Steve didn't. Pity! Most people thought it was fine, and that it would persuade many viewers of Sally's innocence.

A vital audience watches it at Bullwood Hall prison. They are impressed. It increases the sense of her innocence among inmates and staff alike: raises Sally's profile.

'Prison officers tell me that they genuinely believe in my innocence and think my appeal is bound to succeed. One of the fringe benefits of this is that now I am aware that I am not looking for signs of danger as I walk around the prison. That terrible all-pervading sense of fear is beginning to go away. And by this time, I have three friends inside and a number of acquaintances.

'Through sheer hard work, I am now number one in the laundry; then they move me to a job with more responsibility, in the prison shop. This is a more pleasant environment, working with members of staff rather than inmates. It is still hard work, and I have to handle money, but there is a sense of escapism, because what I am now doing is so unlike normal prison life.'

Professor David Southall, an eminent paediatrican colleague of Meadow, makes a complaint to the police, implicating Steve in the murder of his two babies. The opinion is based on the Just TV programme! Coming from such an eminent expert, this has to be taken very seriously. Social Services ask Professor David to investigate – it could mean Steve losing his son as well as his wife to life imprisonment.

How professionally unhealthy an emotional involvement is for a lawyer is brought home to me again, when I write a piece for the Law Society's *Gazette*, the main legal magazine. They bin it, politely. I put it on one side for a week and then read it again. It is awful! A good example of write-rage! Maudlin – I talk about being ashamed to be a lawyer – over the top, ranting at everybody and the system. Strident. No objectivity. I too bin it but forget that I have sent it to a former articled clerk of mine, Walter Merricks.

Margarette Driscoll writes a good piece in the *Sunday Times*, that pours scorn on Meadow's statistic and is highly critical of the conviction, but hers is a lone voice at this stage.

On 13 January 2000, I fly to Manchester to spend the night with Steve and talk to Professor David. We discuss all aspects of the case, mostly going over old ground that was covered at the trial. But one thing is new: he asks if I know anything about a story that Sally made a phone call to a criminal barrister, just before or after dialling 999, on the night Harry died. Steve knows it cannot be true. He was there; apart from anything else, he was only out of Sally's sight for three or four minutes, making Harry's bottle in the kitchen. Even without checking the phone records, we know there could not have been time for Sally to make any phone call. David is puzzled. If it is not true, why would anybody make up such a lie?

Medical experts are often reluctant to go firm with their opinions, so much of medicine is a matter of opinion – even causes of death. This produces a quandary. Without more positive medical opinions it may not be possible to secure a conviction. If an expert is told something confidential about the suspect, which points unequivocally to guilt – it may be true, or may simply be invented – it may persuade him to be more forceful in his opinion. If Sally had had such a conversation, it would be a communication between lawyer and client and probably could not be used in evidence, but the rules of evidence would allow the jury to be told that the phone call was made and the identity and profession of the person Sally called. It would be enough to convince anybody of her guilt. The fact that it has not formed part of the case against Sally proves it is a lie. Steve checks the phone records. They did not instruct Mackey until introduced to him much later by Steve's boss. I tell David this and that there will be no record of it. He will put it in a letter to all the lawyers and others who are involved in Tom's case in the Family Court.

Frank is disgusted by the idea that anybody would stoop so low. This is the stuff of a serious complaint against those responsible. Quite how it could help Sally's appeal is more difficult to say.

On 18 January 2000, I go with Frank to meet Professor Berry at his hospital in Bristol. He wants to be helpful, because he is convinced Sally should never have been convicted, since no credible medical evidence was presented at trial. He says that the medical profession bears a heavy responsibility for what happened to Sally.

We go from him to a meeting with Professor Bernard Knight. He was the most eminent of pathologists; now retired, he does not take on any new cases. He is amazed at the mistake over Harry's eyes:

'Green is a clever man; much respected,' he tells us. 'He is an expert in eyes, but retinal haemorrhages are one of the easiest conditions to identify under the microscope. I could teach you two to do it in half an hour.'

On 27 January I have a meeting with the BBC. Bill Law, a producer of Radio 4's *Law in Action*, plans an item in his programme on Sally. I am to record an interview, on tape, for the broadcast.

Friday, 28 January 2000

My first trip to Bullwood Hall is for a professional visit to Sally. I am officially acting as one of her solicitors; my firm, Batt Holden in Wimbledon, is now the agent for Burton Copeland in Manchester. I am dreading my first meeting with Sally since her conviction. I do not know what to expect. My first surprise is a prison officer, who checks my passport to confirm my identity. As I tell him who I have come to see, he asks, 'What's she doing here?'

This is not an enquiry about why she is in that particular prison; he wants to know why an innocent woman is serving life. I tell him that's what I am there to try to put right. I wait in 'the bungalow' outside the gates while they get Sally.

Hockley, in Essex, is about five miles inland from Southend-on-Sea, It is a *Knotts Landing* type community, with mainly detached four- to five-bedroomed houses facing the main road through the village. The oldest pub for miles is the Bull. Nobody driving through this affluent Essex community would guess that in the woods behind it lies a prison containing lifers and young offenders – and some seriously evil people.

The prison's visitors' hall is a riot of plastic colour. Chairs and tables for four are bolted to the floor. There are many windows, so that the effect is light and cheerful. In one corner is a raised desk for officer observation. In the centre of the ceiling is a black globe almost hiding cameras that point in all directions.

Sally is sitting at one of the tables. My nervousness evaporates as her smile works its usual magic. She makes me feel more like a million dollars than a tongue-tied lawyer not knowing how to comfort a woman who may have to spend the rest of her life in this place. She is a lovely looking lady. She has lost a lot of weight in the last three months. She is wearing a sweater, T-shirt and leggings. 'civvies', not a prison uniform.

'I don't want you doing too much,' she says.

Hang on a minute. I'm not the one sentenced to life!

'No chance of that, Sal. I'm one of the most idle people you will ever meet. How are you?'

I tell her that I am only an hour and a half away from Bullwood Hall so I can come in whenever she wants me to. She is concerned that Steve is still in Wilmslow, his very job in jeopardy and the house unsold:

'There's a sense of unreality about my situation. Everybody who goes to prison expects their first appeal to succeed, to set them free. It is part of the process; the culture. It is almost as if you are not truly convicted until you've lost that first appeal. Every lawyer knows there is no miscarriage of justice until the appeal process has been exhausted. I also learn, very quickly, how few prisoners' appeals succeed.

'I refused an anger management course, simply because it has never been a problem for me. It is required for a murderer to undergo that treatment. They eventually accept that it is ridiculous to force me to go through it. But I am accepting bereavement counselling.'

We discuss the grounds of appeal. I tell her how optimistic we all are about the statistic. She has heard from Steve and Mackey that Bevan is now also convinced that this is her strongest ground. The time passes quickly until

I am thrown out at 4.15 p.m: it seems as if I've only been there twenty minutes. Sally has that effect on people.

Law in Action goes out on Radio 4 on Sunday, 30 January. There is ten minutes on Sally, which is a powerful plea for her innocence.

Solicitor Bill Bache, in Salisbury, has been instructed to defend Angela Cannings, who has been charged with the murder of three of her babies. Bill and his PA, Jackie Cameron, spend the day with me going over everything that happened at Sally's trial and the lessons to be learned from it. He and Cameron are convinced that Angela no more killed her babies than Sally did. There is no evidence that she ever harmed any of them and the evidence is far weaker than in the Clark trial. But they both recognise that Angela's chances of acquittal are slim, because Meadow, who is giving evidence for the prosecution in her trial too, is so believable and juries want a natural and credible explanation for the babies' deaths if they are to reject what he says. I suggest that they find as many experts as they can, who can put forward alternative causes of death and place the credible alternatives before the jury. I tell them that we now have statistical evidence that using Meadow's methodology, the chances of two murders is $1:2,200$ million – thirty times the chance of two cot deaths. Bill agrees that the danger of $1:73$ million, even if there is no mention of it in Angela's trial, is that a member of the jury will remember it from Sally's case and its media coverage in the privacy of the jury room; and Angela has had three deaths! If the statistic is not revealed in her trial for the monstrous distortion it is, she may be convicted and nobody will ever know why.

Steve now has full custody of Tom and travels to Essex twice a month to see Sally.

Friday, 18 February 2000

I see Sally again at Bullwood Hall. There is so much going on in the recruitment of new experts for the appeal, and so much being done behind the scenes by Mackey, Bevan and Kelsey Fry, that she needs to be kept up to speed, and her instructions taken on many issues. She is a lawyer and understands more than most, even if she is not experienced in criminal law.

Thursday, 24 February 2000

Olivia Price, Pat Child and Yvonne Bye are campaigners on the dangers of vaccination. They have no doubt that the pertussis vaccine given to Harry as part of the DPT jab four hours before he died is what killed him. They are persuasive. They give me a mountain of paper to read and tell me to get in touch with Dr Vera Schreibner, a medical researcher in Australia, who has devoted her life to researching the damage done by vaccination. She has written extensively on it and lectures world-wide. She has one problem – no medical qualification. The Court of Appeal is unlikely to listen to an expert without that essential piece of paper to her name. The campaigners give me a copy of the 1979 Vaccine Damage Payment Act and tell me that the maximum amount of damages awarded for injury from vaccination has just been raised from £10,000 to £30,000. Olivia's son was so damaged that he will need 24-hour care for the rest of his life. Does anybody in authority think that £30,000 will deal with his problem?

Schreibner works closely with Dr Archie Karakolinos, a general practitioner in the outback of Australia, who has developed a theory that lack of vitamin C is the cause of many cot deaths. Once called scurvy, this disease has now been virtually eliminated in Western countries, because of improvements in diet. It was, however, still prevalent among the Aborigines for a reason science has been unable to explain.

Karakolinos would often get calls on his radio that a baby had become unconscious; if no treatment was given, the baby would die in a couple of hours. He established a routine that as soon as a baby became unconscious the mother would radio him; he would get in his plane and give the baby a big dose of vitamin C. The baby always recovered. The medical establishment rejected the theory, but one of the political parties decided to look into his claims, found they were true and he got the official seal of approval. He has had some success in the USA but none so far in Europe. None of Sally's experts will give the theory the time of day.

Wednesday, 8 March 2000

Martin Bell – of white suit fame – is Sally's Member of Parliament. He has met Steve and has visited Sally in prison, has followed the case and is convinced that she should never have been convicted. He asks for all the paperwork.

Frank has arranged a meeting with Professor Gordon Stewart in Salisbury. He is a retired expert on the effects of vaccination, who is convinced that the pertussis vaccine had something to do with Harry's death and may have been implicated in that of Christopher, who had his jab three weeks before he died. Stewart cannot help personally, because he has retired.

Tuesday, 11 April 2000

Dr Trevor Rothwell is secretary of the Home Office Pathologists Overseeing Committee. I travel to the Midlands to see him because we want his committee to carry out a full investigation of the mistakes made by Dr Alan Williams, whose findings are contradicted by experts on both sides. He is sympathetic, but says Williams' findings could not have been all that wrong or Sally would not have been convicted. But that is the reason for the complaint. I leave feeling that my journey to the Midlands has been wasted.

Professor Behan is another expert in vaccination whom Steve has tracked down. Mackey and I meet him at Burton Copeland's London office. He is a great bear of a man. He says all the right things and has the perfect qualifications. He explains that the pertussis vaccine causes a disease in the brain, which is fatal in some babies. He thinks Harry is one of them. He suggests we contact Professor Menkes, a paediatric neurologist in Los Angeles, who is the world's leading authority. When Behan leaves, Mackey tells me he is not convinced.

'Let's see what he puts in writing and then make up our minds whether to run with him at appeal,' he tells me.

I get in touch with Menkes. He agrees to write a report.

At Bullwood Hall, surprisingly, Sally is again not apprehensive:

'I am almost relaxed as the date of my appeal approaches because I've been told, repeatedly, by Julian Bevan, by Mackey and by John Batt, that the grounds are undeniable. It is not a case of if, but when I will be home again with Steve and Tom.'

Schreibner is to give a lecture in Ringwood in Hampshire. Olivia Price arranges for me to have a private talk with her beforehand. I have sent her all the necessary paperwork on Harry and Christopher, and she has no doubt Harry was killed by the pertussis vaccine. She shows me an impressive graph illustrating the peak time of death following vaccination; the first is within a few hours – which is Harry; and not far behind it is 21 days – which would fit Christopher. The problem is that none of our experts will support it as a cause of death. The lecture is thoroughly professional, accompanied by flip charts with graphs and statistics. It is a performance listened to with rapt attention by an audience of about a hundred. Schreibner's arguments are persuasive, but she is not from mainstream medicine; she does not have all the letters after her name that are needed to make any headway with the Appeal Court.

Geoffrey Wansell is a journalist who writes feature articles for the *Daily Mail*. Frank will have nothing to do with that tabloid since it published the photograph of Hope Cottage and called it the Death House – but I will talk to anybody who will carry the message that Sally is innocent. I spend half a day with him. I am reasonably confident he will write a favourable article.

I ask for a report on vaccination from Professor John Menkes of Los Angeles. It is very encouraging, suggesting that the pertussis vaccine was a possible cause of Harry's death. I am excited, as are Sally and Steve. But it was not to be. Vaccination as a cause of death is very controversial. Although the Vaccine Damage Act provides for compensation for death or injuries caused by vaccination, there is great controversy over it. None of our other experts agree that it could be a cause of death.

Professor David interviews Southall at some length over his allegation that Steve murdered Christopher and Harry. David satisfies himself that there is no substance in it.

Steve is incensed that he has been subjected to this unwarranted allegation on the basis of a television programme. He makes a formal complaint to the General Medical Council.

The Appeal

Today – 8 June 2000

Mackey has worked prodigiously with Kelsey Fry and Bevan, on the grounds of appeal. The paperwork is impressive and persuasive. I cannot see how the appeal can fail.

Today we apply for leave to appeal, at the Royal Courts of Justice in the Strand. The court has already indicated that leave will be given, but Spencer, still the prosecution QC, is unhappy about this. He launches a full-scale assault on the validity and admissibility of the new evidence, as a result of which there is now to be a full court hearing to address his points.

The judges at the hearing are Lord Justice Swinton-Thomas, Mr Justice Wright and Mr Justice Tomlinson. I get to the courts early because I know Sally will be there at dawn, having been brought in a van from prison. I keep her company in her lonely cell, discussing the latest version of the written grounds of appeal.

Sally takes her place in the dock; just the top of her head is visible. The judges have had to read the transcript of all three weeks of the trial. Almost with the first words, I judge that they are all on our side! They nod sagely at each of Bevan's points, asking only questions that clarify what he is saying.

And they give Spencer a really hard time. Some of his present points do not impress the judges. We almost jump for joy when they reject Spencer's submissions and grant leave for the appeal. Sally is on her way out! She smiles at Bevan, and at Steve, who mouths 'I love you', and she is taken to the cells below.

The decision and its rapidity speak for themselves. The judges have recognised that there are serious questions about Sally's conviction and – if they agree with Bevan that the argument is beyond dispute – they could go on to decide the substative point there and then, but that would require the consent of both counsel and I cannot see Spencer agreeing to that. It could not be a better result and augurs well for the actual appeal.

The new hearing is set down for five days, starting on 17 July 2000.

Spencer has been astute: by taking so many technical points on the question of whether Sally should even be given leave to appeal, he has ensured that this panel of judges will not decide the merits of the appeal. Now Spencer has a 'second bite' and will be hoping for a more sympathetic panel of judges when the full hearing takes place.

Sally is cautiously optimistic:

'My legal team is very confident but I have been let down so many times, I still have a nagging worry. I know that this time Bevan and Kelsey Fry must be right, because I saw the reaction of the three judges who gave me leave to appeal and am sure that, if only they could have gone on to decide the substantive issue there and then I would have been freed. My legal team tells me that "it is inconceivable that the appeal will fail". It may not be a complete acquittal, because the court may order a retrial, but I am sure, knowing what we now know, that I will never be convicted a second time. Those are the thoughts that get me through the summer in prison. And so now I must believe that I am finally going home.

'But now there is another frightening problem: Group 4, who provide the security guards to escort prisoners to and from court, do not want to make the daily journey from Bullwood to London. They have put in a request that I be moved to Holloway for the duration of my appeal. I have managed to hold my own and make friends here but the thought of Holloway fills me with dread. It has a fearsome reputation, especially for people convicted of baby killings. Fortunately, I have been able to build a relationship of mutual respect with the Governor and staff at Bullwood, and they intervene on my behalf so that I am now to be brought back every night to Essex. It means four hours' travelling every day, in high summer, in the sweat box, but at least I will be safe.

'Appearing in public for the first time in ten months, plus the journey and media attention, takes its toll on me physically and emotionally.'

Monday, 17 July 2000: Court of Appeal

I join Sally in her tiny visitors' room underneath the Royal Courts of Justice. I answer all her questions and I tell her again that this is it: she is about to walk.

The courtroom is full as the usher commands us to rise. All bow to Lord Justice Dennis Henry, Mr Justice Stephen Richards and Mrs Justice Joyanne Bracewell. The presiding judge has a reputation as a hard but fair man; on the golf course he always seems to have the most attractive of the women as his partner. Richards is the new boy on the Bench – said to be very bright, on the fast track to the top of the law. Bracewell frightens me: she has thin, pursed lips and a stern, disapproving look. She is a judge of the Family Division, a more practical than academic lawyer, although it is said that she wrote most of the Children's Act.

She is familiar with the skills and knowledge of Meadow, who has appeared before her many times in family cases.

She practised at the Manchester Bar where Mackey got to know her well and at one time had a favourable opinion of her, personally. I do not like what I see. I sense that she is against us.

Legally, our case is watertight. Interestingly, the judgments of the Court of Appeal do not have to be unanimous. If the decision is by a majority, nobody ever knows unless the presiding judge allows a dissenting opinion to be given; this rarely happens.

It soon becomes clear that attitudes are now reversed. For some reason, the judges are giving Bevan a hard time, and smile every time Spencer opens his mouth. Maybe this is simply their way of evening up the odds. Bevan is Mr Big in criminal law, a senior adviser to government, its top prosecutor; Spencer's silk gown still has the maker's label in it. The judges are just making sure everybody understands they are not overwhelmed by Bevan's reputation.

Naïvely, perhaps, Sally is surprised by the manner in which Spencer conducts himself:

'the lengths to which he goes to preserve my convictions. Not content with sticking to the legal points of appeal, he undertakes a character assassination of both Steve and myself, just as he had done at trial. I am surprised they allow him to do that; I was never prepared for such a sustained attack.'

The grounds of appeal are:

1. **The trial judge was wrong in law to order the two cases to be tried together; there should have been separate trials.**

What this amounts to is a challenge to the so-called seven 'similar facts'. Time of night the same, similar ages, same place, alone with the mother each time, Steve either away or about to go away on business each time, leaving Sally to cope alone. And there was evidence of previous abuse in each case.

Bevan does a great job, demolishing any commonsense view that these are sinister similarities.

2. **The judge was wrong to tell the jury they could take account of all the circumstances of both deaths before concluding that either was unnatural.**

This is a strictly legal point, which Bevan had to take, because he is right in law. It is a technicality on which we should succeed, but it is far from our best argument.

3. **The judge wrongly directed the jury as to the law on the statistic of 1:73 million.**

This is supported by new evidence from statisticians Dr Evett and Professor David that 1:73 million is fundamentally flawed and misleading. The judge wrongly directed the jury that they could use it to calculate the odds against Sally's innocence.

That the defence did not call this evidence at trial is explained by the fact that the CESDI Report was only in draft and statisticians would not give an opinion until they saw the whole document.

Evett and David say that, using Meadow's basis of calculation, the chance of two murders, in a family like Sally's, is 1:2,200 million.

There is in fact a thirty times GREATER chance that these were cot deaths than murders. Meadow told Sally's jury that two cot deaths will only happen once every hundred years. He did not tell them that, using the same formula, two murders would happen only once every 3,000 years. If Sally did murder her babies, the last time a mother committed such a double crime was a thousand years before the birth of Jesus!!

Spencer accepts that the statistic was wrong, but says it would have had no effect on the jury; it was not a seminal moment in the trial.

4. **The judge wrongly directed the jury about the significance of Sally's refusal to answer any more questions after being advised to do just that by her solicitor.**

Mackey is keen on this one. And he is right, in law, but it is a technicality that would not have swung the appeal on its own. It is right that it is there, because it adds further weight to the grounds of appeal.

The reason the appeal hearing takes five days is because virtually all the medical evidence has to be raked over again, to demonstrate how perverse the jury's verdict was, given the contradictions between experts.

Bevan wins the argument clearly, on every point, it seems to me. I sense Spencer is worried; he can see the way the case is going, on the law, and that he has no chance of maintaining the convictions. He gets more strident, makes a number of statements with which I disagree factually, but to which Bevan raises little objection. That is the way Bevan is, and maybe it does not matter; he has already won this appeal! The judges continue to smile at Spencer. I persuade myself that it does not mean anything; only that they want to make him feel better being on such a 'losing wicket'. It could not be that they agree with Spencer and are against Bevan, because the law is on our side.

Steve is upbeat:

'The defence team say it is inconceivable that the appeal will fail. The statistics alone make the convictions unsafe. I have talked to dozens of lawyers and they have all said the same as Bevan and Kelsey Fry. However, they also said there would be a new trial, but we feel we have nothing to fear from that. We know the worst they can throw at us and we can discredit all of it, now. So I was confident, when I dressed that morning and made my way to the Law Courts. I knew Sally would be coming home.

'We had had a good couple of days at the first hearing – for leave to appeal. If they had gone on to hear the full case, Sally would have walked then. It seems a strange system that makes three judges spend several days reading everything about the case to then go through a hearing, with counsel arguing on both sides, for three new judges to have to go through the same time-wasting exercise, repeating exactly what the other judges have just done. I am apprehensive because these three are not as positive as the first were. I feel we won at least three and half days of the five days of argument, but I don't like the way the judges are responding. We clearly win the argument on the medicine and the statistics. But today, Spencer attacks both of us relentlessly and the judges seem to be hanging on every word. Yet our lawyers show no concern. Maybe the rules allow Spencer to do such things.

'Another worry is that Bracewell seems only too anxious to help Spencer out when he hesitates in his argument. I begin to dread what this might mean.

'And then, suddenly, everything is put on hold.'

The court reserves its judgment until 2 October. That means another ten weeks inside for Sally, which is a further injustice, but at least she will then be freed. But this is not how Sally is thinking:

'I don't know, instinctively, that my appeal will work. I have no particular feelings, one way or the other. I accept what Julian, Kelsey Fry, Mackey and John Batt say: it is bound to happen. I will be free. They can't all be wrong – again! Not this time. I accept it intellectually, because there is no legal argument against it which holds any water. Although my instincts are not telling me I will be out, I can believe it so easily because I know I have done nothing wrong.

'I am not worried by the prospect of another three months in prison. Ninety days' jail time and then out is rather different than being inside, never knowing if I will ever be released. I've been told, categorically, that as soon as the court reconvenes, I shall be freed. That means I shall have to spend the summer at Bullwood Hall. I can do that. I can serve that time without too much of a bother. I will "batten down my hatches", occupy my time in my mind, planning my life outside. It is the easiest time I will serve.'

Friday, 29 September 2000

Mackey and I are due to meet Sally at Bullwood Hall. Emerging from the Dartford Tunnel, Mackey calls my mobile. He sounds strung out. He has been in a meeting, which was supposed to last five minutes and is still going after four hours . . .

Who cares? Sally 'walks' on Monday.

I see her on my own. It is the happiest of my many visits. I tell her that I believe it will all be over in a trice. They will hand down the written judgment. They won't read it; Lord Justice Henry will say 'The appeal is allowed'; the chances are he will order a new trial.

Sally is firm about one thing:

'I don't want anybody talking about champagne. This is not a celebration. This is about my two babies who died.'

Because the rules insist that all appellants take all their belongings with them to the Court of Appeal, and that is difficult in the sweat box, Sally wants me to take her hi-fi and summer clothes home today. We have a happy hug, I collect her plastic bag and say 'Have a good weekend!'

Monday, 2 October 2000

I get to the Royal Courts early. The forecourt is full of journalists and cameramen. I say nothing. This time Sally is smiling in her small cell and there is an air of celebration among the Group 4 security guards. They, too, know she is going to walk. After a while, I leave so that Bevan and Mackey can give her the good news. By now, they know the result of the appeal, because Bevan and Spencer will have seen a draft of the judgment over the weekend, to correct any factual errors.

Steve has put his worst fears to rest and walks into the Law Courts with confidence. There is only one niggle:

'I phoned Mackey at home, just to ask him about arrangements for Monday and he was very off with me; really strange. I didn't think too much about it at the time. Now I wonder . . .'

In the Great Hall, Frank and Steve have arrived. More smiles; a little nervousness from Frank, but pessimism is a way of life for him. We while away the minutes.

We see Bevan and Mackey striding down the hall. Bevan says to Frank: 'I'm afraid we did not succeed. I'm terribly sorry. What can I say?'

Frank is so shocked I fear he might do something silly. Instead he says to Bevan, 'Don't say anything!'

Bevan appears angry with me. He almost shouts: 'No more television programmes!'

On the morning of her appeal, few people in the prison, inmates or staff, expected to see Sally again:

'Even the Group 4 staff, who had taken me every day in June, asked, specifically, to do it again, to be there to share my joy at release.

'Bevan and Mackey come into the interview room. I can tell from their faces that something has gone horribly wrong. They both look devastated. Bevan has his head in his hands as he says: "It is the most intellectually dishonest appeal judgment I have ever read."

'I am very concerned about him; he looks so upset and despairing on my behalf, as does Mike Mackey.

'I am determined to appear in court with my head held high, as the judgment is handed down. I see Steve mouthing the words "I love you", and shaking his head. I had got to know the staff in the cells really well; they are shocked and sympathetic.'

Steve feels betrayed by the famous British justice system yet again:

'I now know what was bugging Mike: he must have seen a draft of the judgment and knew the result but was forbidden to tell me. I don't know what to say: I am numb. Outside the Law Courts, the traffic still moves, people walk and talk. They have a normality. My world has just disintegrated.'

In a haze I read out a statement to the media – something to the effect that – like the Terminator, I'll be back. Photographers chase me down the Strand. I eventually lose them and make my lonely way home.'

There is another claustrophobic ride in the sweat box for Sally:

'I virtually fall through the doors of Bullwood Hall, crying so hard I think my heart must break. They have allowed my closest friend, Susie B., to greet me. I can see she is genuinely affected by the sight of my devastation. Staff and lifer inmates are there for me. There are a great deal of tears on G Wing. They allow Susie B. to sit with me, in my cell, well into the evening. All I do is cry to the point of hysteria. It is my bleakest moment.

'What now? I cannot believe it. I could not understand the verdict of the jury but this . . . from "three wise men" I respected! My faith in the whole justice system has totally collapsed. I feel let down and betrayed by my own profession.

'I am placed on a 2052 – suicide watch. Every unsuccessful appellant is treated the same, but I have no intention of harming myself. At least there will be somebody to talk to – prison officers on duty – in the middle of the night.'

So what did go wrong? Professor Meadow has given evidence in the family and criminal courts for over twenty years. He is greatly admired by doctors and lawyers in the UK, the Commonwealth and the United States. He often gives evidence before Bracewell in the Family Division. Meadow is an icon in medicine, a knight of the realm, the world authority on child abuse. Do the judges simply feel that an expert of such eminence could not be wrong when he says neither death was natural? He made a mistake about statistics, but he was merely quoting somebody else's work. And if he is so wrong about Sally Clark, that might raise questions about other cases.

It is not a good day for English justice. In my opinion the judges have made fundamental errors in their analysis of the evidence at trial. They will bear a heavy responsibility for their decision.

Copies of the Written Reasons are distributed by the court clerks. They are very pro-prosecution. Bracewell, as the most experienced in family abuse, probably wrote the main part; and Richards, some of the Human Rights issues, of which there was some discussion at appeal. Virtually every medical finding is interpreted from the prosecution's point of view. That experts – even prosecution professors – could not confirm Williams' findings – seems to have had no effect on their certainty of Sally's guilt.

In conclusion, the judgment reads:

> Taken separately there was a strong case on each count. Taken together we conclude that the evidence was overwhelming, having regard to the identified similarities . . .

It is barely credible to me that three judges of appeal consider that these similarities point to guilt. I can understand Mr Justice Harrison missing it at trial. He was almost overwhelmed with submissions before it began. Now three more of our senior and experienced judges make what seem to me to be elementary mistakes in the law; no one judge should get them this wrong, let alone three together.

They say the so-called similarities support the view that there is over-whelming evidence of guilt:

> For all those reasons, we consider that there was an overwhelming case against the appellant at trial. If there had been no error . . . on statistics . . . we are satisfied the jury would still have convicted . . .

Even if the jury had heard that two murders would happen in the one family only once every three thousand years?

> 'The point on statistics was of minimal significance – a sideshow – and there is no possibility of the jury having been misled . . .'

Do newspapers – tabloids and broadsheets, here and all round the world – headline 1:73 million because it has only 'minimal significance' for ordinary people – the sort of people who sit on juries? It is ironic that Bevan's dismissive view of statistics at trial has now received such ringing endorsement by three judges of the Court of Appeal. My arguments – so stridently advanced in 1999 – were obviously poppycock!

An appeal can be made, to the House of Lords, but the grounds are narrow, and this judgment is written to be appeal-proof.

Mackey's expert will also file an appeal to the European Court of Human Rights, which could well be Sally's court of last resort, and will take years to be heard.

Despair is a much over-used word, but there is no other to describe what all of us now feel. Can Sally survive this 'killer' blow?

Friday, 6 October 2000

Four days after the worst day in Sally's life, I don't know what to say to Sally at Bullwood Hall; how to comfort her; how to make her feel there really is something to live for.

Her smile does not disguise her grief. But as always her thoughts are for others:

Sally: Are you all right?
Me: I'm fine. Now tell me about you . . . Really!
Sally: I must let Steve go . . . He must be able to live a normal life – he and Tom. Divorce whatever . . . I am only being realistic . . .

There are quite long pauses.

Sally: I may be in here for twenty years . . . it could be even longer . . . I may never get out, if the Lifer Governor at Styal is right.
Me: Mike is drafting an appeal to the House of Lords. He is using a specialist barrister called Topolski . . . Very hopeful . . .
Sally: Why are you always so optimistic?

That's the question I had been asking myself all the way down in the car. Mackey has been the realist, never failing to paint the other side of the picture; always cautious with the white. That is the prudent, sensible thing to do, but I decided that one of my functions was to give Sally the emotional strength to hang on. Now that credibility is zero, I have joined the ranks of other lawyers whose predictions have proved wrong. And this was the big wrong one.

I say all the obvious things: that I won't stop . . . I don't care what it takes . . . this will not stand . . . somewhere out there . . . I seem to have trouble getting the words out. Injustice, on such a scale, is bad for the emotions, particularly if you know – respect and love, as if she were my own daughter – the client. I could not feel closer to her at this moment – the innocent victim. I apologise to Sally for losing my composure. She leans across to comfort me!

Sally: Why me? Why has this happened to me? What have I done to deserve this?

Me: I grew up under that Cathedral spire in the Close. I believe that there is somebody up there . . . I have no idea what makes Him tick. I don't think you are alone. This has happened to other mothers, dozens certainly, and maybe hundreds, around the world.

Sally: Murder convictions?

Me: Not only . . . False accusations of abuse. You remember Meadow going on about Munchausen's Syndrome by Proxy?

Sally: Yes . . .

Me: I asked Professor David about it. He says it undoubtedly exists, but probably not in as many cases as are being diagnosed. If there is a greater purpose in all this . . .

Sally: If you're suggesting that, when I get out, I should start campaigning for other mothers, forget it!

At least she thinks getting out is possible.

Sally: You've no idea how many evil women there are. I've seen them . . . met them . . .sat next to them . . . evil! Evil! I will never be party to setting somebody like that loose to do terrible things to another baby. Never!

We come as close as we ever have to disagreement.

Me: I accept that, for you, but not for me. I have seen, at first hand, what this has done to you and Steve and Frank and Rosemary. I'm pretty certain I have identified other innocent mothers, who are doing life for murders that never happened. I am a lawyer. I have the brains, the time and the energy to do something about it. I can't sit on my hands . . .

Sally seems to see me in a new light, or is it my imagination?

Sally: I can't stop you but I won't become a campaigner.

Me: That's for you to decide. But I will write the book of your case, and if I get it right, that should make people realise what is going on – how many innocent mothers . . . and fathers . . . are being put through the Sally Clark treatment, when they are innocent . . . how many children have been torn from their parents on false allegations of abuse or Munchausen's . . .

Somehow we get through the two hours. As ever, I feel better for having spent time in her company, whether I have given her any comfort, any hope, I have no means of judging.

Steve is in despair. The decision was such a shock and so unexpected that it is difficult to know where to begin the future:

'I had left Tom with my parents in Derbyshire. I take the train to pick him up. The buffet car is packed so I sit on the floor to read the written reasons again. Scribbling: "That's wrong, that's wrong, that's factually wrong. That doesn't make sense. That's not right. What about our evidence?" How could they possibly say that Dr Le Vin supported Williams? Le Vin is one of the top ten eye men in the world, whom we brought all the way from Toronto. He said that he would be using Williams' post-mortem, in his lectures around the world, as an example of how not to do an autopsy on a baby! Did the judges take no notice of such a condemnation of Williams, the main prosecution witness, on whose findings all the other experts for the Crown depended for their own opinions? The judges' verdict seems to refer to a different case. Judges of the Court of Appeal are supposed to be the most respected intellects in the law. How can they have made such an interpretation of what happened at Chester Crown Court?

'Now, I have to face Tom and pretend that we haven't suffered a devastating blow. I have to make him feel happy and secure. But he has no mum. I am his mum and his dad and that is not right. Neither Christopher nor Harry suffered a moment's harm at either my hands or Sally's, but our surviving son, Tom, is now being abused by the criminal justice system. It may be years before he has a normal home life, with his own mum to tend and nurture him.

'It is worse being a lawyer myself. I know that no system is perfect, but I was taught to believe that, however imperfect, ours is the best there is. And yet, with us, the law has got it so badly wrong: time after time after time.

'It is now apparent to me that if there is ever to be any hope of securing Sally's acquittal I will have to devote my time, my legal skills and abilities in a concerted way. There is no legal aid and I can't afford to pay out any more money. I shall have to do it myself, hopefully, with the help of a friend or two.'

A few nights later, I am in bed. I usually send up a prayer or two just before falling asleep. It's a pretty idle way of worshipping the Almighty, but it may be better than nothing. I am trying to pray for something to happen for Sally . . . I can't seem to find the words . . . I don't know what to ask for. Anything will do. I have reached my lowest point. Yes, I suppose desperation is the word.

I am still struggling for words when a voice speaks to me, in my head. It is not my imagination. The words are not mine. The thought is not mine. I don't know who the voice belongs to. Is it God? Probably one of his minions – sorry, angels. The voice says, 'It will be all right. It will be all right.'

Am I awake or asleep? Awake. Do I believe it was a message from the Almighty? I think the answer must be yes. What do I make of it? If a mate had told me it happened to him I might have said 'Pull the other one.' I can't do that with this; it was too real!

I don't try to rationalise it, because that is not possible, but I can treat it as something I can hang on to . . . something that will let me hope . . . something that tells me that I will have the strength to carry on for as long as it takes; the wit to recognise what Mackey calls the Golden Key to set Sally free.

Walter Merricks is the Chief Financial Services Ombudsman responsible for over a thousand complaints a day on all aspects of the industry. He has watched the Sally case with mounting concern. sensing the miscarriage of justice. He suggests I should contact practising solicitor Sue Stapely, and ask if she is prepared to become Sally's public relations consultant, *pro bono*!

I got to know Sue when she was Head of Public and Parliamentary

Relations at the Law Society. A former BBC programme-maker turned solicitor she is now a director of Fishburn Hedges, a very successful London communications consultancy. Sue realises that she will not be able to spend the time Sally's case needs unless she re-arranges her working life. After some months working as part of the legal team, she gives up her directorship and its secure financial package, and sets up her own business, arranging work mainly with a smaller, niche consultancy – Quiller Consultants. This firm specialises in strategic communications and issues management and, like Sue, has contacts with many important figures in government, the media, the law and industry. This allows her to devote one day a week, and whatever additional time she can manage, outside office hours, to work on Sally's case.

This is a vital piece of good fortune for Sally. Sue is the only UK-based practising lawyer who specialises in handling the media relations of court cases. Before you can persuade the Court of Appeal to overturn a criminal conviction nowadays, you often have first to build a favourable climate in the tabloids and broadsheets, to influence opinion formers. It will not be easy. The main coverage at the time of the trial was of the prosecution case and was unrelentingly critical of Sally, as a woman and as a mother. It is an amazingly generous and costly commitment.

Sue Stapely, quite rightly, insists on reading all the papers thoroughly before committing herself to the work. I arrange for her to meet Sally at Bullwood Hall. The two have much in common: both late qualifiers in the law, both mothers of sons. Sue 'knows' within moments of meeting her that Sally is innocent and has been badly let down by the system. Then begins the long haul, alongside me – as my daily *alter ego* – to clear Sally's name and get her freed. Sue and I have much in common too – television and the law – and become staunch allies and firm friends.

As part of his relentless search for the real reasons his sons died, Steve goes to a lecture at Manchester University, by microbiologist Dr Caroline Blackwell, on bacterial toxins and cot deaths. He talks to her afterwards: she will be happy to carry out tests on any tissue samples he can obtain. But we have real trouble getting them. Spencer can apparently see no reason why we should have them.

Tuesday, 24 October 2000

I see a letter in *The Times* from Professor Brian Lowry, a geneticist at the University of Calgary in Canada. He believes Sally is the victim of injustice. I call Canada. He happens to be in London. He agrees to meet me at the Grosvenor Hotel in Victoria.

He is a quiet Irishman with a charming brogue. He is an enthusiast, and is near retirement. Meadow's statistic is a disgrace, he tells me. I will send him the paperwork. He will see if there is anything he can write a report about that will help. He maintains his interest throughout the following three years and constantly hits the phone or e-mail at the first sign of any new medical development in North America and elsewhere. He tells me his 'references' run to about 30 pages.

Thursday, 21 December 2000

Mackey has briefed specialist barrister Michael Topolski to make an application for leave to appeal to the House of Lords. As I arrive at the Law Courts, he has bad news. The court has just dismissed an appeal with similar grounds to ours. It has scuppered Sally's chances. Our case is called and five minutes later our application, too, is dismissed.

The good news is that Sally's application to the European Court of Human Rights has gone in and been acknowledged; it could have been rejected out of hand. It has passed the first scrutiny. The legal reality is that all Sally's UK remedies are now exhausted. The committal magistrate's first scrutiny decided there was a case to answer on both babies. The jury found her guilty. The Court of Appeal found the evidence of guilt overwhelming. And now even a House of Lords appeal is ruled out. She has run out of options. The future is, in all probability, the rest of her life in prison because she will never admit to killing her precious babies.

It occurs to me that I am about to find out what makes me tick. Will I bow down under this huge weight of legal opinion or will I continue to struggle against what now seem almost impossible odds, to clear Sally's name? I am quite sure Sally is innocent. We have now reached the stage where this can be properly labelled a miscarriage of justice – all legal avenues are closed. I do not have to ponder the problem for long. I am a lawyer, committed – by the age-old reason which brought lawyers into existence – to stand between the overweening power

*of the State and an innocent citizen. However long it takes, however hard it is,
I have no choice but to stay with it until the injustice is recognised and Sally is
set free.*

Steve decides to give up his partnership with Addleshaws in Manchester,
and seek work in London.

There is no place where time passes so slowly as prison. Sally has now spent
over a year in jail. Steve will not give up: nor will Frank or Mackey. We
will have to begin the search for new evidence, which may not even exist,
if we are to stand even the faintest chance of a new appeal hearing. We may
work for years and get nowhere, and be paid nothing. Frank fears that he
may die before his beloved daughter is released. The only certainty is that
nobody will have a happy Christmas.

After the failure of the appeal, Sally now finds a certain degree of
questioning, of previous beliefs in her innocence, on G Wing.

'Nothing is said to my face, but I know there is whispering behind
closed doors. A new hostility builds, unrest and name-calling, mainly
from the other wings, soon stamped out by lifers determined to show
solidarity even if, privately, doubts have begun to creep in.

'The next weeks and months are hard. I still believe my innocence
will be proved, but, for the first time, acknowledge that it is going to
take a long while.

'So far as the prison is concerned, I am no longer an "appeal
pending"; I am going to serve a long prison sentence. This means
probation reports, sentence planning and coursework options. They
may be expecting me to be hostile, but I have to be practical; they are
only doing their jobs. I co-operate fully with everything demanded. I
spend hours with probation, with my personal officer, and I go on
work assessments (these are soon abandoned as I do not fit any of the
criteria).

'As I do not know how many years I will have to spend in prison, I
will make the most of what there is on offer: I request regular
counselling. I do not like the first counsellor, but she is changed and

every week I now see a counsellor in whom I have confidence. This will continue indefinitely.

'It sounds a bit stark to say it, unless one understands the passing of time in prison, but nothing happened in 2001 worthy of note.'

'My day at Bullwood Hall begins with a banging on the wall. To my amazement, I sleep well in prison. The knocking is Sue in the next room, waking me at 7 a.m. "Unlock" is officially at 8 a.m., but by then we need to be showered and ready for the day. I usually go to Sue's room for coffee and sometimes toast. I never make it myself. One of my quirks is that I cannot bear to make my room comfortable; I feel that if I do, I will be tempting providence that I'll be here forever. So I have no curtains at my window – lifers are allowed that privilege. I will not make my cell like home. I intend never to settle in; it will not even be a bed and breakfast for me. And I never touch my toaster. I think of it as bad luck, for some weird reason – prison does such things to you.

'At 9 o'clock, there is "Work Movement". All 180 prisoners move simultaneously to their assigned workplaces. By 9.05 a.m., all are ticked off. My first job, in the laundry, is hard physically, and it is disgusting: all those sheets! In summer, heat adds a horrible dimension. My fellow inmates expect me to regard the work as below me. That's not me. I get my arms stuck in with the rest of them.

'At first, I do not join the "Work Movement". I go early, about 8.15. This is for my protection as I am at risk of serious attack for my "crimes". I work until 12.15 p.m. with the occasional tea break. Then it is back to the cell for a roll check; then lunch. We eat in relays, by wings, and it is varied every week. Dining is cafeteria style. At first the regime is that everybody has to order their food from a menu, a week in advance; ticking boxes. This is gradually relaxed until we are allowed to choose as we get to the counter.

'The food, at first, is not bad. I am not a fussy eater; I will eat anything, but it gradually deteriorates until everything tastes the same – bland. I normally have a sandwich and a piece of fruit, sometimes a pizza, fast food. If I close my eyes, I don't know what I'm eating. It is a fast-moving operation – everybody out in ten to fifteen minutes. I go back to my room and then to the landing, where I make my second phone call of the day to Steve, my first is before I go to work. There is always a queue for the phone. It is frustrating when

Steve's line is engaged, because I have to go to the back of the queue to ring again.

Work is resumed at 2 until 4 p.m., then back again to the room. Tea is at 5 o'clock, again in rotas. This is a more substantial meal, with water the only drink provided. Every prisoner gets one sachet of instant coffee a day. I can buy more but it is pretty horrendous stuff.

'Full association is between six and 8 o'clock, sometimes just half that time if there is a shortage of officers, which happens regularly.

'"Movement" is scary; all those women moving at once. When I finally join the mass movement, I become a bit of a joke, because I walk with my head down, focused on getting to my destination in one piece. I never notice what is going on around me. On one occasion, I walk straight through the middle of two women fighting, without realising it. It is my way of coping with that part of the regime. Every day is mechanical, incredibly controlled, everybody on auto-pilot.

'But as the shortage of prison officers kicks in, Sue B. and I find ourselves working in Reception – doing jobs normally done by officers. After my morning coffee with Sue B., we go off to Reception, wearing our "privileged" red arm bands. That job means we have the chance of working evenings and we both take it. It helps defeat the boredom.

'We are locked in at 8.15 p.m. Generally, I do not watch television or listen to the radio. I spend my time writing letters home and to the many supporters who regularly write to me. Being locked in for nearly twelve hours every day is a bit of a trial, but Sue B. and I discover that we can talk to each other, with telephone clarity, down the plughole of our sinks, which are connected. We spend hours doing it. When officers check on us hourly, I would sometimes say, "yes. I'm on the phone." Other prisoners talk to each other through their windows.

'My room becomes known as the show house, because I am compulsively neat. Sue B's is known as the "lived-in room", because that is how she copes, making it as comfortable as she can.

'Reception work is much more like real work on the outside. It is responsible and I have daily contact with the outside, with Group 4 and officers from other prisons. They treat Sue B. and I as civilian workers, apparently unaware that we are lifers.

'I check all prisoners in and out. I put all their possessions into a box and enter each item on a property card. When they leave, everything is checked and returned. It is partly a system for stopping bullying. If they come in with five gold earrings and leave with only two, they have to account for the missing items. Checking prisoners out was difficult. I could not help being envious of them going to their homes and loved ones. Seeing them walk down the drive with their back packs – going home! I am pleased for them but it is hard for me. The young offenders, particularly, say to me: "Sorry Miss. Next time it'll be you." They called both Susie and I "Miss" – we seem to have a certain aura. Susie is an A grade prisoner and I like to think that being my friend helped with the perception of her. She never has any hassle. Many prisoners would come to me, particularly the young, to talk about their legal situations, because of my qualification. I am always willing to help them. We are all in the same situation. We have to help each other out with whatever skills we may have.

'Envy is not always my reaction when I check girls onto the outside. I checked in one girl for the fourth time! I think why? Why do this? As I checked out a girl for a third time I asked her where she was going. She said, "My Mum's in Holloway, my Dad's in Strangeways and my Grandad's in the Isle of Wight prison. I'm going to my Nan's."

'Some prisoners are very bright; some of the young are much brighter than me. They could be anything: solicitor, barrister, doctor! And yet, here they are, as if in a revolving door.

'My first Christmas at Styal, I was talking about Tom's liquidised food and the fact that we did not have a liquidiser. A young offender offered to teach me how to nick one, from Curry's. As I said, we each have our skills and exchange them with each other! I declined the offer, with grateful thanks for the kind thought, but could not help thinking what a strange skill to have!

'Lifers are treated differently from other prisoners. We are allowed two boxes of possessions and our own clothes, unless we are considered a security risk, in which case we wear a uniform.

'We wear our own clothes all the time. It is a volumetric system. Basically we can have about six tops and six bottoms. Everything has to fit into the two boxes, the same size for everybody. They have to contain any bedding – duvets for instance – and stereo. Television is provided in each lifer's cell and we pay £1 per week each for the privilege. That's a lot of money when you are earning £8 a week.

'One day a girl who is frequently on suicide watch comes to me with a problem: her stereo is broken. Can I lend her mine? We all try to help her. As I rarely use it, I agree; forgetting that lending anything is against prison rules, to discourage bullying. Four months later, her cell is spot searched and my stereo is found. I am up on a disciplinary charge. Everybody else thinks this is hilarious. Sally Clark, model prisoner, caught in a breach of the rules! I am frightened. Other prisoners appear before the Governor on a regular basis; for me it is a first, and very unwelcome. The punishments are fines, loss of wages, loss of television. None of the officers can believe I could be so stupid. I am marched in between two officers. Every other officer and inmate has gathered to watch the fun! I am wearing my T-shirt with "Naughty!" on the front. I try to get off on the right foot by saying to Deputy Governor Hassel: "I don't suppose it will help if I say I like the tie and shirt.' It does not. The charge is read out. He continues: "I have a report here that says Sally Clark is a quiet person on the wing but the officers believe it is the quiet ones who have to be watched, as they are the ones who incite violence and are, potentially, the worst security risks."

'I am horrified. I cannot believe they would do this to me! What have I ever done but act like the best behaved girl in the class! And then there is a great gust of laughter. They have set me up with a spoof report because they know I am terrified. I am let off with a caution.

'The governors are fair. They have a difficult job to do and I do my best not to make it any more difficult for them. Tony Hassel is particularly nice. I shall be exchanging Christmas cards with him when I'm out!'

The worst time in jail for Sally is the random drugs testing, not because she has ever taken them, but because the procedure is so demeaning.

Mackey has read articles by Dr David Drucker at Manchester University, about genetic factors in cot deaths. He is prepared to help but he too needs tissue samples. So far Steve has had no luck getting these out of Macclesfield Hospital and so another possible cause of death cannot be investigated. A parent of a cot death in Belgium contacts Steve and suggests a Dr Liebaars, who is also investigating genetics. He points Steve at a colleague at Southampton University, whom Steve then contacts.

Sue Stapely is quietly networking, alerting all those in positions of authority in the law and government to what she describes as one of the most unforgivable miscarriages of justice ever.

Every day she speaks by e-mail or phone to journalists, television and radio programme-makers, politicians and parents, slowly building awareness of the real issues in Sally's case and the situation other bereaved mothers could face. Sue is approached by Cambridge academic and statistician David MacKay, who was outraged at the misuse of statistics in Sally's case. He offers help. Together they create a campaign website www.sallyclark.org, which David updates daily, and entirely at his own expense. It becomes a global research tool which we all use as a means of talking to experts in related fields all over the world. Each day Sue deals with up to forty e-mails generated by the website, filtering any that might be media-useful, and medical ones, to me.

Martin Bell, MP makes a formal complaint to the General Medical Council about Green and Williams.

Frank makes a similar complaint against Meadow.

Following the jury's question at trial about it, vaccination seems an avenue worth following up. I make contact with a neurologist who has had a lot of experience with babies and vaccination after-effects.

Glimmers of Hope

The Criminal Cases Review Commission (CCRC) was set up by the government on 1 January 1997, to take over responsibilities formerly exercised by the Home Office and Northern Ireland Office to review suspected miscarriages of justice and to refer a conviction back to the Court of Appeal if there is a real possibility that the conviction will not be upheld. It also has power to investigate any matter referred to it by the Court of Appeal, and to consider recommendations for the exercise of the Royal prerogative of mercy – pardons.

The Commission consists of a legally qualified chairman and a board of members with appropriate experience and qualifications, all appointed by the Queen on the recommendation of the Prime Minister. There is a full-time staff of officers, mainly lawyers, who investigate each case.

Mackey begins work immediately, putting together a draft application based on what has already gone wrong. Trying to dredge up technical defects in the trial will not be enough. We have to find more hard evidence to prove how the babies died. But the country's best experts trawled through every medical aspect of both deaths and got us nowhere. What hope can there be realistically? The only thread of a hope we all cling to is that as we are certain Christopher and Harry were not murdered, there *must* be another explanation for their deaths. All we have to do is find it! It will take time. It could take the rest of my life, as well as Frank's.

A miscarriage of justice is dreaded by lawyers. There is no legal aid for the investigations, some of which may be costly and hugely time-consuming. Mackey, as senior partner in one of the busiest criminal law practices, has many calls on his time, both administratively and for clients

in all sorts of trouble with the law. It is difficult to expect his partners –
all of whom have to meet strict financial budgets to keep the firm's
finances sound – to accept that the highest earner should spend so much
time on work for which he may never be paid. His client is in prison for
life and obviously not earning. Steve has paid him all he has. Their savings
are gone. Only if the case is accepted by the CCRC will Mackey be paid for
some of his time. Nonetheless, he steals every possible hour. He works at
home at night and all over weekends, such is his commitment.

How long is life imprisonment? The Lifer Governor at Styal threatened
that it could really mean life. Sally has just had Mr Justice Harrison's
written recommendation that she serve 15 years. That has gone to the Lord
Chief Justice, who has endorsed it 14/15 years. It is now the Home
Secretary's job to confirm the length of time Sally will actually serve before
she can be considered for parole. Some lifers who say they are innocent
refuse to take any part in trying to reduce their tariff – as it is called –
claiming it is a charade. Mackey's attitude, and Steve's and mine, is that
we must do everything in our power to challenge her tariff, in case we can't
persuade the CCRC to reopen the case.

Mackey instructs a legal expert on tariff, Dr David Thomas QC. He is a
specialist in sentencing and author of the seminal work on it. He writes a
highly persuasive piece, citing many cases of infanticide and manslaughter
where a short custodial sentence has been appropriate. Steve's job and mine
is to identify and see character witnesses and take statements that will go
in a petition to the Home Secretary.

Steve and Frank co-author a letter to the hundreds of Sally supporters
on the database collated by the Reverend Pauline Pullen and her husband.
It urges them to make their views known to their Members of Parliament
and the Home Secretary.

A bluntly effective journalist, John Sweeney, takes an interest in the
case. That is something of an understatement. He became involved at the
instance of Pauline Pullen, who is a neighbour of the Clarks. She is slightly
built, a sweet and gentle priest in the Wilmslow parish. She also works for
Martin Bell, helping with his constituency duties. Pauline has visited Sally
in prison and is convinced of her innocence. When she meets Sweeney, she
seizes her moment, when he shows scepticism about getting involved in a
case as open and shut as Sally Clark's. She backs this large, intimidating

man, up against the wall, and – prodding him firmly in the chest – tells him he's got to help get Sally out! (Pauline, of course, denies doing any such thing.)

Sweeney persuades BBC Radio Five Live to commission a programme. We spend a day talking about the case and its ramifications. The main focus of his interest is Meadow, because his flawed statistic of 1:73 million is still being used in other cases and is now part of the lexicon of journalism.

Friday, 12 January 2001

A solicitor acting for the Law Society makes application to the Solicitors' Disciplinary Tribunal that:

> Sally Clark, a solicitor, currently residing at HM Prison Bullwood Hall Essex, may be required to answer allegations . . . and that such order may be made as the Tribunal thinks fit.

So the Law Society, the solicitors' professional body, is asking its own disciplinary tribunal to strike Sally off the Roll of Solicitors because she has been convicted of double murder. It is virtually certain that will happen.

My reaction is anger: ridiculous! The Law Society must protect the public from solicitors who ought not to be practising. Convicted murderers should not be allowed to practise law. Ergo, this is necessary. There is no defence. Nothing can stop it happening. So why do I want to fight it? Because the law is so often a matter of opinion and what else is there to do, at this moment?

Saturday, 27 January 2001

Steve brings Tom to stay the night at our home. Tom, now aged two, is a very good-looking boy with an enchanting manner. He soon has my wife hooked! Steve and I discuss the case and he makes a tape of various matters not covered in his evidence at trial.

Thursday, 8 February 2001

I spend the day with Noni de la Pena, a Los Angeles documentary film-maker, who is funded by a civil rights charity to make a 90-minute programme about false allegations of child abuse. Her particular focus is on Munchausen's and Meadow's theories. Convinced that hundreds of mothers have been wrongly accused of Munchausen, she has examined 350 such cases in the USA. In 150 children she has found that the alleged fabricated symptoms were the same as the known side-effects of drugs either the children or the mothers were prescribed.

The new owners of Hope Cottage complain thay they can smell gas in the house. They have discovered an old red carpet blocking the chimney of the gas log fire in the lounge. Steve asks a fire engineer recommended by Mackey to make an investigation. He says that there was probably a layer of carbon monoxide, and possibly cyanide, at the level of where both babies died in the bedroom directly above the fire. Dr Whitwell tells Steve to contact Professor Forrest, a toxicologist. He needs blood samples from both boys, to carry out laboratory tests; Guthrie cards (which contain four blood spots taken at birth) might do, but it is a long shot, due to the way blood deteriorates. Steve spends hours on the search only to be told, eventually, that the cards have been destroyed.

Thursday, 15 February 2001

Lady Limerick is deputy-chairman and driving force of the Foundation for the Study of Sudden Infant Death, the charity working for mothers whose babies die from cot deaths. She says that one of the main advocates of the Foundation and its events is Professor Sir Roy Meadow! His support is worth thousands of pounds to the charity. She is cross with him for using the 1:73 million statistic, but for her to take up any cudgels on Sally's behalf would be difficult; mainly because the Foundation never gets involved in individual cases, she tells me.

Sylvia Limerick is a compassionate, intelligent, hard-working and effective advocate for mothers suffering the agonies of losing their babies. It is unrealistic to expect her to raise a banner for one particular mother wrongly convicted of murder

– how does she know the jury got it wrong? Slagging off Meadow to her, for what I believe he has done in Sally's case, will not work.

Friday, 9 March 2001

Journalist Bob Woffinden comes to my house. He is an experienced feature writer and author, who specialises in miscarriages of justice. Despite the dismissal of the last Appeal Court case, his book about James Hanratty is a masterpiece of exposition of what can go wrong in a murder trial. He wants to write about Sally for the *Sunday Telegraph* magazine. We spend all day together, and I talk into his tape recorder, answering his questions. He spends hours with Steve. His 6,000-word article in the *Sunday Telegraph* on 6 May 2001, 'Against the Odds', is a masterpiece. It will reach a huge audience, who will now be persuaded of Sally's innocence.

Sue Stapely continues to contact and deal with enquiries from a steady stream of journalists and programme-makers and she and I agree, carefully, which ones we are prepared to talk to. Sue's objective is to generate only thoughtful and well-researched feature articles in the mainstream media. Most days she turns down bids from the more sensationalist press, who want to interview Steve or the legal team or gain access to Sally's prison diary. We are both surprised how many journalists still seem to think they can interview someone in prison, but such interviews are at the discretion of the Governor, and the consent of the Prison Service is required.

Objectivity now definitely takes a back seat. Its place, in my mind, is taken by focus; obstinacy becomes determination to find the golden key that will set Sally free. This means abandoning virtually all my other clients and commitments and working full time for Sally Clark. It soon becomes 60, 70, sometimes more, hours in a week. I am not the only one working endless hours on the case. Steve is indefatigable, chasing every medical, legal or parental lead, talking to everyone who writes to Sally in prison or takes an interest in the case. Sally's father, Frank, calls in all the favours of his long career in the police force, talking and writing to everybody who might be able to help. Ultimately he has 600 corres-pondents and the postage is costing a fortune. Mackey, perhaps, has the worst job of all. The Court of Appeal has written its judgment to be appeal proof, leaving nothing for him to work with on his application to the

CCRC – supposedly. He has to think his way right through the case, from its very beginnings, searching for any loophole which he can make into a new ground of appeal. It entails hours researching the paperwork, which now runs into thousands of pages, and days and nights of thinking time.

One of the first people to contact Frank is Professor Bill Inman. He is the former head of the government's yellow card scheme, on which doctors report notifiable diseases which may lead to epidemics. Bill was paralysed by polio as a young man and is now in a wheelchair. I visit him at his home near Southampton. He knows all about vaccination and is interested in Professor Gordon Stewart's belief that the pertussis vaccine may be linked to both deaths, but suggests that Professor Tom Meade – his successor in the yellow card scheme – may be better. It is to prove a crucial recommendation.

I follow up every lead. Everybody with a qualification or relevant experience who writes to Sally, or contacts her via the website, I call up. Most I see personally, at their place or in London.

I investigate the situation in Japan, where cot deaths were once virtually unknown: babies slept on cotton futons. When Western-style cots were introduced, they began to have cot deaths. There had to be a connection. That led me to Dr Jim Sprott, a toxicologist in New Zealand. I read everything he had written. His theory is that a combination of three chemicals that are present in man-made fibres in modern mattresses generate a gas when the baby's body heats up, and that it is lethal. This theory was taken so seriously by the UK government that it set up a committee, chaired by Lady Limerick, to examine it. The Limerick Committee's conclusion was that as the lethal gas could not be replicated in the laboratory, the theory was wrong – so it did not explain a single cot death.

Sprott challenges that decision, because only two of the three gases were tested in combination. And, in New Zealand, where Sprott has persuaded cot manufacturers to eliminate the offending chemicals, no baby has suffered a cot death on one of those mattresses in seven years. Prior to that, New Zealand had one of the highest incidences of cot deaths in the world.

If mattresses were implicated in Sally's babies' deaths, we shall never be able to prove it because Christopher's was lost by the police and Harry's was thrown out.

Hong Kong has virtually no cot deaths. This is astonishing, since it has some of the most crowded living conditions in the world, and smoking is endemic: both are said to be serious contributing factors in cot deaths in other English-speaking countries. Patrick O'Connor, Steve's old boss, now works in Hong Kong. He gives him the name of their leading paediatrician.

I call Professor Anthony Nelson, seeking the names of experts who might be able to explain this phenomenon and so give evidence helpful for another appeal by Sally. He tells me that the culture is different among the Chinese. Crowded conditions help prevent cot deaths, because babies are seldom left alone, even for minutes. There is always somebody in the same room, looking at or tending them. If a baby stopped breathing it would immediately be noticed and the baby picked up and resuscitated. He recommends Dr Beecroft and Professor Roger Byard in Australia.

I visit old friends in Salisbury: Doctors John and Joan Norris, both GPs. John Norris was my own father's doctor for many years. He tells me that Sally's father once saved his life. When he was held hostage by a madman, Frank negotiated and managed to disarm the man. The Norrises speak of a friend they are meeting for dinner who might be able to help Sally: Dr Glyn Walters, a retired chemical pathologist. I phone and ask if he will try to firm up Professor David's theory that Christopher died of idiopathic pulmonary haemosiderosis, a very rare but sometimes fatal disease involving the blood and the lungs. I do not know it, but Glyn Walters' agreement to help will be one of the most significant contributions in Sally's case.

Professor John Edwardes also offers his help. He is an expert in certain diseases of the heart in babies. He is not deterred by the fact that Harry's heart murmur, diagnosed in the first few weeks of his life, was thoroughly investigated and found to be benign.

I talk to my own doctor and every other I can contact about the frequency of nosebleeds in babies, trying to establish whether Meadow's view at trial has any support in the profession generally. One doctor says he would send a baby with a nosebleed immediately to hospital – that is what he had been taught at medical school. Others say that if a baby did suffer such a thing it is unlikely that a doctor would ever hear of it. Practice nurses and health visitors would regard it as too minor to trouble the doctor!

Friday, 30 March 2001

After rather a lot of hassle, involving researching and quoting the law, the Home Office gives permission for a journalist to interview Sally. Sue

Stapely has persuaded Joshua Rozenberg, a solicitor himself, former legal correspondent for the BBC and now legal editor of the *Daily Telegraph*, to write about her. She takes Joshua to spend two hours with Sally. The resulting article is hugely encouraging for Sally and all of us.

March 2001

Penny Mellor is the daughter of a major in military intelligence. She narrowly missed being blown up, twice, by IRA bombs, and her partner is a Fortune 500 company director. Penny has eight children. A fearless woman, she has boundless energy, high intelligence, a photographic memory and a certainty that many mothers have been wrongly accused of child murder or abuse. A grapevine of such mothers has turned into a formidable array of victims, calling on her for help to find lawyers and experts to help them fight false accusations. I soon conclude that she is a saint, but one in an unholy amount of trouble herself.

Mostly she helps people by phone. One such mother was falsely accused of murdering a baby and Social Services were about to take a five-year-old sibling into care. The grandmother, fearful of what might happen to her grandchild in care, spirited her away – a serious offence. The parents followed them to Ireland. When they eventually returned to England, they were arrested and charged with the kidnap of the child. On the basis of a number of phone calls to the family, none lasting more than 40 seconds, Penny too was arrested and charged with conspiracy.

The others are persuaded to plead guilty in the hope that they will receive non-custodial sentences. Penny fights the case because she has done nothing criminal or wrong, and had no hand at all in the kidnap. Convinced that the mother was originally the victim of false allegations, she argues her case like the tiger she is, and antagonises the judge. The jury convicts her and the judge hands her a savage two-year sentence. The others are also sent to prison. Penny's sentence is reduced to eighteen months on appeal, of which she serves half.

Penny is thought of by many as a martyr to the cause of the victims of false allegations of abuse and murder. As a lawyer I can see that orders of the court must be upheld and those that flout them must be punished. But the problem stems from flawed evidence given by experts which is believed by the judges because of the experts' impressive qualifications and, maybe, eminence in the profession. The judges of the

Family Division get to know them well and rely on them. If some of those experts have theories with weak justification, it may be difficult for judges to spot this unless other experts challenge them. It is said that some judges are simply not interested in scientific research. The secrecy ensures not only the anonymity of the children, but that all other details of the case are kept secret. Any shortcomings of those experts will remain hidden. Justice denied in secrecy is a cancer which, if not dealt with, will spread. The imprisonment of Penny and the others in that case illustrates the collateral damage caused if ordinary people are denied justice in the most emotionally charged area of their lives – their children. Prevented from drawing public attention to their injustice, they may take the law into their own hands and cause even more problems for the system.

Penny, released from prison after 9 months, becomes one of my most valuable sources of information in helping Sally.

Life is not easy for Steve, particularly with Tom:

'The Family Court decides that I am a suitable carer for him and he is returned to my full custody. But in a sense, my problems only then began. I am a dad, not a mum. I don't really even know how to be a dad because we had such a short time with Christopher and Harry. I certainly do not know how to be a mum, but that is what I must try to be. I will learn. I speak to friends who are mothers. I read voraciously. I take Tom to Mother and Baby groups and am constantly on the phone to my mum for advice.

'What I am not expecting is the overwhelming sense of dread every moment Tom is out of my sight. I am responsible for my son: I, alone. His mum is locked away. Two of our sons have died. How can I stop it happening to Tom? How can I stop him having an accident? I can't. At times, the thoughts get so completely out of hand that I am at my wits' end.

My partners at Addleshaws generously allow me to take a fourteen-month sabbatical. I am a single parent, at home all day, caring for my baby. More through luck than judgement or experience, we do alright, Tom and I. He seems to understand that I am trying my best for him. He makes it easy for me – sleeping 12 hours every night, by hardly ever being ill and always smiling at my initially inept attempts to feed him, to change his nappy, to get the words of nursery rhymes right – I am always off-key – and to remember the Teletubbies' names.

Tom and I become a team – he is my little mate, and we develop a strong bond of love; I get closer to him than most dads, but why did it have to be like this? We manage to muddle through together. Sometimes I sit outside his nursery all night – just in case he needs me.

'It doesn't take me long to realise that being on his own with me is not a proper life for Tom. He needs the company of other children his own age, and that means nursery school. I spend days finding the right – the safest and best – one.

'Then comes the morning I take him for his first day. I cannot bear it. I cannot handle the thought of leaving him with strangers. But we walk there together, he holding my hand, sometimes quite tightly. Suddenly, much too soon, we are there. I don't want him to see me crying. But I can't help it.

'I kiss him goodbye and hand him over to a lovely lady, tears coursing down my face. I cry all the way back to the house: it feels strangely empty. What have I done? I sit there, desolate, terrified that something may happen to him. I realise that, somehow, I have to stop thinking like this: for Tom's sake I must be strong, not let him see my anxiety.'

Sally wonders what 2001 will hold for her:

'One positive factor about 2001 is my regular visits with my son and that the bond between Tom and me develops and we become really close. Prison officers remark on the strength of that bond. The next landmark is that Steve gets a job with a top City law firm in London. I am so relieved, because I feared that my situation might have harmed his career for good.

'Some inmates cut themselves off from the outside world because of the pain of what they are missing. I go the other way and am as involved as possible. The house in Essex is not "home" for me. It is nothing like Hope Cottage in Wilmslow. But we have lost all our savings in my defence costs and more modest housing is part of the price we are paying for what has happened to me. I am actively involved in choosing which of the houses on offer Steve should see, and in the eventual choice. I choose the fabrics, colour schemes and furnishings, from swatches and catalogues that he brings me on his visits, but I have never seen them in place. Even when I do, it won't be my home.

'I choose all Tom's clothes from other catalogues and plan his daily menus. I make all the preparations for his birthday party – apart from the actual cooking – sending out the invitations, organising the party games and making up the goody bags. Lesley Kerrigan, our nanny, moves to Essex to be Tom's live-in nanny and brings him in to see me nearly every week. I have him for one day a month in prison on my own – on the orders of the Family Court – and Steve brings him on weekend visits.

'My – by now – good friend, Sue B. wins her appeal and goes home, almost a year to the day after my own appeal failed. It is like losing my right arm, but I am thrilled that she is back with her family. I know a lot about her case. I have studied it, to understand the law involved. Hers are nothing like as strong grounds of appeal as mine and yet she succeeds and I failed.'

Steve's life is impossibly hard. Few non-lawyers could appreciate the amount of time and commitment required by deal-based banking law. So much money is at stake in corporate acquisitions that there is no such thing as a normal working week. Steve begins when the work demands and goes home – if at all that day – when the last document has passed his scrutiny and is on somebody else's desk. Two or three days a month, he will work through the night, sometimes slipping home for a shower and an hour's sleep. But there are peaks and troughs to the work; and in every pause in the workload, Steve works on anything that stands the remotest chance of helping free his wife. The number of his lever arch files is growing.

Turning Point

I discuss the Solicitors' Disciplinary Tribunal with Sally during one of my visits to Bullwood. To fight it I would normally go to the best QC, or the most prestigious firm of solicitors experienced in this type of work, and it would cost a fortune. Sally does not have a fortune; nor does Steve. I tell her that I have one qualification that none of the array of well-qualified 'silks' and others in the legal mile have – I will do this for free. She agrees that I may do it, but without too much hope that it will achieve anything.

Mackey is polite, but thinks I'm mad; it's a waste of time and energy. I think he is right. Neither of us say so, but we are sure Sally will be struck off the Roll and no longer be able to describe herself as a solicitor.

Mackey [*on the phone*]: What can you possibly achieve, that will have the slightest benefit to the client?
Me: I don't know.
Mackey: That's usually the yardstick by which we measure what we do.
Me: I don't think Sally wants to be struck off.
Mackey: Tell me another!
Me: I'm going to ask them to adjourn it.
Mackey: On what grounds?
Me: That the European Court of Human Rights has provisionally agreed to accept her case and there is a reasonable chance that they will clear her.
Mackey: It's your time and money!

I have never appeared before the Tribunal. I have no experience or knowledge of how it works, nor have I knowledge of the applicable law. The last time I was an advocate in court was twenty-five years ago, to defend a friend doing 95 miles an hour on the M1. I got him off. It must have gone to my head! I am helped enormously by Sue Stapely, who, when she was running communications at the Law Society, dealt with the Tribunal regularly and knows many of those involved and those who act as advocates before it.

There are all sorts of problems, not the least being that I cannot say Sally did not murder Christopher and Harry. The Tribunal is not allowed to take an interest in her innocence: her guilt is proved by her conviction and the dismissal of her appeal. Leaving aside the little matter that I don't know what I am doing, I decide that, to back the application for an adjournment, I will need to show what a wonderful person Sally Clark is, through the voices of those closest to her. Steve and I split the job of getting statements.

Lady Jo Benson is not only an old friend, she has taken on Sally's mother's role. Her husband, Sir Christopher, whose name was a big influence in the naming of Sally's firstborn, is a former chairman of Docklands and many big companies. He is Principal of the Inns of Court School of Law, and honorary bencher of Middle Temple and honorary fellow of the Royal College of Pathologists.

Martin Bell, no longer an MP but continuing to campaign, makes a statement saying that, having read all the evidence, he is deeply concerned that it was a miscarriage of justice, and that, in spite of all that has happened, Sally is a fit and proper person to be a solicitor.

Partners in the firms of solicitors where she worked rally round with very supportive statements.

Karen Vernon SEN, SRN, SCM is a community midwife who attended Sally and her babies. She writes movingly about her many caring talents and says: 'In my professional opinion, I do not believe her capable of harming babies.'

Pamela Grieve is also a State Registered Nurse and SCM, with a Health Visitors' Certificate. She tended Sally and her babies. Hers is a moving testament to Sally's exceptional qualities as a mother. To give it took considerable courage because Macclesfield Hospital did not want her to make a statement supporting Sally. Grieve says:

> I have every faith in Sally. Her conviction continues to shock me as being terribly wrong. During all the time I spent with her, I never saw any signs that made me concerned or worried. By comparison with other mothers I have worked with, she was particularly relaxed and genuinely happy. I do not believe that, under any circumstances, she would have harmed her sons.

Solicitor Anne Hardy, Sally's friend and neighbour in Wilmslow says, '. . . I do not believe that she is capable of murder. She was unfailingly patient, caring and good-humoured. I asked her to baby-sit my Rebecca and my Sam, even when the police investigation was going on. I had no doubts about leaving them with her.'

Her next-door neighbours, Peter and Diana McVeigh, say much the same thing.

Carolyn Bradley is a good friend and was close to Sally when both babies were born and when they died. She finds it 'absolutely inconceivable that Sally could harm a baby, because she is one of the most loving people I have ever known, and one of the least selfish'.

Pauline Pullen refers to her situation in prison: 'I am always struck by her air of calmness and serenity, and also by how supportive everyone in prison is. It is almost as if everyone is just waiting for her inevitable release.'

But perhaps best of all is an unsolicited letter to the Tribunal by Dr Stephen Watkins, Director of Public Health at Stockport Health

Authority. None of us has met him, but he says that the real chance of a second cot death is that it will happen about once every eighteen months. Like the lottery, the chance that it will be you is small but the chance that it will be someone is high:

> It was not understood by the Court of Appeal . . . they believed it was a side issue . . . they did not appreciate that it was an event that occurred with predictable frequency. To call it very rare is just as inaccurate as it is prejudicial. The Court also believed that the probabilities were corroborated by the pathology evidence, which is quite wrong. That you should strike Sally Clark off is as unthinkable as that you should strike off a solicitor for witchcraft. You police a profession which coined the statement *fiat justitia ruat caelum* and you cannot ignore your responsibilities to justice and commonsense.

Sally would obviously be the key witness, but that is torpedoed by the Prison Service. They can't afford the sweat box to get her there and back. My wife Jane suggests that we make a video of her speaking to camera, in prison. I would never have thought of it. To my amazement, I get permission to do it. An old friend, Chris Hodgson, a television producer and director, recommends a professional cameraman, Jim Sloss. At Bullwood Hall our passports are checked and we are escorted to a classroom.

I have insisted that Sally speaks her own words. I want the Tribunal to hear what she has to say, but I have not warned her she has to do it from memory or it will look stilted on camera. After two hours and sixteen 'takes', and just before our allotted time expires, Jim Sloss pronounces himself satisfied. Sally sounds and looks exhausted but she has put her case clearly and compellingly.

Steve now has 15 lever arch files of materials, eight counsels' notebooks and has created more than 200 items on his home computer. There are 679 word-processed documents in his office computer.

Thursday, 24 May 2001

The Tribunal sits in a third-floor lookalike courtroom in an office at Ludgate Circus in London. Frank is there, and Steve, as are Jo Benson and many of Sally's friends. The press is in evidence, with the legal heavyweight writers Frances Gibb from *The Times* and Joshua Rozenberg from the *Daily Telegraph*, who have been press-ganged by Sue Stapely. I have Helen, my PA, with me; she has masterminded the paperwork. Sitting on one side is Sue, with Steve beside her so nervous he holds her hand in his. She reads my brief yet again, having pored over it to help me draft it by e-mail and phone.

'You realise that they cannot listen to any of this? Legally?' Sue says.

'Something like that,' I reply, 'But what else is there to say?'

Sue has prepared everything meticulously for the media coverage. This hearing is the first real chance, since the appeal, to mobilise sympathy and awareness through the media. She has organised three television camera crews and more than twenty news and legal journalists to be there. She has briefed all of them carefully, and provided a written summary of the case I will be putting on Sally's behalf. Many of the journalists are themselves mothers and have become concerned supporters.

There is a panel of three with a male chairman. Two are solicitors. Sally's video tape is in a recorder for a large television set.

My application is for an adjournment pending the outcome of the European Court appeal. I produce a letter from Burton Copeland confirming that it is before that court.

Peter Cadman, appearing for the Law Society, quotes the Divisional High Court case of John Shepherd, where it was decided that the Tribunal could not look behind a criminal conviction. He tells me, confidentially, that Sally's conviction troubles him and he will give me every opportunity to put her case in full.

I talk for about twenty minutes, telling them how Green's mistake about Harry's eyes led to Christopher's cause of death being changed from natural to smothering, which led to other, largely imaginary, findings in Harry, which led to Sally's arrest and committal. That by then there was an unstoppable momentum about the prosecution. Nobody was interested that it was set in motion by an elementary medical mistake, which, once it was recognised the day before the trial began, should have led to the case being abandoned. But the prosecution had Professor Sir Roy Meadow and his 1:73 million, and gambled, correctly, that it would be enough to get a majority for guilty. I tell them how important qualifying late was for Sally; and that her qualification is now about the only thing she has left.

They watch Sally's tape. She looks pretty but thin, blonde, nervous. The background is clinically white. She apologises for not being present in person, as she would have liked to tell the Tribunal personally of the events of the last few years; also for having not learned her words. She says:

'. . . We had three children, all of them boys. Christopher, my first boy, and Harry, my second little boy, are no longer alive. My third son . . . is nearly two and a half years old. I see him for two wonderful days every month and then in between, on regular visits with his daddy. Together with my husband, he is the light of my life.

'I grew up in Salisbury. I was an only child, the apple of my parents' eye. I was very close to them and they were loving parents to me. When I was a child, I remember thinking that when I eventually got married, I wanted to have the same loving relationship with my husband as my parents had with each other . . . I had a strict upbringing but corporal punishment had no place in my home, and yet they instilled in me a strong sense of right and wrong. It was through my father's career and my parents' teaching that I developed my firm faith in our system of justice. I dreamed one day of becoming part of it. When I got such a positive response from my applications for traineeship and had the blessing of my family I went ahead. It was tough. I gave up a well-paid job and had no grant. We had to make sacrifices . . . When I was admitted to the Roll of Solicitors, at the Law Society's Hall, by the Master of the Rolls, it was the proudest day of my life.

'My life was turned upside down when I suffered the loss of my beloved Christopher and just as we had started to rebuild our lives, Harry. It is not easy to put into words the utter despair and anguish we felt at that time. The pain and sense of loss were enormous and we struggled to make sense of it all. I went through two years of hell awaiting trial. I now suffer the minute-by-minute torture of life imprisonment, knowing, as I accept only I could know, that I did not harm my little boys. Nothing but love them.

'Following my conviction and then the loss of the appeal, I felt let down by a justice system that I always believed in and worked hard to uphold. I was in a state of shock and disbelief. And yet, as I sit here before you today, I have absolute faith that our system of justice will work in the end and prove my innocence. My fervent wish is to walk free and return eventually to the profession I worked so hard to join and of which I am so proud to be part. I very much hope that you will use whatever powers you have to allow me to remain on the Solicitors' Roll, whilst decisions are taken elsewhere about my future. I have lost everything; none of it of my own doing. I would ask you not to take away from me some of the few remaining positive things that I have left, other than my husband and son. Being a solicitor is such an important part of my life that losing my membership of the profession would be like losing part of myself.'

The silence when Sally finishes tells me she has moved everybody, emotionally, in that room. Most – including the usually stoical Steve – are in tears; anything I say will stop them crying! So I sit down. Sue tells me even hardened journalists reached for their handkerchiefs and a tribunal member is drying her eyes.

The Tribunal adjourns to consider my application.

We wait, anticipating – once again – the worst.

They take 45 minutes about their decision. We all stand and bow. The chairman says that my application is refused. No surprise. We have lost. Ah well! Mackey was right; yet again. I am about to put my papers away when the chairman says, 'Would you care to address us further, Mr Batt?'

It is, of course, always a mistake to ask a lawyer if he has anything else to say! So I start talking again. I feel a bit like a suspect being tortured by the threat of a firing squad – I don't know if there are real bullets or not, but if I keep talking long enough maybe Sally and I will survive.

Me: Mr Chairman . . . Members of the Tribunal . . .

What the hell is there to say? It took weeks; preparing every word, every inflexion, every subtle nuance. Now I am speaking off the top of my head, trying to make some sort of impact, and to what end? They are bound to strike her off!

Me: Two solicitors, at the peak of their powers, earning well, living in a beautiful home . . . we are not talking about the ghettos of deprivation, a mother at her wits' end . . . Sally is described by all her friends as gentle, selfless, a wonderfully loving mother . . . There is a very apposite phrase used by the Court of Appeal about similar fact: 'an affront to common sense'. This whole case and these convictions are an affront to common sense. How did it happen? I will use the words of Dr Watkins: 'It was and is a predictable miscarriage of justice.'

The Shepherd case, which says that you cannot look behind these convictions, contains an interesting qualification: 'except in exceptional circumstances'. If those words having any meaning, it must be that you can take such circumstances into account in mitigation of any penalty you, in your discretion, choose. I would urge you to use that discretion with humanity.

They adjourn for a further 15 minutes. I am writing in my notebook, 'struck off' when the chairman speaks:

Chairman: Mrs Clark is in prison. She cannot practise law in there. She poses no risk to the public. We see no reason to strike her off the Roll. Our decision is that she will be suspended.

My hearing is not too good. I whisper to Sue: 'What did they say?' She is holding Steve's hand hard. Both are close to tears. 'You've done it!' Sue whispers back. 'Done what?' I whisper again. She says, 'They've suspended her. She's not been struck off.'

How can that be? With a double murder conviction! I had not even asked for suspension. If I had thought of it, I would have dismissed it as pie-in-the-sky impossible. And yet, it makes perfect sense.

Outside, in Ludgate Circus, Margaret Gilmore interviews Frank for BBC News. He is marvellous. Then she asks me what I think. *Big mistake, Margaret!*

Sue Stapely makes endless calls to the media on her mobile while standing in the street outside the court building.

Sue now has something she can work with. She gets the story on the front page of the *Daily Telegraph*, and on television it is the lead story of both the lunchtime and evening news. That is simply astounding. It is a morale-booster for all of us. The media now goes into a frenzy. Sue gets thirty to forty e-mails a day from all over the world. Each one gets a carefully considered response. She talks to Mackey or Steve or me about nearly all of them. Even Mackey is now beginning to see that the press can be a tool to help put right the injustice to Sally. Part of the legal establishment has said, aloud, that there is something seriously wrong with Sally's conviction and the Court of Appeal's extraordinary decision. There is no other interpretation of the refusal to strike off a solicitor convicted of double murder, whose guilt has been so emphatically endorsed by the second highest court in the land.

With skill, charm and endless patience, Sue makes this day the turning point in the Sally Clark case. The story leads the Twelve, Six and Ten o'clock News bulletins and is on the front page of most of next day's papers. Over the coming months, Sue will cajole, urge and steer journalists, editors and legal writers, advising them how to make new stories out of the Sally Clark case. It is a job requiring endless stores of patience, hours of persistence, every day; work at night, at weekends. Whenever a deadline has to be met, Sue will be there with a new angle, somebody else to talk to. The daily e-mails increase. Steve, Frank, Mackey and I drop everything to respond, making ourselves available for interviews or TV appearances. Sue is turning back the tide.

I remember that night in bed when a voice in my head said 'It will be all right. It will be all right.' Was it hallucination? Was it just chemicals in the brain producing a reaction? Or was it . . . I lived my 'Jesuit' years in a cathedral. I think it was Him; and now, I am beginning to think He was not kidding.

It is a big fillip for Sally:

> 'I thought the Tribunal was a lost cause, and was marginally unenthu-siastic about fighting the decision. Yes, my career means the world to me but I could understand why they would want to srike me off, particularly as I had lost my appeal. I was almost inclined not to fight my corner, but John Batt persuaded me. He reminded me what my career meant to me; I realised I was becoming defeatist and almost giving in to what the press said about me as a career-oriented woman. It was as if I was ashamed to admit that my career meant that much to me. But I soon knew it was worth fighting to remain on the Roll of Solicitors of the Supreme Court. Now, reading the press reaction, there is no doubt that the Tribunal has done my morale and my situation in the eyes of the public the world of good.'

Steve and Frank are thrilled with the decision. It gives them both hope.

Monday, 11 June 2001

Nearly half of another year has passed with Sally still in jail.

Sir Christopher and Lady Benson hold a reception in the gardens of Middle Temple. Many people are interested in Sally's case; two guests in particular, both barristers, Deborah Eaton and Maureen Baker QC, offer to look at the evidence. I copy them all the transcripts.

Steve learns about two firms of solicitors in north London who are pursuing claims for damage done to babies by vaccination. He spends half a day with them in Camden making notes for our experts.

Monday, 18 June 2001

Sharon Patrick, a journalist with ITN, survives the Home Office screening process for interviews with prisoners and can now see Sally at Bullwood Hall. She is researching an item that will be shown on *Tonight with Trevor McDonald*.

Wednesday, 4 July 2001

Campbell Malone, a Manchester solicitor specialising in Court of Appeal cases, arranges a conference at the Conway Hall in Holborn. Mike Mansfield QC, a well-known criminal law campaigner, is the main speaker. His theme is that the CCRC was set up to help put right miscarriages of justice. It went well at first, with most of the referrals leading to quashed convictions. Now the tide has turned and more cases are being dismissed by the Appeal Court, than allowed. What is going to change? Either the CCRC will have to raise its hurdle or the court will have to lower its own. Mansfield also bemoans the fact that, too often, that court seems to make up its mind in advance and then write its way round the law to fit that presumption.

I have been asked to talk about Sally. At the end of the meeting I am approached by a number of other solicitors involved in miscarriage cases. We commiserate on how it has taken over our lives. I pick up some valuable tips.

John Sweeney asks Steve to give him a TV interview for a documentary he is making, *Cot Deaths: The Witchhunt*.

Thursday, 5 July 2001

There is a 'council of war' at the Goring Hotel. Sue Stapely has arranged for Steve and I to meet David MacKay, the mathematician and statistician at Cambridge University whose outrage was provoked by the Meadow statistic. A friend of his had lost a baby to cot death.

The website set up by David is building on Sally's network of helpers from all over the world, many of whom become friends. Everything that happens in the case appears on the website. The first Court of Appeal judgment appears verbatim. The correspondence proves illuminating and time-consuming. Experts contribute e-mails or copies of medical papers. Mackay forwards every one to Steve or Mike Mackey, Sue or me. Every worthwhile lead – of which there are hundreds – is followed up.

I am not a machine-friendly man; I am inclined to think that computers are just a fad that will go away! But David MacKay changes my attitude. Now I know that not only is it a very useful tool, but in a case of miscarriage it is indispensable, almost the 'weapon of choice' in the battle to put it right. It also makes known the advances and reverses to a huge audience of informed opinion, at the press of a button. We will never know how influential it is; the only certainty is that without it Sally would have had a lot more trouble making the world aware of the enormity of the injustice wreaked upon her.

Steve has also been trying to track down the CONI records kept so meticulously by Sally. Strange that they should go missing.

Steve visits Macclesfield Hospital to try to sort this and chase down other leads. When he tries to talk to various health professionals they refuse, saying they have been instructed by their superiors not to talk to him.

Noon: Sunday, 15 July 2001

John Sweeney's BBC Radio Five Live programme is broadcast. He calls it *73 million to One*, and quotes Meadow's aphorism, from the *ABC of Child Abuse*, of which he is the editor, that 'one cot death is a tragedy, two is suspicious and three is murder until the contrary is proved'. Sweeney calls it Meadow's Law.

The programme focuses mainly on Sally's case, but also highlights what may be dozens of other miscarriages of justice, where mothers have been convicted of baby murder, or lost siblings into care, because of Meadow's Law and this speculative new theory about cot deaths.

Paediatrician Dr Ian Rushton, with forty years' experience of sudden infant death, is interviewed by Sweeney. He says that 'a few years ago such cases as Sally's would have been treated as unexplained deaths. But Meadow's Law, now adopted by a number of doctors, means that mothers have to produce medical evidence as to how their babies died, if they are to escape conviction for murdering them. No such evidence exists.'

Statisticians and geneticists say the chance of a second cot death may be as low as 1:4 !

Sweeney reports the rumour that a member of Sally's jury has been quoted as saying: 'Say what you like about Sally Clark, you can't get away from 73 million to one.' It is probably just that – a rumour. But it would fit my observation of the jury reaction at the trial. The Court of Appeal said the statistic was a 'sideshow'. But would that jury have convicted Sally Clark if they had known the real chance of a second cot death could be just 1:4?

Sweeney interviews Frank: 'for murder to be true of my daughter, she would have to be a monster. Everybody who knows her, knows that is not true.'

Dr David Drucker, Reader in Microbiology at Manchester University, with whom Steve is in contact, believes he has discovered a cot death gene. He says his research is in the very early stages: 'We have just opened a door and taken one step into that room. We don't know what else is in there yet.'

Sweeney quotes an editorial in the *British Medical Journal*, written by Dr Stephen Watkins, entitled 'Conviction by Mathematical Error'.

Sweeney asks me what I think goes wrong. I tell him: 'A jury sees a mother in the dock, there are two dead babies (which she cannot deny), and a professor says the deaths were not natural. If she can prove how her babies died they will let her off, otherwise they will believe the professor, and convict her as a murderer.'

Sweeney concludes his programme by urging the Home Secretary to consider a new slogan: 'One cot death is a tragedy, two cot deaths is a tragedy and three cot deaths is a tragedy!'

Steve is following up Meadow's assertion, at trial, that nosebleeds do not occur in very young babies. He contacts Professor Jean Golding, an epidemiologist at Bristol University. She has conduced research which shows that they are not uncommon. She is also interested in Meadow's statistic, which she says has no validity at all.

I have no means of knowing how significant my next telephone call will be. I have made so many every day for over two years following up every lead, however implausible.

Marylyn Stowe is senior partner and head of the Family Law Unit at Grahame Stowe Bateson in Leeds. Her specialist field is 'Big Money' divorce cases, many of which involve forensic investigation and analysis. She has offered her services to Steve, free, because – as a mother and fellow solicitor – she is incensed at Sally's conviction and the dismissal of her appeal.

Steve asks me what part she could play in the continuing search for proof of Sally's innocence. My reaction is to ask her to work on Macclesfield Hospital. We are making no progress on a number of fronts:

- Despite a number of requests, we have been unable to get the medical records for toxicology, to follow up on possible carbon monoxide poisoning.
- They say they cannot find the original apnoea monitor, about which the jury asked a question, nor can they find the CONI records which Sally kept meticulously every day of Harry's life, and we can't get tissue samples for Professor Oxford at the London Hospital for testing for a lethal form of influenza, in the case of Christopher.
- Steve has also been trying to get health visitor Ann McDougal to make a statement correcting a wholly misleading interpretation put on a statement of hers. She said Steve was downstairs making supper when Harry died, not making a bottle. Mrs Justice Bracewell, at the Court of Appeal hearing, pointed out that this was another lie told by Sally and Steve, confirming her guilt. Ann has already confirmed to Steve that nobody told her Steve was making supper, she just assumed it! She told Steve she would make a statement correcting it but when he sent her a letter suggesting the wording, she was reluctant to put anything in writing.

Frank has had a call from Ed Smith, a manufacturer of apnoea monitors, concerned at the so-called malfunction in Harry's case. Marilyn Stowe meets him and takes a first draft statement. Steve takes over and spends hours on the phone, elaborating and simplifying what he can say. When first introduced they did have faults but these were soon corrected. Since 1990 there have been virtually no reports of faults because they now incorporate a fail-safe mechanism. When the alarm attached to Harry's body sounded continually it was NOT due to a faulty connection. It was a signal that Harry's breathing was being interrupted and should have been rushed to hospital. Harry was suffering multiple apnoea attacks.

The reaction by the CONI representative that the constant sounding of the alarm was due to a faulty connection is not surprising. Many doctors have doubts about the medical value of apnoea monitors except as a comfort to parents. That view is at least nine years out of date and yet still it persists.

Had the jury been aware that those alarms were signalling the real thing, would they have found Sally guilty of murder?

Marylyn Stowe is a formidable lady. She applies herself with diligence. At first she is given a hard time, and forbidden to talk to 'low grade' hospital employees without permission from the press officer. Stowe ignores this.

She makes heroic efforts to find the original monitor fitted to Harry. The monitor should be in Harry's medical notes. Further efforts to find them are frustrated by more obstruction by another hospital manager. Stowe spends days on this search, travelling all over the North from her Leeds base.

Tuesday, 31 July 2001

Dr Zakaria Erzinclioglu is a renowned forensic scientist and author. Paralysed by polio, his three young children tend him and bring a welcome note of charming informality to my meeting at his home. They serve me a sumptuous lunch, as if I was visiting royalty.

His particular interest is Meadow's evidence and his written academic papers. He tells me that Meadow's theory is like that of a man who sees a field full of horses and, observing that they all have four legs, concludes that all animals have four legs.

Thursday, 9 August 2001

John Sweeney and an editor of BBC TV's *Newsnight* call, for a full briefing on the latest developments. Sue Stapely has already given them the bare details and has formed the opinion that they can be trusted and will help.

Professor Tom Meade is prepared to make a full investigation of vaccination in both babies. He thinks there is little prospect of it having infected Christopher, but it must have something to do with Harry's death, which occurred so soon after immunisation. He puts me to work on obtaining statistical information from the Committee for the Safety of Medicines. He is about to go into hospital for an operation, but will start work when fit again. He is positive about Harry and I am very hopeful that this will impress the Criminal Cases Review Commission.

Friday, 24 August 2001

I take Sharon Patrick from ITV with me to visit Sally. I spend the first hour bringing Sally up to date with my investigations and taking her instructions. I then let Sharon conduct her interview.

Tuesday, 28 August 2001

Leslie Hawkins, a toxicologist in Guildford, agrees to carry out tests on samples of Christopher's and Harry's blood. Tissue samples or slides will be needed, which are also required for toxicological tests for possible carbon monoxide poisoning at Hope Cottage

Mackey, Steve and I try to get them, without success. The hospital, on legal advice, refuses to authorise their release.

Steve is following up a number of new leads including the following:

- It was said during the trial that petechiae were evidence that Harry had been smothered. Dr Mellon, at Newcastle University, has done research showing that petechiae are common in babies and can even be caused by sneezing.

- Dr Carpenter is an expert in interpreting rib fractures. He is prepared to make his new technique available to us if we need it.

Steve continues to chase Macclesfield Hospital on a number of other points.

The Law Society enforces its order against Sally for the costs of the Disciplinary Tribunal. Steve pays up. The Society then serves notice of appeal against the decision of the Tribunal to suspend Sally. They say the Tribunal failed to give proper weight to her conviction for two murders and to the dismissal of her appeal; that suspension alone is wholly insufficient; that it failed to exclude my plea of Sally's innocence and finally:

> The maintenance of the reputation of the solicitors' profession and the sustaining of public confidence in that reputation requires the striking off of the Respondent . . .

I do not believe the Law Society's appeal will succeed because the Tribunal made it quite clear that they had carefully considered all the issues required by law, and exercised their discretion accordingly. The Court of Appeal has laid down the principle that it will not interfere with a tribunal decision merely because it might have reached a different conclusion itself; it has no power to substitute its own discretion for that of the Tribunal.

I think this is a mean-spirited thing for the Law Society to do and one which will aggravate most of its members, who will wonder why such action was taken against one of their own members. It also hurts Sally, although I think I convince her that they will not succeed in overturning the Tribunal decision. I was a naughty boy in bending the Tribunal's rules, making such play of Sally's innocence, but they made it clear that that did not influence them. I believe the Tribunal saw through the legal niceties to the real justice of the situation and did a public service in sending out a message that something was seriously wrong with this conviction, if not with the criminal justice system.

Sue ensures that the situation is quietly and correctly reported in the legal press. I do not think it sensible to spend time and effort fighting this. I tell

Peter Cadman (acting for the Law Society) that until the European Court of Human Rights rules on Sally's appeal, it would be premature to waste the time and resources of the court. I think the appeal should be adjourned until after that happens. He persuades the Law Society to agree.

Thursday, 30 August 2001

Dr Michael Baden is an American pathologist who gave evidence for English nanny Louise Woodward at her trial in Boston, when she was convicted of the murder – reduced by the judge to Murder 2, manslaughter – of Mathew Epan. Baden is staying at the Savoy Hotel and has agreed to see me. I wait for 45 minutes in that impressive foyer in the Strand. I am a patient man; time means nothing to me in this case. Baden is a tall, grey-haired, impressive man. I feel that I am not someone of importance in his life.

He is prepared to write a report. He will need all the medical evidence, for both sides. His secretary will let me know his fee when he has had a look at the papers. He asks me for a brief résumé of the medicine. When I mention that there was a nick in Christopher's fraenulum he says that can only mean that the baby was abused. End of story. I thank him for his time and tell him I will be in touch with his secretary. I will not.

Ted Davison, alerted by Sally's website, contacts David MacKay who puts him on to me. Davison, a fellow of the Royal Statistical Society, is offended by the way the Meadow statistic will mislead the public and medical experts alike. He kindly buys me lunch at Gemini Restaurant, in Tadworth. I give him the Meadow transcript. He will make something happen.

Bullwood Hall watches *Tonight with Trevor McDonald*, as does the rest of the country. Sally is apprehensive:

> 'There's a noticeable shift in the way elements of the press are treating my situation. With every piece of positive publicity comes a gradual shift in public opinion. I am still receiving fifteen to twenty letters a day, as I have been throughout 2001; in fact, during the whole of my time in prison. The positive attitude in the prison also increases.'

September 2001

Marilyn Stowe receives a phone call from John Glynn, in the Legal Services Department of Macclesfield Hospital. He has at last located the medical notes of Christopher and Harry and has them in his desk, 'in case they go missing'. According to Glynn, the results of certain tests on Harry are not legible. Stowe's statement recording her work, says:

> He said the original was with the pathologist and he was trying to get hold of it . . . A lot of people were interested in the enquiries the family was now making and he had even been contacted by police . . . who had been alerted by Williams.
>
> I subsequently received a bundle of documents from Mr Glynn . . . He confirmed that the blood document was a fairly poor copy and the Pathology department may have a better copy.

Only on a detailed consideration of the voluminous medical notes Glynn handed over did Stowe discover that the blood test results were not included. But Glynn subsequently passes a legible copy to Steve Clark.

The fair copy turns out to be not the toxicology tests that Marilyn was looking for, which would have shown whether either baby had been affected by carbon monoxide, but something entirely different. It is a microbiology report which we didn't know existed. This is the one originally commissioned by Williams at the time of the post-mortem on Harry. It reveals *Staph. aureus* in Harry's body. It does not mean a thing to Steve. He decides to bin it.

Lord Parry Mitchell is a friend of Frank's and has agreed to speak in a House of Lords debate, led by Earl Howe, on false allegations of child abuse and murder. Sue Stapely knows him well from their time together as politicians in the Social Democratic Party. She gives him a briefing in the hope that the media will make contact and report his speech. I meet Mitchell at his office on Wimbledon bridge and fill in the legal details he will need.

Wednesday, 17 October 2001

Steve, Ted Davison, Frank and I go to the House of Lords debate. Howe is very good, as is Parry Mitchell. A government minister and a bishop take the establishment line that there is a procedure for dealing with mis-carriages of justice and no reason to believe it is not working.

The Minister is playing it by the book – but a bishop toeing the government line? Where is he coming from!

Tuesday, 23 October 2001

The hard work and research of Ted Davison bears fruit in a news release with the heading: THE ROYAL STATISTICAL SOCIETY CONCERNED BY ISSUES RAISED IN SALLY CLARK CASE. Squaring the incidence of one cot death to arrive at the frequency of two is statistically invalid:

> Not only is there no such empirical justification but there are very strong reasons for supposing that the assumption will be false. There may well be unknown or genetic factors so that a second case becomes much more likely. The well-publicised figure of 1 in 73 million cannot reasonably be justified as a 'ballpark' figure, because the error involved is likely to be very large. The true frequency of families with two cases of SIDS may be very much less incriminating than the figure presented to the jury at trial.

In a stern condemnation of the misuse of statistics the RSS continues:

> Society does not tolerate doctors making serious clinical errors, because it is widely understood that such errors could mean the difference between life and death. The case of *R* v. *Sally Clark* is one example of a medical witness making a serious statistical error, one which may have had a profound effect on the outcome of the case. The Society urges the Courts to ensure that statistical evidence is presented only by appropriately qualified statistical experts, as would be the case for any other form of expert evidence.

November 2001

Sally's closest friend, Susie B., has had a new trial and once again is convicted. Sally writes:

'Yet again my faith in the justice system takes a severe battering. Not only as a lawyer, having read her case, but having got to know her, I feel strongly that she is innocent. I also feel guilty that part of me resented her going home, and now, a tiny part of me is glad to have her back.

'For a time all my problems fade into the background as I concentrate on getting her through these crucial weeks – she did the same for me when my appeal failed. I am glad of the distraction because my own case is proceeding so slowly. The utter despair I felt at the rejection of my appeal, returns as I cry for Susie. When she was freed, my father told me I would make new friends, but Bullwood Hall is not like school. It is not as if there are many other friends to make. I say to Susie: "I believe in your innocence, but one thing makes me think you must be guilty: you are in the cell next to mine. I cannot believe that two innocent people are in prison next door to each other, and the only one I can be completely certain about is me."

'By now she is used to my sense of humour.

'Our roles are now reversed. In July, when she was freed, everything looked rosy and optimistic for Susie, whereas for me they could not have been more bleak. Now she is back in prison, but my application has already gone in to the CCRC. For me there is hope. For Susie, none.'

Steve has been making a thorough investigation of other cases in which Williams has given evidence. He now has three overflowing lever arch files. Their information is needed by Martin Bell, who has made a complaint against Williams and Green to the General Medical Council. When Bell loses his parliamentary seat, George Osborne becomes MP for Tatton. He speaks in the House of Commons about Sally's case as one of the worst miscarriages of justice of recent times.

Friday, 9 November 2001

Mike Mackey's weeks of working nights and weekends pays off in a comprehensive and carefully argued application to the Criminal Cases Review Commission.

It is an impressive analysis of the main issues that went wrong and runs to over 20 pages. The main grounds are that the defence can now produce fresh evidence as to:

- the competence and credibility of Williams, on whose findings the whole prosecution medical case is founded;
- the competence and credibility of Green;
- the competence and credibility of Meadow;
- the fact that the Court of Appeal was misled on the basis on which statistics were admitted at trial; and
- the fact that the Court of Appeal was misled as to the definition of Sudden Infant Death Syndrome.

Mackey refers to other cases in which Williams has been criticised.

Green's credibility is attacked because the computer legend suggests that his notes were not made on the dates he claimed. This could mean that there are questions over his evidence. Mackey makes the point that if Green's evidence at committal was the whole truth, the contents of his statement of 30 July 1999 cannot be right. There are further points relating to attendance notes, which cast doubt on their reliability. He refers to a letter to Crown counsel – discovered accidentally by Steve – in which Green admits that the evidence he had given was scientifically unconvincing.

Meadow's statistic is attacked because it was inadmissible at trial, if only because at no time did Sally claim that her babies had suffered cot deaths – so the statistic had no relevance to any issue in the case.

The grounds are backed up by extensive quotations from the transcripts of both trial and appeal. The arguments are, in my opinion, persuasive, although there is no clincher. I still expect the application to succeed; how long it will take the investigating officers to reach that conclusion is another matter. Mackey has given them a lot of homework to do.

December 2001

Sally and Susie B. help each other through Christmas:

'I have the best job at Bullwood: working in Reception. For Susie a new job is "created" as governor's orderly. We are both now respected and we keep ourselves to ourselves, while at the same time maintaining good relations with the remainder of G Wing.

'Time passes so slowly in prison. It already seems days and months since the CCRC application went in, and still there is no news. The trouble is that a day inside is like a week, or more in the outside world, and you are always seeking news.'

Sally has now spent over two years in jail; every minute of every one of the 730 days slow torture. Will it ever end? There is no sign, yet, of the single fact – the golden key – that will set her free.

The New Year 2002

Steve's search and mine for new medical evidence continues unabated, so far without a major breakthrough; surely the sheer volume of work and contacts, world-wide, will reveal something.

Every day Steve or Frank calls: some days several times. I call Steve usually to get instructions from Sally about some new development. Discussions with Frank keep him up to date; sometimes we need his opinion on police matters, and all sorts of people are writing to him with suggestions for new evidence which have to be followed up. Most days I talk to Sue by e-mail, which she has insisted I learn how to use, or by phone – much more user friendly for me. She continues to orchestrate the right kind of media interest and keep her wide network of opinion fully informed. She also feeds Steve or me daily with new offers of help from the website.

Dr Douglas Fleming, in charge of research at the Royal College of General Practitioners, offers his help. He reads the post-mortem reports on both babies. His theory is that most cot deaths are probably forms of influenza, or something to do with the lungs. He is very interested in Williams' original finding of a lower respiratory tract infection. He goes to work.

A couple of weeks later, he produces a graph. It shows that Christopher died in a peak week for influenza in babies in the five-year period 1996 to 2001. Harry died at a similar but lower-peak week. To prove it one way or the other, Douglas Fleming has asked Professor John Oxford, a noted virologist, to carry out tests. For that we need blood or tissue samples for both babies. The prosecution continue to prevaricate about supplying the samples we need.

Frank and I are invited on to Channel 4's Richard and Judy programme. Sally is the top story of this five o'clock TV programme watched by millions. The infamous statistic – 73 million to 1 – and the evidence that two cot deaths can only happen once every hundred years is blown away when Frank reveals that over forty parents, who have suffered two or more cot deaths have already contacted the family offering support. One of them, Susie Sale, from Bristol, had two babies die at about the same ages as Christopher and Harry. She was treated with sensitivity and respect by Bristol police. Unlike Sally's sons, her babies' post-mortems were done by a paediatric pathologist – Professor Peter Fleming. He found no evidence that any harm had been done to her children; but nor could he find any cause of death. No 'hawk' of child abuse was involved. These were typical, tragic cot deaths suffered by a loving caring mother. Dr Douglas Fleming broke the news that Christopher died at a six-year peak for lung infections. The support of Richard and Judy was a great help to all of us.

Monday, 11 February 2002

Susan Batt, our son Charlie's wife, dies of breast cancer today. It is an expected but devastating blow to the family. She leaves three children: Derek, 14, Lizzie, 12, and Janie, 7. Jane and I fly to America for the funeral.

I have been more fortunate over Susan's terminal illness than my wife, who has had to bear the brunt of Susan's slow death, mainly by telephone, through our son and younger daughter, Joanna, who has been over there, caring for the family, for four months. I have had the distraction of Sally's case to occupy my mind.

Steve has second thoughts about the microbiology report. He retrieves it from the wastepaper basket. It mentions certain tests on Harry. It means nothing to him but it might to Professor David. He had carried out extensive and painstaking tests on both babies and his reaction was immediate: 'Eureka! This shows bacteria throughout Harry's body. Noboby knew that. You need a specialist pathologist, and also a microbiologist should be asked for an opinion.' He suggests Dr Caroline Blackwell. Steve talks to her – she is prepared to help, saying that Professor

James Morris, consultant pathologist at Lancaster Royal Infirmary, is an expert in SIDS and bacteria. Steve calls him and then sends him the report. Morris says it discloses a cause of death for Harry.

Mackey and I take it over.

Morris is prepared to write a report. He will need everything: all the medical evidence, all the reports. We tell Steve. He asks, 'Am I allowed to get excited about this?'

It takes a while for my PA, Helen, and I to put that together. A day or so later, Morris calls. 'I can tell you this much without reading too much further,' he says. 'Harry died of natural causes: an overwhelming staphylococcal infection; no other cause of death is sustainable.'

Steve still has trouble sleeping; wondering what would have happened if Waste Disposal had taken that report!

Dr Glyn Walters in Salisbury, who is already helping on Christopher, is a chemical pathologist. It occurs to me that this should be right in his area of special expertise. I call him. He confirms it:

Walters: Send me everything. This is it for Sally!

Mackey – ever the cynic – does not believe me when I tell him Williams failed to disclose a Microbiology report which shows that Harry died of natural causes. It could not happen in a murder trial with so many experts involved. One of them would have spotted the omission. It *has* to be a red herring!

He goes to see Morris for himself, at Lancaster. He phones me on his return. Morris has convinced him this report is 'the business'.

On Friday, 8 March 2002, Morris' report concludes:

. . . on the basis of the evidence I have seen, the most likely explanation for the death of Harry Clark is overwhelming staphylococcal infection. This is natural disease. Given that there was a pure growth of S.aureus in the CSF [cerebrospinal fluid] with polymorphs, no other conclusion could be sustained.

Walters has also now written a report, which concludes:

The above considerations lead me to conclude that Harry Clark died from a disseminated staphylococcal infection.

Both of these statements have a certainty which, in my experience, is unusual with experts. That neither I, nor anybody else, had to lean on either of them to induce these doctors to write these unequivocal diagnoses proves that you don't have to do more than put all the facts before experts to get firm opinions from them.

Mackey instructs Dr Caroline Blackwell, sending her all the medical reports. She adds her weight to what Morris has found.

Mackey tells me Sally's conviction will definitely be quashed: 'That's not pie in the sky – that's a fact!'

He explains the law like this:

1. 'The jury asked questions about blood tests on Harry. Although the microbiology report showed the results of swab not blood tests, the question was asked by a lay jury and Williams should have disclosed the report.
2. The jury was told 57 times that there was no evidence of natural disease in Harry. Every time it was untrue.
3. The fact that two properly qualified pathologists have certified that Harry died of natural causes means, at least, that a possible natural cause of death for Harry was withheld from the jury.

   Ergo: The conviction must be unsafe.

It does not take long for Mackey to put these reports and the discovery of the microbiology into new reports to the CCRC. They respond within a couple of days, seeking a meeting.

Angela Cannings' Trial April 2002

At Winchester Crown Court, Angela Cannings, also from Salisbury, is on trial for the murder of two of her three sons. (The stipendiary magistrate at the committal hearing threw out the charge in respect of the first baby, accepting that there was no evidence that the death was unnatural.) The presiding judge is Mrs Justice Heather Hallett, who is also the daughter of a police officer.

I have included some details of this apparently unrelated case because it has resonances for Sally's situation. The charge is the same – the murder of two baby sons – and Meadow gives evidence for the prosecution again which has a direct bearing on what he said at Sally's trial. But most interesting is the judge. By one of the strangest of many coincidences in this saga, I will be sitting in court when Mrs Justice Hallett hears another case.

Angela is a very different character from Sally, but there are uncanny similarities in the two cases. Angela is totally supported by her husband, family, GP and all health professionals as a good and caring, loving mother. There is no evidence that she ever harmed her own or anybody else's babies. There is very little medical evidence but Meadow, and Dr Ward Platt from Newcastle, are giving evidence against her.

Professor of Epidemiology Jean Golding gives evidence for the defence that Meadow's study of 81 cases thought to be cot deaths, which he claims he proved were murder, has no scientific justification because there were no 'controls'. He did not examine the behaviour of mothers of genuine cot deaths against that of baby-murderers; he therefore had no means of knowing if the behaviour he had described as typical of baby-killers was not also true of mothers of babies who died naturally. Golding likens his paper to 'stamp collecting'.

In cross-examination, Meadow says:

The paper you refer to . . . is really a clinical descriptive paper: it is not an epidemiological survey or statistical survey; it is actually, in my terms, a rather minor publication . . . it came about because . . . people said 'put down the slides you are showing . . . in a paper' . . . All it does is describe the features of 80 children who had been found to have been smothered . . . It is not a . . . scientific work in that sense . . . it shouldn't be viewed as accurate in that sort of epidemiological sense . . .

This admission has far-reaching consequences. It means that every time that study, in a family or criminal case, has been interpreted as scientifically or epidemiologically accurate, it has misled the judge or the jury as it must have misled the magistrate in Sally's committal, and their decisions and verdicts may therefore be unsafe. It has been repeatedly reported as accurate scientific research and this has given entirely the wrong impression to all those outside the courtroom as well as those within. All those cases will have to be investigated as possible miscarriages of justice.

By agreement between prosecuting and defence counsel, there is to be no reference to Meadow's 1:73 million. This worries both Angela's solicitor and myself. We fear that somebody on the jury may have seen the publicity given to it during Sally's trial and may believe it to be true. If it is not made clear to the jury that it is totally wrong, or that the chance of two murders is actually 1:2,200 million, there is a risk that a jury member will raise it in the secrecy of the retiring room; it might convict Angela and nobody would ever know. Angela's counsel rule it out: it breaks the golden rule of advocacy that you never introduce evidence damaging to your client's case, just to bring other evidence contradicting it.

At the conclusion of the defence evidence, Mrs Justice Hallett sends the jury out for a break and invites Mansfield to make a submission. This means that the judge is worried that there may not be enough evidence on which it would be safe for the jury to convict. She is inviting arguments from both counsel on the point.

Such submissions are often made by defence counsel, at the conclusion of the prosecution evidence. I do not know of another case in which the judge has taken the initiative, and invited defence counsel to make a submission so late in the trial, after all the witnesses have given their evidence.

Mrs Justice Hallett hears the arguments and rejects the submission!

That, too, is extraordinary. She finds against the submission she herself instigated. There could be two explanations: the obvious one is that prosecuting counsel persuades her that she is wrong, but there is another: that instead of instructing the jury to find her not guilty she decides to be merciful to Angela, letting the jury pronounce her not guilty, rather than have it appear that she got off on a technicality.

After the judge's summing-up, which is fair – if anything, leaning towards a not guilty verdict – the jury retires.

Angela's supporters in the foyer begin the celebration of what they 'know' will be her acquittal. They get so boisterous that ushers have to tell them to 'keep it down'.

The jury returns.

The Clerk of the Court rises:

Clerk: Members of the jury . . . have you agreed upon your verdict?
Foreman of the jury: Yes.
Clerk: On the first count on the indictment do you find the defendant
   guilty or not guilty?
Foreman: Guilty.

There are shouts from the public gallery.

Clerk: On the second count on the indictment do you find the defendant
   guilty or not guilty?
Foreman: Guilty.
Clerk: And those are the verdicts of you all?
Foreman: Yes.

Gusts of protest ring out from Angela's supporters. Angela looks as if she
will faint.

*Something very strange has happened. Virtually everybody in that courtroom –
including the officials and backroom people, who usually have a good nose for jury
reactions – was certain Angela would be found not guilty. Did Meadow's infamous
statistic enter the secrecy of the jury room? Did a member of that jury, sworn to give
a verdict only according to the evidence heard in court, say to the others: 'You know
that the chance of two cot deaths is 73 million to 1. Angela Cannings had three.'
No member of the jury heard that number from anybody in that court. It was never
referred to. Did the jury use knowledge acquired outside the trial, from newpapers
or other media, to convict Angela? That is the only conclusion I can reach. In my
opinion, evidence given by witnesses at her trial – even though Angela did not make
a good witness in her own defence – could not have done it alone.*

The Golden Key Fits

I fly from Gatwick to Manchester for a meeting with Mackey and Criminal
Cases Review Commission investigator Angela Flowers. Her opening
words, after the politenesses, are:
   'If it is all right with you, we propose to go straight to see Dr Wills, the
hospital microbiologist. We will go ahead with the new ground of appeal
and leave the other grounds lying on the table.'
   The rest of that two-hour meeting was concerned with technical

details. The CCRC will pay for any extra experts they decide to instruct. Flowers has an appointment to see the microbiologist at Macclesfield Hospital. She did not think that there was any point in the CCRC instructing an independent pathologist; Morris and Walters are both independent and well qualified.

She adds a note of caution: 'If we refer the case back to the Court of Appeal, you will have a clean slate; you can put in any grounds of appeal you like, but you should know that the only references of ours that have been unsuccessful have been those where the lawyers chose to go with different grounds from those on which we acted.'

The decision is not for Angela Flowers to make, but Mackey and I have no doubt that the members of the Commission will back their officers. Sally is on her way to the Court of Appeal again.

What will be Spencer's reaction? Mackey and I agree that he is a good lawyer, and that he will recognise that the failure to disclose the microbiology report is all we need to make Sally's conviction unsafe; and then we have 57 factually incorrect statements about infection to the jury. Spencer must surely acknowledge the force of the legal argument, and concede.

Friday, 28 June 2002

One of the experts I have been working with is Professor of Mathematics Ray Hill. He gives a paper at a conference organised by the Department of Child Health, University of Leicester.

In it he demolishes the statistics given by Meadow. His calculations show that, having had one cot death, the chance of a second is either $1:60$, or $1:400$. He asks the questions: How many instances of second SIDS can we expect a year in England and Wales? Answer: 7.68. Meadow told Sally's jury it could not happen more than once every hundred years. He goes on to say that if a tragic second death occurs, '. . . justice gets turned on its head and the mother is expected to prove her innocence. How can she do that when SIDS, by definition, is a death for which no adequate explanation can be found.'

Tuesday, 2 July 2002

The CCRC decision is 57 pages long, plus appendices. Its main thrust is the non-disclosure of the microbiology report containing a natural cause of death for Harry. But it goes on to make a number of new and interesting points none of us had thought of:

- The new medical evidence [Morris and Walters] undermines – so as potentially to destroy – the similar fact evidence, in particular the Crown's central argument that there was no natural cause of death for Harry;
- The Commission notes that, in evidence, Professor Green told the Court (on considering Christopher) 'there was nothing in the slides that I saw, or what Williams told me, to suggest that there was any natural disease present'. This was in direct contradiction to what Williams told the Court, i.e. that Christopher was suffering, at the very least, from pleurisy.
- Put bluntly, Mrs Clark would never have been charged with murder had not Harry died subsequently. If her conviction for Harry's murder is unsafe, then her conviction for the murder of Christopher must also be unsafe.
- The jury was seriously misled by Williams' answer to the jury question about blood tests on Harry.
- The police did not interview the Clarks until a month after Harry's death. Mr Clark's inaccurate recollection of the time of his arrival home could just as easily be attributed to the lapse of time as to a desire to mislead.
- The Commission has considered a report by Mr Edmund Smith which suggests that the sounding of the monitor alarm at night . . . would not have been due to any defect in the monitor.'

The CLRC concludes:

> The Commission considers that there is a real possibility that the Court of Appeal will find that the new medical evidence renders Mrs Clark's convictions unsafe. Accordingly both convictions are referred . . .

The language is conservative and conditional, but that is the nature of the CCRC, whose role is only investigative. This is the best possible result for Sally. It gives Spencer no room to manoeuvre. He will have to concede.

Sally is ecstatic:

> 'The relief is overwhelming. Yes. I do believe it. No I can't believe it – I can't believe that such an important document should have been kept

secret. But there is another relief – all I have ever wanted the experts to tell me is why my darling boys died. I thought I knew that Christopher died of a lung disease. That seems to be in doubt, but now the CCRC say pleurisy may have played a part. But with Harry, Steve and I now know why. We know he had a fatal infection. We know – fighter that he was – that he fought it; the polymorphs in the spinal fluid prove that. But most amazing of all is the certainty. Two well-qualified independent pathologists, both experts in this very narrow speciality, say with complete conviction: this is why Harry died. He wasn't shaken. He wasn't smothered. It was nothing you did or Steve did or failed to do. Lethal bacteria invaded his tiny body and try as he obviously did, he was no match for it. At last I can look forward to getting my life back.'

Steve has worked so hard for this moment. He has had to bring up Tom on his own, move house alone, apply for and secure a new high-powered job suited to his talents and experience; work his socks off in every spare minute, chasing every medical and other avenue for evidence to get his wife cleared of a miscarriage of justice that has led to her imprisonment for life.

That night, Steve lets the tears flow. He has held himself in for so long, mainly for Sally. He tells me:

'Our daily phone calls are the only things that keep her in touch with the real world. I have had to be staunch, unyielding in my faith that she will be freed, while all the time I am terrified by demons and doubts that anything would beat the system that had jailed her. I have been her only lifeline to sanity. Now some of that load has eased. This is not spurious science. It is not speculative theory. This is medical fact. Morris even says there can be no other cause of death: I have never heard a doctor say such a thing, so positively.'

Steve has had to be the anchor for Tom, and support for Frank, but now, at long last, after three years of misery and frustration it now seems it is finally going to be put right. 'And let there be no doubt,' he says. 'People are going to answer for what they did to my wife! But that can wait, just until I get my darling Sally back.'

It is frustrating that he cannot leap in a car and go straight to Bullwood

Hall and take her in his arms, tell her how much he loves her and bring her straight home. But it does not work like that and he knows it. He phones me and Frank and his friend Andy. He gets calls from radio, TV and newspaper journalists wanting comments. He does a gruelling round of television interviews. Sue Stapely is fantastic, getting unbelievable coverage all over the media.

Sue knows and admires Clare Montgomery QC, who she thinks is the best criminal lawyer at the Bar. I agree with her. Sue writes, urging her to take on Sally's advocacy. Mackey has never worked with her but is prepared to. He would want her junior to be Jim Gregory, a senior and experienced barrister, based in Manchester, with whom he has worked for years. We are all agreed that a new team of barristers is needed.

All my friends in the law tell me that Clare was the brightest brain of her generation at university and this will give Sally the best chance. Sally and Steve are both in favour. Mackey phones her clerk, who says she is in a case until October, and after that it is doubtful if she will be able to take on ours. I know somebody else who knows her: Charlie Benson, barrister son of Christopher and Jo Benson.

He and his barrister brother, Julian, grew up with Sally. Both are committed to her innocence. Charlie is a highly sought-after junior at the Criminal Bar. He recently recommended Clare Montgomery as his leader in a big case; in the event, he could not be her junior, which would have earned him a lot of money, because he was halfway through another case. Clare owes him. He will try to collect on the favour.

Journalist Sweeney is livid. The editor of *Panorama* has refused to commission a programme about Sally. 'She has been convicted by a jury and her appeal thrown out by the Court of Appeal.' Sweeney is more successful with BBC 2 and his programme, *Cot Deaths: The Witchhunt*, is broadcast tonight. 2 July. It is the product of the time and effort expended by all of us to ensure that it will focus as powerfully as possible on the real facts of Sally's case

Sweeney breaks the news of the failure to disclose the microbiology report, and this programme is the first to announce that the CCRC has referred Sally's case back to the Court of Appeal.

Sweeney cites a number of cases in which Meadow has given evidence that mothers have abused or poisoned or smothered their babies. In each case, Meadow's opinions were challenged. In one case – call it Baby Haynes (not its real name because it cannot be identified by court order) – the cause of a baby's death was disputed. One crucial piece of evidence related to the Glasgow Coma Scale, which is a means of measuring a baby's viability, its chances of survival in serious illness:

Sweeney: . . . the experts were divided. The majority thought the baby had died a natural death, but the precise cause was unknown. Sir Roy Meadow said the baby died because of the delayed effect of smothering . . . But by the time the parents left the hospital, that night, the baby scored 14 out of 15 on the Glasgow Coma Scale . . . How could the mother – by then at home – have killed the baby if he was improving? At first Professor Meadow was at a loss.

Meadow [*from transcript of the Family Court case*]: 14 is near normal and it does not fit in with the other observations. It is discrepant and I cannot explain it. I am not sure what she means by the Modified Glasgow Coma Scale. I am unfamiliar with using the scale on young children, and it certainly was not the practice in our hospital ['Jimmy's' in Leeds]. It sounds like a system that they have found helpful, rather than an internationally or indeed scientifically standardised test.

Sweeney continues his commentary:

Sweeney [*to camera*]: Dr Lorcan Duane is a consultant in paediatric medicine at Manchester Children's Hospitals. [*To Duane*]: How much do you rely on the Modified Glasgow Coma Score?

Duane: I would say . . .100 per cent, as an assessment of their coma level.

Sweeney: Would you be surprised that a paediatrician does not use the score?

Duane: I would find it hard to actually comprehend . . . on a busy A & E department it is used all the time for the appropriate children. It is a standard working tool in most paediatric emergency departments and most paediatric wards.

Sweeney [*to camera*]: The Modified Glasgow Coma Score is the standard test in children's hospitals around the world, and has been used in Sir Roy's old hospital, St James, in Leeds since 1996.

The judge in the Baby Haynes case did not know the truth. He accepted Meadow's opinion. When that mother's second baby was born, it was taken away at 25 minutes old. Mrs Haynes has never seen her daughter again and the child has now been adopted. This story is told another three times on BBC Television.

The CCRC decision to refer the case back to the Court of Appeal leads to a media frenzy and hours of extra work for Sue Stapely. Many bids for interview are rejected as not fitting the careful strategy we have agreed. She arranges radio and TV interviews for Steve, Frank and me with broadcasters all over the country.

The Key Turns

The CCRC decision is the talk of Bullwood Hall:

'Support and enthusiasm is high, and I feel sure now that I will be home for Christmas, because I am sure that there is no way the prosecution can or will oppose the appeal. Throughout this entire nightmare, we had retained the same solicitor, Mike Mackey, but we have agreed to change our barristers. I am thrilled when John Batt tells me Clare Montgomery has agreed to act for me with Jim Gregory in support.'

Thursday, 1 August 2002

Over two and a half years have slowly passed for Sally in jail. But at least now there is real hope and the days will begin to speed up.

Bevan makes a call to Clare Montgomery, offering to give evidence at Sally's new appeal, to explain his role. It is a generous and compassionate offer. It is a selfless gesture, typical of the high ethical and moral standards which guide this man's career. She gratefully declines his offer.

Clare Montgomery is short, her dark hair cropped, and is free of make-up. She wears spectacles and looks businesslike. She is wearing the legal uniform of a black suit. She makes me feel as if I know what I am talking about. It is a much-appreciated compliment.

She has already read everything and I suspect she has a photographic memory. She agrees that a new report by statistician Ray Hill should form the basis of a new ground of appeal. We discuss a number of other issues she wishes either Mackey or me to follow up. I ask her what she thinks of Sally's prospects:

'I shall be astonished if this appeal fails,' she tells me.

It doesn't look much, on the page; but when I hear it from her, it sounds more like fact than opinion.

The grounds of appeal make the most compelling and satisfying reading. Mackey files them with the court.

Spencer replies, almost immediately, with a 52-page skeleton argument. He has three experts who say our doctors are wrong: Harry did not die of any infection. The microbiology report was never concealed, it was with the prosecution papers throughout the trial and first appeal; the defence cannot complain now if they failed to ask for it.

Montgomery is not impressed, discounting the response as disingenuous, misleadng and untrue. The admission that the vital microbiology report was in the papers and yet it was not disclosed is astonishing in the light of the jury's repeated questions about Harry and the answers he and Williams gave the judge and jury.

Mackey is relaxed. The appeal is about two basic points of law: the failure to disclose that report, and Morris' and Walters' opinions giving a possible cause of death. 'If we focus on those we will win. We don't need to do any more,' he tells me.

Mackey is right, in law; but we have been here before, at the first Court of Appeal, with unanswerable grounds, and Sally wound up back in prison for life. I want two belts and three sets of braces to make sure that does not happen again. Steve and Frank agree. And then begins the most frenetic phase of our lives as all of us search the world for other experts to back up Morris and Walters.

Steve calls Professor Whitwell, who suggests that we contact Professor Roger Byard, who has written the leading textbook on Sudden Infant Death. Steve finds an address for him in Adelaide, Australia. Byard's book featured in another Williams case. The book contained 20-year-old research contradicting Williams' opinion about a heart condition from which a dentist's young patient suffered. She died.

Professor David says there are other experts we can go to for an opinion on the microbiology report.

I call Byard, who is a forensic pathologist, and give him brief details of the microbiology report. He says: 'If I find *Staph. aureus* in two sites, I know I have a probable cause of death; if I find it in three, I know I have an actual cause of death. In eight, with polymorphs in the CSF, it is game set and match!'

I send him an expensive mountain of paper by courier.

Dr Sam Gullino is a forensic pathologist in Florida, working for the state, who has only ever given evidence for the prosecution. David warns me about him: 'He is forthright in his opinions. If he does not like what he sees in the medicine, you will be in for trouble.' The American doctor is pleasant, highly complimentary about David's skills but non-committal about Harry Clark. He tells me he works for the prosecution. He once did a report for a defence team but heard nothing further from them. I get the message that he will be a hard man to convince, but still say I would like to send him the papers. He promises to give them priority – as a favour to Tim David.

My PA, Helen, hits the photocopier again and the courier takes away another expensive package.

Both reports come back saying that there is no doubt that Harry died of natural causes.

Steve tells me he has been talking to an expert in *Staph. aureus*, Dr Jenkins at Leicester University. I give a brief explanation of the microbiology to Dr Jenkins. This is right where his research is at the moment. He will write a report. Another package goes off by post.

Mackey has his hands full with all the written paperwork that goes with an appeal. Hundreds of pages have to be checked and copied several times.

Steve persuades Professor Jean Golding, who gave evidence at the Cannings trial, to write a long report on the Meadow statistics.

I ask Montgomery how much medical evidence she is prepared to read, because I have files stuffed full of papers and studies on SIDS from three years of working through the world's writers on the subject. She says: 'Send me every report you can get.'

Mackey briefs Whitwell and Rushton on the microbiology. They write reports for him. Microbiologist Caroline Blackwell writes a further report, commenting on what the prosecution experts are saying. It is positive and on our side.

I contact professor Peter Fleming at Bristol University who has already been in touch with Frank, voicing his concerns over Sally's conviction. He is the UK's leading authority on SIDS and the first author of the CESDI Report. He writes a report for us supporting bacterial infection as the cause of Harry's death.

Then a new 'bombshell explodes' on my desk: Professor Tom Meade's report. He says vaccination could have killed Harry!

I tell him what all the other experts are saying. He says, not unreasonably, that his expertise is vaccination, and he has no doubt that the pertussis vaccine could have killed the baby. But a cause of death is not an exact science; it can only, ever, be a matter of opinion. If the vaccine did not kill Harry, it would have exacerbated the effect of the bacteria.

The prosecution then begin serving us with more reports of their three experts and this leads to the most time-consuming, stressful and hectic part of the case. Every report has to be read by Clare Montgomery and Mackey, and by every other expert. Each has to write a report on that report, and the recipient has to write a new report on that report. Each report we file leads to the prosecution experts shifting their ground, requiring further reports from all of ours. The permutations drive us to distraction. Through all of this I keep Steve, Sally, Mackey and Sue informed of what's going on, so that they can help with the bits of the jigsaw for which they are responsible. We all e-mail and talk to each other virtually every day – often late at night, when travelling, and usually when tired out.

Dr Glyn Walters, in Salisbury, is bombarded with reports: the subject is at the heart of his fifty years' medical experience as a chemical pathologist. He works non-stop and full time for months. His reports now top 100 pages.

Clare Montgomery and Jim Gregory have a conference at Bullwood Hall with Sally. She is nonplussed when Gregory says: 'You must have known you would be convicted.'

Sally does not know what he is talking about. 'You are an intelligent woman. You must have worked out that no jury would vote against odds of 73 million to one!'

Sally is not persuaded:

'That was not the way of my thinking at all. The statistic had nothing to do with me. We never said we had two cot deaths. So it had no relevance. That, for me, was a complete answer, both to the statistic and to a jury reaction. OK, I was also so convinced that I could not be found guilty because nobody murdered my babies.

'I had complete faith in Julian Bevan. I recognised his commitment and I relied on him totally. I still believe that nobody could have done more to secure my acquittal. Clare is quite different. There are no mannerisms, she is neither over-confident nor apprehensive. She is very bright, but carries her intellectual brilliance with charming modesty. When she tells me that legally, the appeal must succeed; that which Spencer has produced has no effect on what the law says about withholding the microbiology report and the cause of death it reveals, I believe her.

'I have high hopes of being home for Tom's birthday in November and, of course, for Christmas, my most favourite time of the year. I shall be able to spend it with my little boy for the first time.'

Friday, 1 November 2002

I visit Sally at Bullwood Hall. She has now served eight days short of three years in prison. I have good news, but also some bad. Sally is more impressed by the bad:

'I shall never forget John Batt's visit. In actual fact, he has come with considerable good news at the progress of the appeal and the new medical evidence, but it all seems irrelevant in my eyes. The devastation at being told I shall not be home for Christmas supersedes any good news. I cry so much that I frighten John Batt. I feel so sorry for the poor chap; he has come to the prison to give me good news, but for the timing, and has not anticipated my reaction. When he starts talking about bail – because there might be a possibility of getting out, pending the hearing of the appeal – I get angry. I will not walk out of this place until I am declared innocent. Nor am I prepared to run the slightest risk of having to come back in here again, however remote that risk may be.

'I sob and sob until I can sob no more. When I go back to the wing in that state, everybody assumes that my appeal has failed.'

Bail is an option open to her and only she can make that decision. Montgomery is pleased with her refusal to apply for it, mainly because it would mean talking about her tactics in advance, giving the strategy away to Spencer. Then there is the psychology of an appeal. An appellant in jail, arriving in the sweat box, is, even to judges, a more poignant figure than someone living at home on bail.

This delay is, in effect, another miscarriage of justice, sentencing Sally to further months of imprisonment unjustly. The lawyers for the prosecution must know that, in law, these convictions are unsafe. If a jury hears 57 untrue denials of infection on the most important issue at a murder trial – no Court of Appeal will uphold the conviction. I have no quarrel with lawyers who express views about the law that differ from mine. I condemn views that any lawyer should know are wrong. The prosecuting lawyers' refusal to acknowledge the obvious strength of the legal argument against them, in effect, imposed that additional sentence on Sally. They should be called to account for it.

Christmas 2002 is probably the most difficult for Sally – even bearing in mind the first one at Styal:

'I can sum it up by saying that it is the first year that Tom can really understand the magic of Christmas. John Batt has told me that my appeal will now be heard on 28 January 2003. But I have been scarred so much in the past, and I know – whatever John says – that there are no guarantees; there is nothing anyone can say that can console me. It is a miserable Christmas, but yet again, Susie and I get each other through it.

'It is strange. In 2000, going to appeal, I had no doubts; I was going home. As we know, that was not to be. Here we are in 2002, with a far stronger appeal, and yet I feel somehow that, no matter what we produce in court, nothing will get me out of this place. The situation between Spencer and me has become personal. Why is he trying so hard to keep me here? It seems ironic that I now have far less confidence that we will win.

'My legal team are all incredibly optimistic, but can I take what they say at face value, given what happened last time? I can't be sure. I try to appear calm and optimistic in prison; only Sue B. is privy to my misgivings. Surely it couldn't happen a second time, surely they couldn't deny me this! The date of the appeal is her birthday, which we feel is a positive omen. Even if my legal team are right, I may still face a retrial. Will I be able to handle that? Letters from supporters continue to come in from all over the country and abroad.'

Thursday, 21 November 2002

I fly to Manchester for a conference with Jim Gregory, Clare Montgomery's junior barrister. In his fifties, he is a large, greying man, with a wise smile of experienced compassion on his face. I immediately take to him.

He is talking to Mackey and Steve about statistics as I walk through the door:

Gregory: Any criminal barrister knows that if you mention odds of 100 to 1 to a jury, the case is lost. Spencer would have known it; but why should he care if neither the judge nor Bevan objected? The jury should never have heard it.

We review the evidence in the new appeal for three hours. Gregory advises no hasty optimism. There is a long way to go:

Gregory: Every appeal is a lottery. It depends so much on the constitution of the court. They hate overturning juries' verdicts. You must take nothing for granted. Every effort must continue to be made to seal any possible loopholes. I have been against Spencer many times. He is ruthless and tenacious; he is also obsessive about detail. Get one detail wrong and he will be all over you.

The weeks run away as Steve, Frank, Mackey, Clare, Jim Gregory, my PA, Helen, and I work all the hours, and make and take continual telephone calls with experts and others. Glyn Walters seems tied to my umbilical cord!

The website continues to generate all manner of offers of help and messages of love and support to Sally and Steve from other parents, also tragically bereaved. The media interest continues unabated. Sue Stapely visits Sally in prison with Steve and Tom to help prepare her for the appeal hearing and the inevitable media deluge, whatever the outcome.

Sally – with help from Sue Stapely – has drafted a statement she hopes to be strong enough to read if the appeal succeeds. She also wants another, in case she is not successful. It would be tempting providence not to prepare for the worst. Sally makes Sue promise that she will stand beside her outside the court and be ready to read her statement for her if her courage or voice fails her. She wants her words read by a woman, not by a man.

Sally has now counted down the 1,100 days of her three-year imprisonment.

Friday, 10 January 2003

At Mackey's office in Manchester there is a conference with Montgomery and Morris. The morning is spent scanning paperwork dealing with the latest allegation from the prosecution: that the microbiology report was disclosed to the defence in the unused material.

This is a serious allegation. It is the duty of the defence to examine all unused material. Spencer is now claiming that Mackey's failure to ask for it means that the appeal must fail, because it is a mistake by the defence. The idea that an innocent woman could spend the rest of her life in jail because of such a technicality may strike some as a mockery of justice. But it could happen.

Mackey has carried out a detailed investigation of the unused material, with the police present at which each side had witnesses. Every piece of paper was examined, with meticulous care not to disturb their sequence. At the end, the police officers agreed that the microbiology report was not in the unused material disclosed to Mackey. And so another false allegation by the prosecution is nailed.

Professor Morris joins us in the afternoon. Montgomery goes through his report with him, making sure she understands the nuances of his opinion.

Mackey has now filed with the court, and served on the prosecution, reports from eleven experts – the joint effort of Mackey, Steve and me – each a leading specialist in Sudden Infant Death, supporting the opinion that Harry died of natural causes.

The prosecution has responded with three experts. Reports from Keeling, who gave evidence for the Crown at trial, and two new experts, saying that Harry did not die from septicaemia or meningitis.

Monday, 20 January 2003

I visit Sally to brief her on what will happen at her appeal on 28 January.

Will it be the last time?

Until now, I have always played the optimist; that is my nature. I think it is a reaction to my mother, who was sure that, if the end of the world did not come tomorrow, it was certain to come the day after. Every time I have been optimistic with Sally, I have been proved wrong. So, against all my instincts, I urge Sally to take the appeal one day at a time: 'Make no assumptions. Control your hope. There is every reason to believe we will win. Clare – and I refuse to believe there is a better lawyer anywhere – says the appeal must succeed.'

The Court of
Appeal – Again

Tuesday, 28 January 2003

The Royal Courts of Justice are awash with cameras and reporters. Court Number 5 is the majestic oak-panelled room where we were before, in July and October 2000, with such disastrous consequences. Are we in for a repeat performance?

Steve feels worse than he did last time we were here:

'We have an even stronger appeal than the first one. In Clare, we have the best barrister we could wish for and Sue has ensured a vast amount of positive publicity. Yet I am still terribly afraid. My naïve faith in British justice was destroyed by the first Court of Appeal. Had they made up their minds – from the outset – not to free Sally, but instead to believe the reputations of the prosecution experts and protect the sanctity of the jury system.

But there is hope this time. Mrs Justice Hallett made it plain, when sentencing Angela Cannings, that she did not know why she was imposing a life sentence, as Angela presented no threat to anybody, least of all her family. I read that as saying she believed the jury got it wrong. Her presence on this appeal bench gives me hope.

Yet I am still frightened, particularly by the way Spencer has behaved since the CCRC decision. The first court hung on his every word. Will he manage to make these judges do that? And his experts have changed their positions so many times in the last six months, it is almost unbelievable. Spencer has caused Sally to serve more months of imprisonment filing Skeleton Arguments that seem to me to fly in the face of the obvious law. He must surely know Sally's convictions are unsafe.

'I have confidence in Clare. Her Skeleton Argument is a masterpiece and yet . . . and yet . . . If it goes wrong this time, then all hope is abandoned. We are at the mercy of this bench of judges. They can put right the terrible wrong done to Sally or they can destroy my family forever. There will be no turning back – it is our last chance. If we lose here, Sally will be in jail for the rest of her life: there is no way she will ever make a lying confession just to get out. My family will cease to exist. But for Tom my heart cries out to him. He is not yet old enough to understand the lies they have told about his mum, but any day now he will and others will, too. What other children will say to him is too worrying to think about.'

Frank is beside me. He does not know if he will be able to sit it through, he is so nervous. Sue Stapely, immediately behind me, is armed with briefing material for the press. Steve is next to her. Again they hold hands. Mackey stands by the door, as usual, waiting for a quick exit to have a cigarette. Jo Benson is in the back row. Martin Bell, who has continued to work for Sally, long after he ceased to be a Member of Parliament, is there, as is Pauline Pullen and many other friends and supporters.

We all rise and bow as the judges take their places.

Lord Justice John Kay – whose son, Ben, plays rugby for England – is a large man who looks as if he could acquit himself well in physical contact sports. He has a fearsome reputation for not suffering fools. I wonder how he will deal with Spencer. Even more intriguing is how he will treat Clare – as an intellectual equal?

Mr Justice Holland is an older, grey-haired man of whom I know nothing. I don't know why, but I quite like the look of him. He has a kindly face.

The third judge is Mrs Justice Heather Hallett. She and Sue Stapely have known each other for years on the legal circuit. Sue maintains that she is fair and sensible – as every judge should be.

Mrs Justice Hallett's involvement is an extraordinary coincidence; and it can only be a coincidence. When, at Sally's first appeal, Mrs Justice Bracewell appeared on the bench, I thought it was deliberate policy to use judges with experience of the Family Division in appeals on baby-murder cases: it would seem sensible. But I was assured it was impossible: the choice of judges has to be random; whoever happens to be available. The length of all cases is unpredictable. It would be a nightmare to try to choose any panel of judges in advance.

There are not many judges who have tried mothers for what John Sweeney has described as 'imaginary murders'. Mrs Justice Hallett has already tried a case that may well be a miscarriage of justice; is she about to play her part in putting right another?

The courtroom is packed, the press benches full to overflowing. Sharon Patrick is there. So is Joshua Rozenberg of the *Daily Telegraph* with Margarette Driscoll of the *Sunday Times*. Sweeney is perched on the end of the bench. He looks up at me expectantly. For other journalists, it is standing room only.

Sally enters with a guard. She is wearing black and looks pale and tiny in that huge courtroom. She looks, finds Steve and mouths an endearment. She smiles at me, then disappears as she sits. I look at the top of her head.

Spencer is still determined to fight it all the way.

Montgomery: For three years after the death of Harry Clark, Sally's lawyers believed there was no evidence of any infection or natural cause of death. But there was evidence of infection, which had been known to Dr Williams since February 1998. He had kept the results secret from Sally Clark and her advisers.

This is a clear case of non-disclosure, which has caused a serious miscarriage of justice. In all likelihood, he died suddenly, in reaction to the *Staph. aureus* bacteria with which his stomach, lungs and spinal fluid were riddled. It is obvious that these results should not have been kept secret and had they been made known at trial, Sally Clark would never have been convicted of the murder of Harry or his brother Christopher.

It is a matter of regret that the prosecution has failed to accept that there has been material non-disclosure and that, instead, an attempt has been made to minimise those results. This has wholly failed. Each of the prosecution experts has conceded that it is possible Harry died in this way; the only disagreement is the degree of likelihood of that possibility.

She then deals in great detail with the law and the medicine, but Justice Kay interrupts her:

Kay: There has been considerable media interest in this case and we have a number of members of the press here. Could I ask you to deal with these matters in non-technical language, so that the public can more readily understand what the appeal is about?
Montgomery: Of course, my lord.

And without a pause she changes gear, to the language of the layman.

I am impressed with this. I know how much time and effort she has put into her opening: not only the countless hours of reading everything that has the remotest bearing on the appeal, but she must also have drafted and re-drafted every word. To be able to switch to colloquial language is a mark of the serious advocate she is.

Mr Justice Holland interrupts:

Holland: Is the non-disclosure admitted?
Montgomery: Yes, my lord.
Holland: And it is material?
Montgomery: Yes, my lord.
Holland: Isn't that an end of the matter?
Montgomery: I believe so, my lord, but I think my learned friend may have something to say about that.

Mr Justice Holland has just confirmed our understanding of the law and the prosecution's unreasonable prevarication leading to this appeal.

Spencer nods vigorously.

Has one of the judges made up his mind that this appeal must succeed? What about the others?

It is agreed, between counsel and the court, that the issues will be narrowed to non-disclosure, the materiality of the microbiology document and therefore the credibility of the possible cause of death, which means the credibility of the experts propounding it. It is agreed that only one witness will give evidence for each side.

Steve lets out a big breath: 'They are not against us – that's the most important thing. I believe they are on our side. Dare I hope . . . ?'

Montgomery continues her trawl of the grounds leading to what she says is the inevitable conclusion that both convictions must be unsafe. When Montgomery is talking about the jury's questions relating to blood tests, Spencer interrupts:

Spencer: The jury only asked the question about haemosiderosis in relation to Harry. I'm not suggesting that the defence experts are not reputable, but it's only theory.
Kay: You may have a hard job persuading us that it is not genuine.

Montgomery goes on to say that non-disclosure must have been deliberate; the prosecution must have asked such questions as 'Are there any test results for Harry that have not been disclosed?' They must have been told, wrongly, that there were not. The Police Authority, in April 1999, gave an assurance to Mackey that all autopsy reports had been disclosed. The responsibility for that lies with Dr Williams. His claim, to the meeting of experts, that there was no evidence of infection in Harry was untrue. His present position is equally incredible. As to a retrial, Montgomery quotes Dr Byard:

'The Clark brothers demonstrate difficulties that may arise if cases are not fully investigated with all the results clearly summarised. Trying to clarify circumstances of death at a later stage may simply not be feasible due to a wide variety of possibilities other than inflicted injury.'
Montgomery: In addition, the prosecution chose, for forensic reasons, to introduce and emphasise after conviction, and at the first appeal, the suggestion that Sally Clark was abusing alcohol. Not only was the evidence introduced without any defence opportunity to challenge it, but it also served no purpose other than ensuring maximum publicity, the trial judge having ruled that alcohol played no part in the deaths of the children. There must be considerable doubt whether these irrelevant factors may not be so widely imprinted on the public consciousness as to jeopardise a fair trial. In which circumstances it would not be an appropriate case in which to order a retrial.

Montgomery calls Morris. In his fifties, grey-haired, an open, slightly ruddy complexion, and with reasonableness written all over him, he is impossible to dislike. In a soft, almost musical voice, he gives a comprehensive review of his investigation of the medical possibilities and concludes: 'The most likely cause of Harry's death is *Staph. aureus* septicaemia . . . in other words, meningitis, which can cause sudden death . . . It was most likely a sudden circulatory collapse.'

The court adjourns overnight. Montgomery makes no application for bail for Sally, who has to travel back to Bullwood Hall in the sweat box.

Sweeney and his production team adjourn to the pub, with Steve and his friends. Sally calls him on his mobile. She cannot believe it when Steve says: 'You're coming home tomorrow, my love.'

'At Bullwood Hall, nobody expects to see Sally again. I walk down the corridor, open Susie's door and say: "The things I do to be with my friend on her birthday!" I can't quite believe it, but by this stage everyone is indicating that the appeal is a foregone conclusion. It is just a question of whether I shall face a retrial. When I leave Bullwood Hall the next morning, Susie and I sense that I will never return.'

Spencer's only hope of winning this appeal is to prove that Morris' theory is so off-the-wall, and his reputation so controversial, that it is not credible. Instead, to astonishment on our side, Spencer cross-examines Morris on the viability of his theory of Harry's meningitis. Morris is one of very few experts on this quite narrow subject; every question Spencer puts to him, Morris answers effortlessly, proving the very expertise that Spencer should be trying to destroy. What does Spencer think he is achieving?

Dr Nigel Klein is a consultant paediatric microbiologist. He sits next to my PA. He is small and round. Klein goes into the witness box and takes the oath. Extraordinarily, he removes his jacket and stands before the judges in a black open-necked shirt. He has eighteen years' qualified experience. He gives a highly technical explanation as to why Harry could not have died of meningitis, or toxic shock or *Staph. aureus* septicaemia – basically because the expected symptoms are not present. There is no sign of infection to the naked eye or under the microscope, and there was simply not enough time for any fatal disease to overwhelm Harry's immune system and kill him.

Montgomery cross-examines him with lethal acuity. She puts to him that all the early signs of meningitis were, in fact, present in Harry: off his feed – the empty stomach proves that; evidence of vomit on Steve's shoulder when he picked him up; and Harry was unusually lethargic and sleepy for several hours before death. Klein is astonished. The prosecution had not give him any of this information.

Eventually and reluctantly, Klein agrees.

That is a 'cool' piece of advocacy. To get a microbiologist to make the one admission he has been called to refute, required exceptional skill.

Mrs Justice Hallett tells Klein that she understands that he is a specialist in illness in children but queries if he is an expert in Sudden Infant Death. He says he is not.

Lord Justice Kay tells Spencer that as Williams is the man who failed to disclose the material document, and has been heavily criticised by counsel for Sally for 'keeping it secret' from all the other experts and the jury, he should have the opportunity to come to court to explain himself. Otherwise the court may feel obliged to criticise him.

The court adjourns.

Spencer has a big problem. If Williams comes to court and gives evidence, Montgomery will attack him as the main, if not only, cause of Sally's wrongful conviction and imprisonment. There is no knowing where cross-examination might lead, or what other unfortunate matters Montgomery might get him to disclose, if he feels too much blame is being heaped on him.

As the remains of both babies have now been cremated, there is no way another post-mortem can be carried out to prove or disprove meningitis; and alcohol, which played no part in either death, has been widely publicised. A fair new trial is therefore not possible. Will Spencer accept the inevitable, at long last?

After two hours, the court reconvenes. Spencer rises:

Spencer: My lords, Dr Williams has decided not to appear as a witness.
Kay: So be it.
Spencer: . . . And my lord, the prosecution no longer seeks to uphold these
   convictions.

Kay: Very well, Mr Spencer. That leaves the matter of a retrial.

Spencer: I have spoken to my learned friend, and we have agreed that a fair trial would be difficult, as there are no remains of Harry Clark to enable further tests for meningitis. The Crown does not seek a retrial.

Steve punches the air and mouths 'I love you' at Sally. He is trying to stop the tears. Many journalists are also openly weeping, as are the Clarks' many friends who have travelled to court to give them both their support. My handkerchief appears to be wet.

But inside, Steve is different. 'It is something towards which we'd been building for so long and I thought that by this point I would be highly emotional. I half realise I am crying and yet I feel strangely removed from everything going on around me. I suppose I have been exhausted by the whole process. In the end it was such a formality, there was no great clap of thunder or pronouncement. It is very confusing.'

Sally knows from Steve giving her the thumbs up repeatably – that she is free and that she does not face the horror of another trial. But she is confused. Is it really all over? Is it OK to stop feeling numb? Will she *ever* stop feeling numb? The key to the gates of five years of hell – the Golden Key – has just been turned by three learned judges who have given her permission to rejoin the world, and her family. Her thought is: 'Dare I believe it?'

Lord Justice Kay delivers a brief judgment. The full written reasons will come later.

Kay: . . . most of the so-called similar facts do not point in any way to guilt. They are conditions that would apply to any mother at any time. The two cases should not have been heard together. The statistic 1:73 million is clearly inadmissible in law, could not have failed to mislead the jury, and should never have been allowed in evidence. Had that point been argued before us, we might well have found it a sufficient ground, on its own, to make these convictions unsafe. Dr Williams is responsible for failing to disclose a material document, which must have affected the outcome of the trial and is a serious matter. The appeal is allowed, with costs. There will be no retrial.

The judges retire.

It takes two hours for the formalities to be completed – the Court has to fax the prison; they have to acknowledge by fax; then formal permission is given to set Sally free:

'Everyone is in very high spirits but I am not. The Group 4 staff are really pleased. When the fax arrives from Bullwood Hall it carries a message from the Governor: "We all knew you would do it, Sal." Group 4 have never seen such a thing before.

'Clare Montgomery comes to see me. I ask her, "Are you sure that's it?" She tells me it is. After she has left, I become very emotional because I forgot to thank her properly.

"As I come up from the cell, I find Steve, Frank and three of our friends. One of them, Andy, is shaking and crying. I am asked by Sue Stapely if I can manage a statement for the press. I think the adrenalin must have started work because I say yes, although I have no confidence in my ability to do anything at this moment.

'I did not expect anything like the number of cameras which were outside the court or the police cordons to control the crowds. Journalists are shouting "Smile!" They don't understand. I say to Steve: "I can't smile I don't want to celebrate." We've lost two precious babies. We can't celebrate that! I can't see it as a victory of any sort. I am told I can say anything I want, to the cameras. This is the first time for three years I have been allowed to say anything not controlled by my legal team or the Prison Service.'

For Sue Stapely, this is the culmination of one of the most sustained and successful media campaigns; hardly a week or day has passed, in over two years, when there has not been an article, news item, feature or leader, every one initiated by her.

Clare Montgomery, the architect of this success, has disappeared. She does not like the limelight.

Sally's father, Frank, who has been unwavering in his support for his daughter, stands to one side, out of camera range; he does not want to steal any of his daughter's thunder. His has been a traumatic experience that no father should be put through. That he is a retired, very senior police officer heaped the humiliation on him in a way that would not have applied to anybody else. That he has emerged relatively unscathed is a tribute to his staunch belief that, ultimately, the justice system would prevail, and to his own strong character.

Steve is a man in a million. I do not know how he has kept his rage under control. He has had to keep himself sane, hold down one of the most demanding jobs in the law and maintain his wife's spirits, in the depths of her despair, chase up countless leads to Sally's Golden Key, bring up his son without a mother – and has remembered to send his wife a single rose every three weeks for over thirty-six months. His hair, which went grey when Sally was first charged, makes him look older than his forty years. A crowd has assembled in the main hall of the Law Courts while Sally is processed out. Frank, Steve, Sue and I wait outside the cells while Sally's belongings are put into black plastic sacks and handed out to us.

Sue orchestrates the crowd of print journalists inside the building and advises Sally to let them hear her statement free of traffic noise and camera shutters.

Sally is a remarkable woman. She went from the 'lowest of the low' in prison, to become one of the most respected people in Bullwood Hall, holding down a responsible officer's job without once proclaiming her innocence. Her instinct and character alone worked the magic. Uniquely, the stops were pulled out by officialdom, to prevent her suffering time in Holloway during her appeal. Never once did she contemplate suicide or pleading guilty to a lesser offence to gain her freedom. Even now, she will not condemn those who put her through this hell. Only an exceptionally strong and brave soul could have achieved that. Today, her prison pallor is clearly visible, the pain of her ordeal is deepset in her eyes.

We all walk through the Great Hall into the open air and the waiting mass of cameras and even more journalists anxious to capture every moment of this now world-wide story.

Sally emerges on the steps of the Courts. Mike Mackey stands proudly beside her for the best moment of his professional career. The flashes from the cameras are dazzling but, calmly and quietly, Sally reads her own words into a dozen microphones:

'Today is not a victory. We are not victorious. There are no winners here. We have all lost out. We simply feel relief that our nightmare is finally at an end. We are now back in the position we should have been in all along and plead that we may now be allowed some privacy to grieve for our little boys in peace and try to make sense of what has happened to us.

'I would like to thank the hundreds of people who have written to me since my conviction to offer me their support. These letters have been my lifeline, a source of great comfort, especially during my blacker times, and I have read and re-read every one. Not only is it incredibly kind and thoughtful of people to take the time and trouble to write to me, but a number of them have been courageous enough to share very personal memories and relive painful experiences in the hope that it might be of some help. I told them that one day their faith in me would be seen to have been justified. That day has come.'

Television news cameras are taking this, live, from Fleet Street, as Sally battles against the noise of the traffic only feet away. It is beamed on BBC News 24 and Sky News around the world. It is the lead story on all the news bulletins and on the front page of every paper. Sally continues:

'I would like to thank the Governor, staff and inmates of Bullwood Hall prison, for their compassion and understanding. Be in no doubt, it was a tough experience to be in prison, but the support that I received whilst I was there made it much more bearable. They say that friendships are often forged in the most unlikely situations. I leave behind a number of acquaintances and two close friends who have lived every moment of this ordeal with me. I would not have made it this far without them. It would not be appropriate to mention them by name. They know who they are, but my promise to one of them that I will do all I can to ensure that justice is done for her as it has been done for me today, still stands. I will never forget them.'

Sally wavers for just a moment. Steve strengthens his grip on her shoulder. She glances at him and continues:

'I would like to say a particular thank you to my legal team: Mike Mackey of Burton Copeland, and John Batt, my solicitors, without whose tireless hard work, commitment in the face of adversity, and ceaseless belief in my innocence, none of this would have been possible. Clare Montgomery QC for her amazing grasp of the detail of my case and her peerless advocacy. Marilyn Stowe for helping us trace that crucial medical report. The same goes for Sue Stapely and David McKay who kept the world informed of the injustice I had suffered and whose advice and guidance were invaluable throughout. There are so many others, too numerous to mention. I only hope that they will not be offended that I haven't mentioned them all by name. Each one deserves my personal thanks.'

Steve has not seen Sally's speech, which she wrote and Sue Stapely helped her with:

'It is very moving. I cannot count the number of press. I had not expected such a huge crowd, so many cameras. I knew Sue would do her best to get the maximum coverage but this is beyond anything either of us could have imagined.'

Sally continues:

'I am also grateful to the members of the Solicitors' Disciplinary Tribunal, who in May 2001 had the courage and sufficient faith in me to allow me to remain on the Solicitors' Roll, and offered me the first glimmer of hope for many months.

'Thank you also to all my friends out there, many of whom have been in court today, who have shown me unwavering and unconditional support and loyalty. It would have been understandable perhaps for them to have written to me, when all this first happened, but then to have felt that they had done all they could and that it was time to move on. But no, they have been at my side throughout. Their friendship means so much.'

Sally takes a deep breath to steady herself and then carries on:

'The same goes for my family and, in particular, my dad. For as long as I can remember, I have always wanted him to be proud of me and have tried to live my life respectful of those in authority and in accordance with the morals and values taught to me by my parents as a child. Despite my innocence, there have been times throughout all of this when I have felt that I have let him down in some way. Yet he has stood by me, and not only that, worked tirelessly, alongside my legal team, to secure my release. Not what he had planned for his retirement. I only hope that he is proud of me today. I am certainly proud of him.

Finally, my husband, Steve, who together with our little boy, is my life. He has stood by me and supported me throughout this whole nightmare, not through blind love or unthinking loyalty, but because he knows me better than anyone else and knows how much I loved our babies. He has been my rock and I love him now more than ever. Being separated from him for so long has been a living hell. Being deprived of three years of being a mum to our little boy has been even worse. And yet somehow, despite our separation and against all the odds, we have managed to remain a family and stay close. My little boy knows that he has a mummy and a daddy who love him very much and love each other very much and that's what counts.

'May we now be allowed the privacy to rebuild our lives, to move forward and to learn to be a proper family again.'

Freedom

Journalists are frequently portrayed as intimidating, uncaring snoopers, only interested in the sensational soundbite and then on to the next tragedy to turn into a story. Why then are there so many handkerchiefs in evidence today? They can't all be those belonging to Sally's friends. The truth is that journalists are sons and daughters and mothers and fathers. What happened to Sally could have happened to any one of them if they had had two tragedies like Sally's. They cry that there has been a happy ending – if ever the deaths of two babies can have such a closure. A mother who did nothing but love her baby sons more than life itself, is now known to be innocent! And they will tell the world. She has been freed from a life in hell behind bars, and given a second chance to be like them – normal; part of her family. Sally even spots a policeman holding back the crowd but surreptitiously wiping away a tear. They go back into the Great Hall of the Law Courts.

At the back door, a taxi is waiting. Sally and Steve watch a journalist on a motorbike follow them. Steve explains the problem to the driver. He spots a policeman and draws up alongside. The policeman nods. He waves down the motorcyclist and gets out his notebook. Sally and Steve were going to a friend's flat in north London but change their minds and go to the home Sally has never known:

'Flowers begin arriving There are eighteen bouquets in the kitchen and

nine next door. I am fretting about vases. I find it overwhelming –
again! I do not want to watch television. I confess to being disappointed
in our new home. It is so different from beautiful Hope Cottage, in
Wilmslow. Many of my things are still in storage because there is not
enough space. It is disconcerting to find my belongings in places where
I would not have put them. It doesn't feel like home, in spite of all the
effort Steve has put into it.

'The following morning I insist on going to Tesco's. I tell Steve that
if I do not do it now, I never will. The adrenalin is still keeping me
going. All I want to do is push a trolley round a supermarket and buy
things for myself. I look at newspapers and see my own face staring back
at me. I do not know it at this moment, but it is going to get more, not
less, difficult to go out into the real world.'

I phone Steve's mobile. Sally answers; the first time in three years I have
been able to call Sally. I ask her where she is:

Sally: Tesco's, and do you know what?
Me: No.
Sally: Nobody recognises me. Isn't that wonderful!

Sally has a constant fear of recognition.

Two days later, Steve travels to his parents' home to pick up Tom, who is
now four years old. Sally can't wait to see him and his reaction to his
mother being at home and not her 'other home'.

'The press are gathered outside. I ask them what they are there for. They
say they are waiting for Tom. I tell them the court has forbidden any
photos of him. They know that. They just want to see him arrive.
Amazing! I tell Steve on the mobile. He tells me to call the police to
make them go away. I can't do that. I am sure they will leave as soon as
they have seen him come back home to me. I tell Steve not to cover
Tom's head in a blanket – to let him walk in normally.

'The taxi arrives. Steve and Tom get out. The press stand by, watch
and then go away.

'Tom walks into the house, sees me and says 'Are you my
surprise?'

'I ask him if that is OK. He says: "Yes. Can I have some juice?" His normality is wonderful.

'He does sometimes ask about Mummy's other home, but this is usually when I am making arrangements to visit my friend Susie, who is still at Bullwood Hall.'

In its Written Reasons for quashing Sally's conviction, the Court of Appeal says:

'We discount the possibility that Dr Williams deliberately concealed the information that Harry died of natural causes . . . We gave Dr Williams the opportunity to give evidence and explain his apparent shortcomings, but he did not avail himself of that opportunity. His statement of 5 September 2002 said:

'It is not my practice to refer to additional results in my post mortem unless they are releavant to the cause fo death, as the specimens were referred to another consultant.'

We find that explanation wholly unacceptable . . .

A terrible lethargy creeps up on Sally:

Everything is new. I find it difficult to unlearn habits developed in prison. I put letters in the postbox without sealing them; every letter I wrote there was read by them. Going shopping is not the pleasure I expected – it is the huge choice; the range of decisions is too difficult to cope with. I am drained by it. Large groups of people are frightening. I avoid them.

'I do go to a Woman of the Year lunch and an awards ceremony but the main reaction is bewilderment. There were more people in the Royal Lancaster Hotel than I had seen in three and a half years. I become very quiet and take a back seat in everything.

'Trains and tubes are difficult. I feel like a schoolgirl being taken to London for a treat. There is a sense of being naughty if I am not home by 10.30 p.m. The whole world is so huge. As time has gone by since my release, things have got worse, not better. In the first few weeks I seemed to be adjusting well. Now I am devastated that I seem to be going backwards. I have to stop what I am doing, over and over. I can't cope.

'I am still very concerned about people recognising me. I don't think, for a moment, that 100 per cent of people think I'm innocent – after all the things that were said about me in the press, when I was convicted. People remember these things. From my perspective, I have never really proved my innocence. John Batt tells me that that is every innocent person's reaction. Because of the way the legal system works, appeal judges do not say "We proclaim Sally Clark innocent of all crimes". They just say "Her convictions are unsafe". But John tells me that it amounts to the same thing, in law; only last year the Court of Appeal confirmed that anybody whose conviction is quashed is, in effect, declared innocent; every citizen is presumed innocent unless convicted of some crime. Is that what everybody thinks? Ordinary people?

'I do not recognise myself now compared to the confident and assured new mum/lawyer I was in 1996. I am a different person.

'I left Tom a baby. When I returned to him he was a toddler. We bonded through breast-feeding, my contact when he was with foster carers and in prison visits. But my natural instinct, as a mother, has been bred out of me by my time away from him. Quite soon after my release, Tom had a sore throat. Other mums would know the difference between that and something serious. I did not. I just do not know how to react to certain situations. There are occasions when he runs to Steve or to his nanny, rather than me; and that hurts. But they had their routine with him when I wasn't there. It is hard to assert my position. It does not come naturally. Mornings are particularly difficult. He always calls out "Daddy"; never Mummy. And then one day he does. I shall always remember that first early morning "Mummy".

'At first, Tom was very surprised to see me in bed with Steve.

'One day I do face painting with Tom, who is now five. He says: "Mum! That's terrible!" It hurt, but if I was only able to be intuitive, I would have accepted it with a laugh.

'On a day in June I am alone in the house. I come across papers Steve is working on, making a complaint about something that happened at my trial. As I read my cross-examination by Spencer, it all comes flooding back. My world begins falling apart. I am back there, in that terrible nightmare. And I cannot escape!

'Life is also difficult for Steve and me. I am not the person he married. He still cannot talk about Christopher and Harry. I want to talk about the good times with them. He can't bear it. When Christopher died, I was the one who fell apart. Steve took control. This was a major change in our relationship. Today, he is much more in control than I am. He has taken charge of the compensation claim. He is the driving force in the family. It used to be me. He has had to be since May after my release, when things began to go so badly wrong inside me. Our relationship is, in some ways, even closer, but it is different. There are things I just know nothing about; quite ordinary things.

'As to work: there is a local firm of solicitors who do some company work, and I sometimes walk past their door, wondering what it would be like to have a seat there. But I know it is too soon, and maybe never.'

I make a formal written application and Sally Clark's name is restored to the Roll of Solicitors:

'But I don't know if I will ever be strong enough to practise law again. Before the arrests and prosecution, I know I would have gone back: the only question was, how soon. After Christopher died, my plan was to return to work after six months. Having served three and a half years in prison, I do not feel I can work at all, for the foreseeable future. My priority is Tom; getting to know him properly, which he and I were denied all that time; getting him used to having his mum here, all the time. If there had been no prosecution I would not necessarily have gone back to the demanding position within corporate law. I would probably have tried venture capital work. My female friends have had to juggle the various demands of career versus family: I would have liked to work towards the ultimate goal of a partnership.

'Despite what the legal system has done to me, it hasn't lessened my love of the law. I am almost afraid to go back to work, because of what was said about me by Robin Spencer at the trial – and repeated in all the newspapers – that I was career obsessed. It was never true. You can love a profession without being so in thrall to it that you do terrible things. It is true that I would feel a sense of loss if I could not pursue a career that I feel so passionately about.'

Fourteen months after her release, I don't know if Sally will ever be fit enough to do a proper job in the law or elsewhere.

'I have all sorts of letters, offering a return to the profession. However, my age and lack of experience – I have been out of the law since 1998 – will make this very hard. And I have been so damaged by what happened; my self-confidence has been so destroyed that it may be a pipe dream.

'We are now looking for a new home, in the same area because Tom likes his school so much. Our plans may prove unrealistic because of the extent of our financial losses arising from the case. Payments into our pension funds were stopped for five years. Steve's hope of early retire- ment at fifty – you can only take so many years at the very top pressure – is out of the question. He will have to work at least another five, maybe ten years, to make up for the lost contributions.

'Steve and I will have to consider carefully whether to have another child. What has happened raises obstacles. Could either of us take the risk of being alone with a new baby, for fear that if something happened . . . Neither of us could ever harm a baby, but we now know that you can be as loving and devoted a mum as anybody ever born and still wind up in prison, maybe for the rest of your life, for something that never happened.'

Steve is still feeling numb:

'Getting Sally out was only the beginning: she is so damaged by what has been done to her. All our lives have been so badly affected. We've been kept apart for what could have been the best three years of our marriage. Sally still has to build a relationship with Tom, and with me, and me with her. She is not the person I married. I am not the man she said those vows to in St Thomas's Church in Salisbury.

'Sally has good days and others when she can't face anything. I am, if anything, even more exhausted now than I was at the second appeal. We are still trying to come to terms with the effects of five years of fighting for our very lives. We have both had extensive counselling. I'm not sure how long that will last: probably years, judging from current lack of progress. The big difference is that we are now together but that creates its own issues. I am holding down a difficult and stressful job, working crazy hours, when part of me says that if I was only doing nine-to-five I would have more time to help Sal. Sometimes I ask myself: "Did it really happen? Why did it happen? Maybe it was just a bad dream and I will wake up." The main problem is that neither of us was able properly to grieve for Christopher and Harry while we were fighting the prosecution. And we seem unable to do so now because so many issues confront us: adjusting to being together again; Sally learning to be a mum to Tom, having not been there for his formative years; being recognised and pestered by journalists for a quote every time another case hits the headlines; fighting to recover £150,000 of legal costs which are still being denied us by the bureaucrats. Proving Sally's claim for compensation for the miscarriage of justice she suffered is itself a nightmare, having to live it all again. Finally – and I admit that this is our choice, but I feel it has to be done – ensuring that the General Medical Council holds properly to account those experts whose evidence brought about this miscarriage. We definitely want to move on but we seem to be swirling in the aftermath.

'I suppose if it means that no other family will have to suffer what we went through, some good will have come of it. Maybe, as John says, it was meant to be . . . not that I believe in such things, but you can't help wondering. Maybe it was down to use to stop it ever happening again.

'I can only hope that none of this will have a long-term effect on Tom. How will we be able to explain it to him? Will other children give him grief for it in the playground? But what does he think of his mother, whom he can plainly see is not well. What does he think of me? That I should be able to make it all right? Dads are supposed to be able to do that, but I don't have a magic wand.

'Over all, I think I'm more angry than bitter, but I also feel justified. From the outset, I knew Sally was innocent of everything they accused her of. There is some satisfaction in being part of the defence team that, against all the odds, was able to fight back and prove some of the most powerful doctors and lawyers wrong.'

Some of the little things are hard for Sally:

'Spencer quoted part of a letter I wrote, as Harry, saying "because you know how Mum likes a tidy house". He said I killed Harry because he was messy and disruptive. If anybody comments on how tidy my home is now,

I cannot take it as a compliment; only that some people think it is a motive for murder. Will that legacy be with me for life? Will that be yet another part of the price I will pay for what my accusers did to me?'

'Why Me?'

In the depths of despair, following the rejection of her first appeal, Sally asked 'Why me?' I suggested she might have been 'chosen' because she was an ideal candidate to be the pathfinder to breach the dam behind which such a volume of aggrieved parents was building. Their only hope was that somebody with the right friends and the requisite knowledge would suffer the same injustice, and do something about it – breach the dam. On 29 January 2004, Sally Clark did just that. The first rumble in the walls was when pharmacist Trupti Patel – charged with the murder of three babies and the attempted murder of a fourth – was freed by a unanimous jury, in 90 minutes after a six-week trial. Then, Angela Cannings (who had three babies die and was convicted for the murder of two of them) was freed, on appeal, her convictions quashed, in a landmark judgment handed down by Deputy Lord Chief Justice Judge, in the Court of Appeal. And the dam did indeed pour forth all the waters.

Margaret Hodge MP, the Minister for Children, immediately announced that 5,000 cases of possible injustices in the Family Court were to be investigated. Lord Goldsmith, the Attorney-General, announced that 258 convictions for the murder, manslaughter or infanticide of babies would be urgently reviewed and 54 more people, still in jail, would be looked at and – if the Cannings' Judgment tests were met – fast-tracked back to the Court of Appeal. A day later, Harriet Harman, the Solicitor-General, announced that the Director of Public Prosecutions would personally examine 15 cases awaiting trial, to see if any failed the Cannings' tests.

But nobody has yet thought to highlight the impact of the media coverage of criminal trials, the way in which cases are reported with the allegations of the prosecution always given first and sensational prominence. This prejudices the minds of jurors and of opinion formers generally. The other side of that coin is that the media performed a vital public interest role in bringing to light the injustice visited upon Sally and the many others in the dam behind her.

Sally Clark is the innocent mother whose wrongful convictions, shame and degrading imprisonment were, perhaps, necessary to cause a revolution in the thinking in the criminal justice system and the Family Court. For the first time in over twenty years, there is public recognition that something has gone horribly wrong. It gives hope to hundreds, maybe thousands, of ordinary mums and dads innocent of any wrongdoing, damned when justice was looking the other way.

Aftermath

The shame and daily degradation of nearly three and a half years in prison does serious psychological damage to any innocent woman. It is impossible to forecast how long it will take Sally to recover fully from what she has suffered. The successive hammer blows of the death of her mother, the deaths of Christopher and then Harry, her arrest and conviction as a serial baby-murderer and the rejection of her first appeal, followed by three and a half years of a life sentence as the 'lowest of the low', do terrible damage to the psyche.

I fear she may still be in prison, in her head. No sum of money can compensate her for what she went through. I hope that, in time, she may see that there was a purpose in her suffering.

I detect resolve in the judiciary and the government, that nobody should be allowed to go through such a trauma again. There are signs that the message is getting through to the United States, where there are probably thousands of cases of miscarriages of criminal and family law justice. In Australia, Kathleen Folbigg was convicted of very similar charges to those which Trupti Patel's jury so summarily rejected: I have alerted her lawyers to the Angela Cannings judgment. They will base their appeal on it. It should succeed.

However difficult it must be for her, Sally should be immensely proud that her suffering has resulted in such benefit for so many of her fellow human beings.

Her claim for compensation will have to be backed by a professional psychiatric and employment specialist evaluation. The emotional and financial drain of instructing lawyers is not over. Sally and Steve must re-visit their respective private hells for days on end with a new legal team and new experts. Is she fit enough to stand it? Is Steve? Would anyone be? No amount of money will begin to compensate this family for the emotional and physical devastation these events have caused. Even recouping the bare financial losses may involve further lengthy and stressful battles.

To be near his wife in prison Steve had to give up his equity partnership in his Manchester law firm, move and, effectively, begin his career again, five years back down the ladder of promotion. It has cost him a seven-figure sum. He will have to work many more years to make up his lost pension contributions.

Nobody knows the effect on Tom of being deprived of his mother's nurture for the first four years of his life. Steve made a wonderful, unbelievably good fist of bringing him up single-handed, but it is not the same as the mother's ever-present touch.

Postscript

Steve has formally asked the Bar Council to investigate the prosecution of his wife.

The General Medical Council is instituting disciplinary proceedings against Williams, Southall and Meadow. Although Green could not be said to have been solely responsible for Sally's arrest and trial because he made such a mistake about Harry, he was a major contributor to it. No proceedings are being taken against him by the GMC; he said sorry.

Frank has asked The Police Complaints Authority to investigate the story that Sally called a criminal barrister before or immediately after she dialled 999 for Harry. They do so but the file is put away for want of evidence. What Professor David told us has been denied by everybody interviewed.

Harry Clark died of natural causes, an overwhelming staphylococcal septicaemia – a form of early meningitis. Eleven of the world's leading experts on SIDS said so. That does not make it 'God's truth' but it gets pretty close. There is a respectable body of medical opinion that denies this, saying that meningitis cannot overwhelm a baby's immune system to kill it so quickly, and that if it had, the infection would have been visible histologically, i.e. to the naked eye, or under the microscope; microbiology alone is not enough. I have no quarrel with those who hold that opinion. What is unacceptable is that parents may be convicted of murder – in the criminal or Family Courts – by reliance, only, on the opinion of those experts who believe meningitis can't kill so fast.

Dr Roger Byard, who wrote the leading textbook on SIDS, says: 'If the results of microbiology, which suggest a cause of death, are going to be ignored, why bother to do them!' If Sally had lived a few miles further north, in Lancashire, Harry's post-mortem would have been done by Professor Morris, a genuine expert, experienced in Sudden Infant Death, who would have recognised that the baby died of natural causes. No murder trial would have ensued. Sally would not have spent over three years in jail. That is not a justice system, it is life imprisonment by lottery – postcode lottery.

Many doctors offered their services and opinions for nothing because they knew, instinctively, that there was something wrong with Sally's conviction. Doctors have saved my life on more than one occasion. They do a fantastic job against intolerable bureaucracy, with modest rewards and inhuman hours, and are frequently at serious risk of physical injury. That the NHS is subject to such criticism is not the fault of the doctors. I would not do their job for any money. My criticism is of a tiny minority of medical experts who do not measure up to the standards of their peers.

But there is another objectionable commonplace in medicine: the culture of cover-up. To turn a blind eye to the incompetence of other doctors is a denial of the Hippocratic oath; its consequences are harm to the sick, and death to some, among them babies, as has been seen in recent cases. Every doctor I have spoken to believes that any criticism of a professional colleague could get him into disciplinary trouble. It is not what the GMC rule book says but it appears to be what many doctors fear. Whistle-blowers are frequently pilloried for doing their ethical and professional duty in exposing malpractice and incompetence. If the profession does not voluntarily agree to address this issue urgently, the government should consider taking regulation away and giving it to an independent body. Such cover-up is not only immoral and unethical, it may well be criminal conduct. The Director of Public Prosecutions should bring criminal charges against anybody who knowingly allows – or conspires with – others to inflict harm, injury or death to a patient.

The other problem that calls for the most immediate attention is the scandalous lack of paediatric pathologists, those specially qualified to carry out post-mortems on babies. The newborn are not miniature adults. Using a pathologist whose expertise is in adult deaths runs the serious risk that wrong diagnoses will be made and natural causes of death missed. The present regulations for an ordinary pathologist to become paediatrically qualified are so difficult that most reject the option. That means things can only get worse for mothers who suffer the tragedy of a baby dying.

Wrongful convictions and Family Court decisions will cost millions in compensation and wasted legal and court costs not to mention the emotional devastation to parents. It would be more humane and considerably cheaper, to make paediatric qualification more accessible.

The Court of Appeal on 19 January 2004, giving its reason for quashing, without retrial, the conviction of Angela Cannings, whose three babies died, has dealt what should have been the death knell for any new prosecutions for this type of imaginary murder. They say that there is no justification for any expert believing that the deaths of three babies in a family must be murder and that no jury should be invited to convict a mother because she cannot explain why her babies died. The final paragraphs of one of the most academically impressive judgments ever handed down by the Court of Appeal say:

> . . . where a full investigation into two or more sudden unexplained infant deaths in the same family is followed by a serious disagreement between reputable experts about the cause of death, and a body of such expert opinion concludes that natural causes, whether explained or unexplained, cannot be excluded as a reasonable and not fanciful possibility the prosecution for murder . . . should not be started . . . If the outcome of the trial depends exclusively or almost exclusively on a serious disagreement between reputable and distinguished experts, it will often be unwise, and therefore unsafe, to proceed.
>
> In expressing ourselves in this way, we recognise that justice may not be done in a small number of cases where, in truth, a mother has deliberately killed her baby without leaving any identifiable evidence of the crime. That is an undesirable result, which however, avoids a worse one. If murder cannot be proved, the conviction cannot be safe. In a criminal case, it is simply not enough to establish even a high probability of guilt. Unless we are sure of guilt the dreadful possibility always remains that a mother, already brutally scarred by the unexplained death or deaths of her babies, may find herself in prison for life for killing them, when she should not be there at all. In our community, in any civilised community, that is abhorrent.

Appendix

Summary of the Written Reasons for quashing Sally's Conviction

The grounds of appeal made two essential points: the failure to disclose microbiological evidence that rendered the convictions unsafe, and that the statistical information overstated, very considerably, the rarity of two SIDS in the same family.

The Nature of the Prosecution Case

The seven similarities said to be beyond coincidence were:

(i)   Both babies died at about the same age;
(ii)   Both discovered unconscious by the mother in the bedroom;
(iii)   at 9.30 p.m. shortly after a successful feed;
(iv)   Mrs Clark alone with each child when discovered;
(v)   Mr Clark either away or about to go away;
(vi)   Evidence of previous abuse;
(vii)   Evidence consistent with recent inflicted injury in each case.

As to (i), (ii), (iv) and (v), we fail to see how they can be thought to be any significant indication of murder. Some are open to real criticism. The suggestion that Mr Clark was out or going away has some significance we cannot accept. If a successful feed in each was relevant, it needed to be treated with caution. Christopher had vomited and Harry's stomach was empty at post-mortem. As to inflicted injury there was no evidence that either child was being abused during his life.

[The whole of the medical evidence for prosecution and defence, at trial, is then reviewed.]

The first Appeal Court, following its analysis of the statistical evidence, concluded that there was an overwhelming case against Sally Clark. But they were wholly unaware of the existence of evidence to suggest that Harry might have died from natural causes.

The Evidence Discovered since the First Appeal

It is not necessary to recite in great detail the evidence at this appeal of Professor Morris or Dr Klein. The former concluded that 'overwhelming staphylococcal infection is the most likely cause of death' and that no other cause of death could be sustained. This was mainstream medicine and not a maverick view. It seems to us to be of the utmost importance that no sort of suggestion was made to him by Mr Spencer QC that his view was other than respectable medical opinion, which others might share even though it was not the opinion of doctors on whom the prosecution relied.

The approach of the prosecution puzzled us. There was no way the evidence relied on by Professor Morris could have been obtained by the defence prior to trial. As there was no suggestion that his opinion was other than respectable, and in the light of the House of Lords guidance about a jury being deprived of the chance of considering such evidence, the conviction had to be viewed as unsafe, we asked Mr Spencer how the prosecution could invite us to uphold the conviction.

Mr Spencer, recognising that the Court could not second guess what impact it might have had on the jury, [said] he would limit himself to just calling Dr Klein, so that the contrary opinions were, at least, in the public domain.

Dr Klein's evidence – which was also mainstream medicine – was that the history, clinical and pathological features and investigations were not consistent with Morris's cause of death: it 'did not fit with anything I have seen'. Dr Klein said in one of his reports:

> 'The hypothesis that staphylococcal toxins may in some as yet unexplained way lead to SUDI (Sudden Unexpected Death in Infancy) is interesting and clearly warrants further research.'

Morris and Klein were equally impressive witnesses but there was nothing in Dr Klein's evidence to suggest that there was no prospect of the jury believing that Professor Morris's evidence was right. The verdict on that count has to be viewed as unsafe and must be quashed.

It follows that no safe conclusion can be reached that Christopher was killed unnaturally. The conviction in his case is also unsafe and must be quashed.

Failure to Disclose Microbiology Reports

Professor David said:

'It is a matter of great concern that this wealth of laboratory data was not disclosed. Had these results been available I would have investigated them in relation to both deaths. What is so extraordinary is that these results were actually sent away for further testing to Colindale, which is the national reference laboratory for microbiology.'

Professor Morris found it astonishing that the results were not included in Dr Williams' report. It was an 'error of judgment'.

At trial there was no mention of microbiological results by anyone. No one knew there was material of potential importance available. Yet it was clear that the jury were interested in these matters. Dr Williams told them:

'Samples . . . taken from Harry were submitted for toxicological examination and some of it would have been sent for viral studies.'

His answers were factually correct but . . . it is remarkable that he did not seize this opportunity to draw these matters to the attention of the prosecution.

We discount the possibility that Dr Williams deliberately concealed the information that Harry died from natural causes. It seems that he genuinely believed that Christopher and Harry died from unnatural causes. We do not believe he was knowingly party to putting forward a false case. We gave Dr Williams the opportunity to give evidence to explain his apparent shortcomings. He did not avail himself of that opportunity. His statement of 5 September 2002 said:

'It is not my practice to refer to additional results in my post-mortem unless they are relevant to the cause of death, as the specimens were referred to another consultant.'

We find that explanation wholly unacceptable. His practice is completely out of line with what other pathologists accept as standard. It is likely to mislead others . . . who will be denied the opportunity of considering the material . . . It runs significant risk of a miscarriage of justice . . . We reject his contention that there was an onus on the defence to ask questions to reveal the existence of the information.

Finally, on this aspect it is pertinent to record the view of Professor Byard:

'There appear to have been significant and ongoing problems in the investigations of these deaths. Standard protocols were not followed and essential steps such as routine dissection and histology were omitted which prevented verification of alleged autopsy findings. As well, a number of potentially important diagnoses and conclusions were altered over time. Christopher's initial cause of death of lower respiratory tract infection was withdrawn, observations of no significant haemorrhage within his lungs were changed to marked haemorrhage and documented damage to his cervical spinal cord was not found. The finding of retinal haemorrhages in Harry which was vital to sustain the diagnosis of shaken impact syndrome was altered to no haemorrhage, brain lacerations were found to represent post-mortem artefact, swelling in the spinal cord was not present and bruising of the para-spinal tissues was not able to be substantiated. This is not a unique situation with statements in the literature in recent years that "investigations into the pathology and circumstances of sudden infant death are often scanty and inexpert, with significant omissions being documented when cases are audited." The Clark brothers demonstrate difficulties that may arise if cases are not fully investigated with all the results being clearly summarised and discussed in the autopsy report. Trying to clarify findings, diagnoses and circumstances of death at a later stage may simply not be feasible due to a wide variety of possibilities other than inflicted injury.'

These observations substantially mirror our own views. The fact that further tests could no longer be carried out is a result of the failure of Dr

Williams to disclose the microbiology that lay at the heart of the Crown's decision not to seek a retrial. They were also properly aware of the publicity and difficulty in obtaining a jury free from the influence of such publicity. We endorse their decision not to seek a retrial. In any event we would have taken a great deal of persuading that any jury could properly have been sure that either or both of these children were murdered.

Statistical Evidence

It is unfortunate that the trial did not feature any consideration as to whether the statistical evidence should be admitted and whether its proper use would be likely to offer any real assistance to the jury. The jury were required to return separate verdicts on each count yet 1:73 million encouraged a package. If the jury considered that one death was a SIDS but the other not, then the statistics were wholly irrelevant. It was tantamount to saying to the jury that without consideration of the rest of the evidence one could be just about sure that this was a case of murder. If 1:73 million was accurate then the whole of the CONI scheme was effectively wasted effort. We suspect that the graphic reference of Professor Meadow to the chances of backing long odds winners of the Grand National may have had a major effect on the jury's thinking notwithstanding the judge's efforts to down-play it.

The Court of Appeal on the last occasion would, it seems to us, have felt obliged to allow the appeal but for their assessment that the rest of the evidence was overwhelming. It would never have reached that conclusion if the evidence in its entirety, as it is now known, had been known to it.

It seems likely that if statistics had been fully argued before us it would have provided a quite distinct basis on which the appeal had to be allowed.

We are aware that there is public speculation as to whether other convictions of mothers for killing their babies where the babies have died sudden deaths are similarly unsafe. The matters to which we have referred are directly referable only to this case. If any other case is brought before this court, it will receive the same anxious scrutiny by the court that we would like to think we have given to this case.

The Meningitis Research Foundation Helpline is: 080 8800 3344

Acknowledgements

Many people helped me write this book, most notably Sally and Steve Clark and Frank Lockyer; their patience and revealing honesty knew no bounds. Helen Killner was my right hand. Sue Stapely spent days on a masterly edit. Mike Mackey knew many things I didn't and corrected my legal and factual inexactitudes. Dr Jock Smallwood provided a most helpful general practitioner's overview. John Banfield had no insider knowledge of the case; he gave me the valuable insights of a 'virgin' reader. My family, Jane, Gina, Charles and Joanna, gave not only essential support in the writing but in the more difficult emotional times of the last four years. The partners at Batt Holden kindly allowed me to do what I felt I had to do.

I am particularly indebted to my publisher, Fiona MacIntyre, who edited the book with reassuring respect for the original text. Jonathan Lloyd, of Curtis Brown, gave me the benefit of his amazing skill as an agent and adviser. There are many more; they know who they are.

Thank you so much – all of you.

I wrote the manuscript of *Stolen Innocence* months before the Cannings appeal, which, so dramatically, changed the legal landscape in which I was writing. I faced a choice: re-write certain passages – mainly wish-lists – to avoid the charge of hindsight prophecy, or leave the manuscript as written. I chose the latter.